EVERYTHING IS BROKEN

EVERYTHING IS BROKEN

THE UNTOLD STORY OF DISASTER UNDER
BURMA'S MILITARY REGIME

EMMA LARKIN

GRANTA

Granta Publications, 12 Addison Avenue, London W11 4QR

First published in Great Britain by Granta Books, 2010
First published in the United States in 2010 by The Penguin Press,
a member of Penguin Group (USA) Inc.

Grateful acknowledgment is made for permission to reprint excerpts
from the following copyrighted works:
"Everything is Broken" by Bob Dylan. Copyright © 1989 Special Rider Music.
All rights reserved. International copyright secured. Reprinted by permission.
Metta: The Philosophy and Practice of Universal Love by Acharya Buddharakkhita. Used
by permission of the Buddhist Publication Society, Kandy, Sri Lanka.

Map on page vii copyright © Jeffrey L. Ward, 2010

Photograph on page 1 copyright © Greg Constantine, 2008
Photograph on page 87 copyright © Nic Dunlop, 2007
Photograph on page 175 copyright © Emma Larkin, 2008

Designed by Nicole Laroche

A CIP catalogue record for this book
is available from the British Library.

1 3 5 7 9 10 8 6 4 2

ISBN 978 1 84708 180 3

Printed in the UK by the MPG Books Group

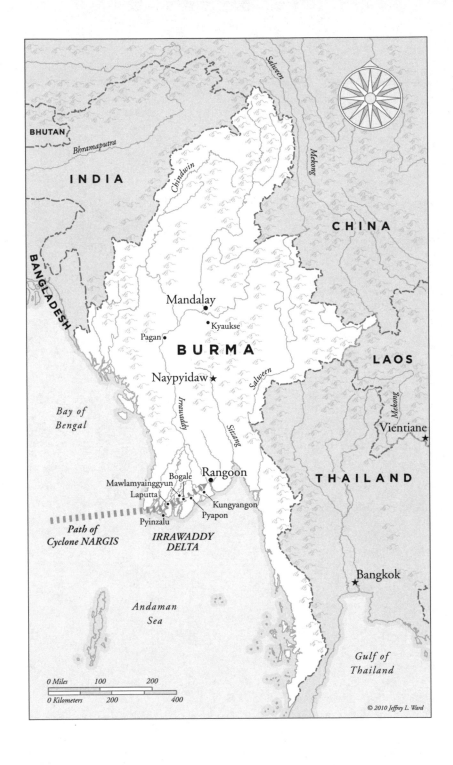

CONTENTS

Broken cutters, broken saws,
Broken buckles, broken laws,
Broken bodies, broken bones,
Broken voices on broken phones.
Take a deep breath, feel like you're chokin',
Everything is broken.

—BOB DYLAN

AUTHOR'S NOTE

The ruling military regime exerts control over all media in Burma and suppresses any versions of the truth that are contrary to its interpretation of events. As a result, official sources of information are often unreliable; most government statistics and publications are little more than pro-regime propaganda, and government staff are forbidden to talk to foreigners without prior permission. Burmese citizens who leak information to international news, or other, organizations do so under threat of imprisonment.

To research this book, I relied on the same truth-seeking methods used by people living in Burma. In addition to my own experience and impressions, I recorded other eyewitness accounts whenever possible. In order to protect my sources I have had to give people false names and limit certain biographical details that might make them identifiable to the authorities. During meetings in which anti-government sentiments are expressed, names are often not exchanged for reasons of safety and some people mentioned in the book remain anonymous. I also read between the lines of government propaganda, analyzed anecdotal evidence, and took into account the many rumours that are continuously circulating throughout the country. In a place where the truth of events is obscured by heavy censorship and propaganda, rumours act as an alternate source of news and, in some instances, can become as important as hard facts.

PART ONE

SKYFUL OF LIES

MAY 2008

IT WAS DARK and Ma Pyu couldn't see anything, though she could sense something unnatural about the quietness around her. Ma Pyu, a teenage girl from a village south of Bogale town in Burma's Irrawaddy Delta, had been knocked unconscious during Cyclone Nargis. When she awoke a short time after the storm had passed, she found herself lying alone and naked on a muddy stretch of ground. Afraid to disrupt the heavy silence, she lay totally still and waited.

After what felt like an eternity, a hazy dawn began to break over the shattered landscape and Ma Pyu could see that she was surrounded on all sides by snake-like shapes. Her panic subsided momentarily when she realized she was lying among the gnarled roots of a mangrove forest. As more sunlight filtered through the knotted branches, she saw that there were other people lying nearby and noticed that they too were keeping absolutely still, even though some of them lay with their limbs twisted in uncomfortable-looking positions—one man's leg was flopped next to his ear, another lay facedown in the mud with his arms neatly folded across his back. As Ma Pyu looked up toward the sky she saw that there were also people hanging in the trees. Their bodies were like oversized dolls, lazy and limp among the branches.

Unable to bear the appalling silence for a moment longer Ma Pyu called out, "Where am I?"

There was no response. Not one of the bodies so much as stirred. She called out again, louder this time, "Where am I?"

Again, there was no response and Ma Pyu started to crawl frantically through the butter-soft mud, heading toward the light at the edge of the mangrove forest. The events of the night before came back to her in disjointed flashes: the wind that kept getting stronger; the flood that swallowed up her home; the boat she climbed into with her parents. She remembered the boat crashing into a tree and breaking apart. She saw her father disappear beneath a wave and her mother clutching a piece of wood spinning away from her in the water, calling out her name.

Ma Pyu emerged from the forest onto a sprawling plain and, not knowing what propelled her forward, she began to walk. She walked past the broken pieces of people's homes—floorboards, palm roofing, cracked mirrors. She found a piece of cloth wrapped around the oar of a boat and used the wet fabric to cover her nakedness. The same stillness of the forest had infested the fields she walked through. A dog lay against the trunk of a coconut tree; its eyes were open but it wasn't breathing. There were buffalo scattered across the land like toy animals and people were lying there, too, but Ma Pyu tried not to look at them. At one point, she came to a river. She felt like she hadn't eaten for days and didn't have the energy to swim. There was a pig floating in the shallows and she nudged it with her foot. It didn't move so she put her hands around its belly and kicked her way across. She thought to herself, There is nothing left. This is the end of the world and I am the only one here.

Still, Ma Pyu carried on walking and, after some hours, she was startled to hear a male voice say, "Sister! Sister! Who are you?" She couldn't work out *where the voice was coming from but she responded with the names of her parents and asked, "Who are you?" A man's head emerged from behind a grounded boat. There were two other men with him and they politely identified themselves and the villages they were from. They explained that they couldn't step out from behind the boat because they were naked: their* longyi *(the sarong worn by Burmese men) had been ripped off as they tried to swim through the raging waters the previous night. Ma Pyu duly averted her gaze until they had found scraps of cloth to tie around themselves.*

Though none of them knew where they were or where they were going, they agreed to walk together and, eventually, they came to a place that must once have been a village. There was the wreckage of a monastery and huge piles of timber and thatch. A one-story cement building remained standing and scores of people clad only in wet rags or torn rice sacks were gathered in and around it.

As they approached the group, someone pushed a coconut against Ma Pyu's lips and she drank the juice and gnawed at the flesh inside. She listened to the people talking about a big storm, a storm bigger than anyone could ever have imagined possible. People came up to her and asked her where she was from and if she knew what had happened to their father or uncle or daughter or brother. Lots of people were crying, though there was one man who giggled oddly whenever anyone approached him. A young girl clasped a jerrican as tightly as if she was still using it to keep afloat; she had not uttered a word to anyone and no one knew who she was or where she was from. There were injured people, too; in the churning waters limbs had been crushed by logs and loose zinc roofing had sliced through flesh.

Ma Pyu spent two nights among this gathering of the shell-shocked. She searched for fallen coconuts to drink from and scavenged for dead animals that might still be edible. Someone managed to light a fire and they were able to roast the meat but it had to be shared between so many people that there was only ever enough for a few mouthfuls each. There was no way of knowing how to get help or where to go; some believed that the entire world had been engulfed by the monster storm.

But Ma Pyu needed to find her parents so she joined some people who had decided to walk to Bogale town, where they hoped they would be able to find help.

Ma Pyu's odyssey is not unique. Many survivors walked for days after Cyclone Nargis in search of food, shelter, and lost family. Some died along the way, of dehydration or open wounds. Some were picked up by boats. Others just kept walking through the wasteland. They ended up in one of the bigger delta towns—like Bogale or Laputta—where they sought shelter among the thousands of survivors who had crowded into school buildings and monastery compounds. Ma Pyu made it to Bogale in the end and there she told her story to anyone who would listen, but she never found her parents or learned what had happened to them.

ONE

A few days after Cyclone Nargis made landfall at the southwestern tip of Burma's Irrawaddy Delta on Friday, May 2, 2008, NASA released a set of before and after pictures taken by satellite.

In the image taken before the cyclone, the delta's myriad waterways were perfectly etched upon the landscape, like dark and delicate veins. Toward the lower edges of the delta, in the coastal stretches, these veins broadened and merged into the inky blue waters of the Andaman Sea. Large swaths of vibrant green indicated fertile rice-growing land. Deforested areas and urban centers, like Rangoon and its surrounding sprawl of slums, showed up as dun-colored patches. In the delta, towns such as Laputta and Bogale were barely visible amid the pastoral palette of greens, browns, and blues.

The satellite image taken shortly after the cyclone depicted a landscape that had been changed dramatically. The fact that the area around Rangoon was now a marbled swirl of aquamarine suggested that it was heavily flooded. The waterways of the delta, so distinct in the earlier image, had become blurred and hazy. The blue of the Andaman waters showed up as a luminescent turquoise that had seeped onto the land, an indication that parts of the delta now lay underwater. Comparing the two images, it was as if a bucket of water had been sloshed across an ink drawing; the carefully marked lines had been erased and the paper beneath was buckled and distorted.

These images showed that Cyclone Nargis had altered the landscape significantly, and caused substantial damage. Yet, in those first days after the cyclone, hardly any news emerged from Burma. The storm severed phone lines and electricity cables, and it was almost impossible to get information from inside the country.

The cyclone had been brewing in the Bay of Bengal for almost a week. When the tropical depression developed into a cyclonic storm, the Indian Meteorological Department named the storm "Nargis," a moniker taken from a list of names provided annually by each of the countries in the cyclone band of the Indian Ocean (contributed by Pakistan, *nargis* is an Urdu word for the narcissus, a flower more commonly known as the daffodil). By the time Nargis reached the coast of Burma, it had grown into a category four storm with wind speeds of up to 135 miles per hour. Cyclones of this magnitude can trigger a storm surge that would be high enough to engulf a two-story house. The storm charted a path across the Irrawaddy Delta, the vast flood basin of Burma's main river that is populated with hundreds of farming and fishing villages, and directly over Rangoon, the country's largest city and former capital, before finally dissipating in the mountains along the Thailand–Burma border. With the help of regional and international weather-monitoring services, this much was known.

What was not known was what had happened on the ground and what had become of all the millions of people who must have been in the cyclone's path.

Over the following week, news began to trickle out from Burma, as generators were activated and electricity and phone lines were restored to some parts of Rangoon. Photographs of the city looked as if they had been taken in the aftermath of a massive explosion. Roads were blocked by fallen trees. Cars had been crushed by logs and telephone poles. Cement walls had caved in and pavements were cracked open. The destruction in the city was catastrophic, but it soon became apparent that what had happened in Rangoon was nothing compared to the devastation of the Irrawaddy Delta. Toward the end of the week, an e-mail from Burma circulated some photographs taken in the delta; these were among the earliest harrowing glimpses of what had happened there.

The first image was a picture of two dead girls. One girl wore shorts and a bright orange T-shirt printed with a cheerful floral pattern. The other had on only a frilly pale green top. They lay on their backs in a nest of sodden palm fronds with their eyes closed and their heads turned away from each other. They looked as if they had fallen, or been flung, from a very great height.

The next photograph showed seven bodies floating in water, perhaps a pond. One grouping looked like it could be a family—a woman with two children on either side of her. The children were face up with their arms flung out, as if reaching for their mother. The other figures could be seen only in parts: an exposed chest, a red T-shirt, a billowing blue *longyi* beneath which a pair of legs disappeared into the still, brown-gray surface of the water.

The most gruesome photograph captured a row of bodies scattered across paddy fields. They were swollen and black from sun exposure. Rigor mortis had locked the bodies into crooked postures; their legs and arms were spread wide, and they lay entangled in grotesque and awkward embraces.

Within just a couple of days, the Burmese regime announced on state television that as many as 10,000 people could have been killed. The very next day, an official death toll was released that was more than double that figure, with over 22,400 people declared dead and more than 41,000 people missing. The majority of these lives were lost across the delta region, with Rangoon reporting only a few deaths.

From these initial snatches of information, it was clear that Cyclone Nargis had been a disaster of epic proportions. In the delta, tens of thousands of people were dead, and many hundreds of thousands were trying to survive without food, water, or shelter. As the horrendous scale of the disaster became apparent, foreign governments offered aid and assistance. Astoundingly, the Burmese government turned them down.

In neighboring Thailand, the U.S. government had loaded a C-130 cargo plane with lifesaving relief supplies that would have taken just under an hour to reach Burma, but the craft was not given clearance to land at Rangoon's airport. The United Nations World Food Programme had three planes ready to fly in from Bangladesh, Thailand, and Dubai in the United Arab Emirates. The planes were loaded with vitamin-fortified biscuits for hungry survivors who might not have eaten for some days and would be in need of instant nourishment. These biscuit-laden planes were also denied clearance. A flight from Qatar carrying relief materials and aid workers managed to land at Rangoon airport but was immediately forced to take off again without unloading any of its contents.

As international emergency response mechanisms kicked into action, UN staff and aid workers experienced in disaster response were mobilized from around the world. Few of them were granted visas to enter Burma. Many aid workers assembled in Bangkok, Thailand, a practical stopover for processing entry visas. The Burmese embassy, however, was closed on the Monday after the cyclone for a Thai public holiday. When a UN team of four experts was finally allowed to travel to Burma toward the end of the week, two were sent back after landing in Rangoon, despite having valid visas.

In addition to preventing aid workers from entering, the regime was also restricting the movement of foreigners already inside the country. International aid agencies that had been working in Burma before the cyclone had switched to emergency mode, but their foreign staff were not allowed outside Rangoon; only Burmese employees were able to travel to the delta to begin distributing supplies and look for ways to set up reliable delivery routes. It is an established procedure in Burma that foreign aid workers at international nongovernmental organizations (NGOs) must apply for permits to travel outside Rangoon (a process that can take weeks, sometimes months); it was hoped that the authorities would expedite travel requests after a natural disaster. Instead, they did just the opposite by slowing down the process and setting up checkpoints on exit routes out of the city. Policemen were posted at the bridges and jetties along the Rangoon River where cars and ferries depart for the delta, and prohibited foreigners from crossing over to the other side.

It was, by all accounts, a situation unprecedented in the annals of disaster response. The UN and international aid agencies started to issue frantic and strongly worded warnings. The UN Office for the Coordination of Humanitarian Affairs, OCHA, said that "thousands more could die" if assessments were not carried out that would enable the UN to respond effectively. Save the Children issued a press release stating that around 40 percent of the dead were children and that more would die if food and water did not reach them soon. A World Health Organization report warned that there was an immediate risk of waterborne diseases such as cholera and typhoid. UNICEF stated that one in five children already had diarrhea. The Food and Agriculture Organization highlighted the bigger picture, saying that the area affected by the storm was the source of most of the country's food (65 percent of the rice and 80 percent of the fishery products) and that Burma could face a food crisis in the near future. "We are on the cusp of a second wave of tragedy," the chief executive of World Vision told the press. "It's a race against time."

Efforts were made to reason with Burma's ruling generals through the highest diplomatic channels. UN Secretary-General Ban Ki-moon stated that he had been trying to contact the country's leader, Senior General Than Shwe, to arrange a meeting; insiders at the UN said that the general was simply not returning Ban Ki-moon's calls. George W. Bush, then the president of the United States, announced that the United States was willing to help and that U.S. Navy assets already present in the Southeast Asia region could be deployed to assist with search-and-rescue missions and aid distributions; first, though, the Burmese generals would have to allow U.S. disaster assessment teams to enter the country. The French foreign minister, Bernard Kouchner, went so far as to invoke the "responsibility to protect" principle, a UN proposal that would allow for the delivery of aid and assistance without the consent of the host government.

The generals were impervious to these pleas and threats. On May 9, a week after Cyclone Nargis, a statement was released in which the Ministry of Foreign Affairs said that the country was "not yet ready to receive search-and-rescue teams as well as media teams from foreign countries." According to the statement, the government was willing to accept provisions but would take charge of distributing them "by its own labors to the affected areas." Officials indicated that bilateral aid, assistance given government to government, would be welcomed, but that meant placing a large amount of supplies directly into the hands of a rogue regime—a setup that was unacceptable for most Western donors, who require accountability, transparent procedures, and the ability to track the delivery of the goods they donate.

As if to further infuriate those who were trying to provide help, the regime announced its plans to go ahead with an upcoming national referendum to vote on the newly drawn up constitution. Scheduled for May 10, the referendum had already been dismissed as a sham by most Burma experts. Having ruled the country for almost fifty years, the military government has established a well-earned reputation for being willing to do whatever it takes to stay in power, and the referendum seemed just another piece of trickery, a grand subterfuge designed to give the appearance of democracy without actually delivering any greater freedom to the people.

Indeed, the ruling generals have shown little interest in democracy and human rights. The regime's current incarnation came into being after a nationwide uprising against military rule in 1988, during which soldiers shot into the crowds and killed an estimated three thousand civilians. In the years that followed, the regime continued to quash any form of dissent. To this day, people perceived as a threat are imprisoned, and all criticism of the regime—be it spoken or written—is systematically silenced. Most prominent among Burma's political prisoners is the country's iconic symbol of democratic values, Aung San Suu Kyi, who came to the fore during the demonstrations in 1988 and who has spent the majority of the intervening years under house arrest.

Efforts made both inside and outside the country to unseat the junta or coax out its softer side have so far failed. When Aung San Suu Kyi and her party, the National League for Democracy, won a landslide victory in general elections held in 1990, the regime discounted the results and continued to rule. Economic sanctions imposed by the United States and Europe have been ineffective in eliciting any substantial concessions from the generals. So when the regime launched its so-called Road Map to Democracy in 2003, no one held their breath in anticipation of great changes. The Road Map, which includes the referendum as part of its seven-step plan, is expected to lead to another general election in 2010 and culminate in what the generals refer to as a "discipline-flourishing democracy"—a phrase that sounds distinctly *un*democratic, especially when used by a military junta that has demonstrated its enduring ability to rule against the will of the people.

After the cyclone, UN Secretary-General Ban Ki-moon issued a statement urging the regime to postpone the referendum and concentrate on the relief effort, but the generals ignored him. Such was their determination to proceed with their plans that preparations for the referendum continued in the wake of the worst natural disaster in the country's recorded history.

An impending sense of anarchy seemed to emanate from Rangoon. With no electricity, whole neighborhoods were plunged into total darkness each night. The cost of fuel was rising rapidly, and long queues had formed outside petrol stations as people raced to fill up their vehicles before prices became too high. Most parts of the city had no running water, and many residents had to purchase water from the owners of neighborhood wells. In the markets, people who could afford to were buying up large amounts of food to stockpile at home. Commodity prices were spiraling ever higher, and there was talk that the city was running out of medicine, food, and water.

In the tumbledown outskirts of Rangoon, and farther afield in the Irrawaddy Delta, there was untold devastation. Everyone thought that the death toll was sure to be much higher than the figures issued by official sources. Boats transporting aid to the delta were encountering waterways clogged with dead bodies. Weak and shocked survivors whose homes and villages had been obliterated by the cyclone were beginning to congregate in bigger delta towns, where they sought shelter in monastery and school buildings that were ill equipped and poorly prepared for such large crowds. Thousands were camping alongside the roads. In the delta town of Laputta, shopkeepers and residents were said to be bolting their doors as gangs of survivors roamed the streets wielding machetes and demanding food.

An ominous story emerged from Insein Prison in northern Rangoon. A sprawling prison complex built by the British colonial administration in the late nineteenth century, Insein (pronounced "insane") is the country's most notorious lockup and holds hundreds of political prisoners along with other inmates. The cyclone had ripped off parts of the roof in the prison and some one thousand inmates were moved by prison guards into an assembly hall. Wet and shivering, the prisoners lit a fire to warm themselves, but the fire raged out of control and the prisoners panicked. Unable to quell what was threatening to explode into a full-scale prison riot, the guards called in armed soldiers who reportedly shot into the crowd, killing thirty-six prisoners and injuring at least seventy others.

The story of this prison massacre was like a microcosm, a bloody prediction in miniature, of what could happen on a far larger scale in Rangoon and across the delta. There was already speculation that riots would break out soon. If people began rioting, the soldiers would be deployed and—as reportedly happened in the prison and has happened many times before in Burma—the soldiers would start shooting people.

Given the ruthless track record of Burma's soldiers, many thought the mounting turmoil could only end in bloodshed. But among the voices prophesying doom, there were also hopeful ones. Some believed that the regime would have to back down; this event was too big, too overwhelming, and sooner or later the regime would relent and accept foreign aid and assistance. The most hopeful went so far as to predict that the end result of all this mayhem would be the fall of the regime and the installation of a democratic government in Burma.

In the chaotic days after Cyclone Nargis, the mood of the country seemed to teeter wildly between abject despair and a deliriously irrational sense of hope.

IT WAS AROUND that time, just over a week after the cyclone, that my request for a tourist visa for Burma was granted. I had been there many times before and, in the early 2000s, I had spent more than a year traveling back and forth to the country researching a book on the links— both factual and fictional—between Burma and the British writer George Orwell, who had been posted there as an imperial policeman in the 1920s, when the country was part of the British Empire.

Though my travels to the various towns Orwell had lived in some-times attracted the interest of government spies curious as to what a lone female was doing so far off the usual tourist routes, I was never caught or questioned and have remained mostly below the radar. During the time I was there, I went to considerable lengths not to draw attention to myself; I conducted my research slowly and carefully, I was openly in-terested in the country's history, took Burmese language lessons, and spent time hanging out in tea shops with Burmese friends. If there ever was a file kept on my activities at the time, I like to think it was filled with non-incriminating observations by bored spies ("the foreign woman has just ordered her *third* cup of tea this afternoon"). I also disguised people's identities in my previous book, as I have done in this one. As a result, I have been able to travel there over the intervening years to visit friends, conduct further research, and write the occasional article.

Now, in the aftermath of Nargis, I wanted to return again to see what I could do to help and to try and catalog events from inside the country. Though I was doubtful that I would get in at a time when so many ap-plications were being turned down, I applied for a visa through a travel agency in Thailand, where I live. Three days later I received a call telling me that I could pick up my passport, which was now stamped with a four-week tourist visa for the Union of Myanmar (as the regime renamed the country in 1989). My travel agent told me I could choose the day and time of my travel as, perhaps not surprisingly, commercial flights to Burma were mostly empty.

By then I was in fairly regular contact with friends in Rangoon and had received various requests and recommendations as to what I should pack. The most important thing to bring was water purification tablets, wrote one friend in an e-mail, as the city was going to run dry in a matter of days. Another person advised me to fill my suitcase with dry noodles in case the shops started to shut down. Yet another told me to bring candles and matches, as there were none left in the city.

Many Burmese people I knew in Rangoon were organizing aid convoys. They were loading food, medicine, blankets, and drinking water into private cars and hired trucks and driving to the outskirts of Rangoon and down into the delta. Mass e-mails were sent out requesting critical supplies to be carried in by anyone who was able to get a visa. There were endless lists of medicines that were either unavailable or sold out in Rangoon, but the most insistent requests were for cash. There are no international banks in Burma, and there are no credit card or ATM facilities, aside from those at a few of the bigger hotels, so money must be carried in by hand. Nervous and bewildered by all the demands, I ended up packing my suitcase with a mixture of my own survival kit (peanut butter, dried fruit, water purifying tablets, and a headlamp), over-the-counter medical items for friends who were administering aid (electrolytes, Imodium, gauze), and hard cash (hundred-dollar bills stashed between the pages of a novel and hidden in boxes of pills).

On the day my plane landed at Rangoon airport, the runway was empty. After a major disaster, a working airport situated in the disaster zone would normally be crowded with fraught officials trying to organize the off-loading and onward transport of aid and equipment being flown in. But the airport was spookily quiet. It was a gray, overcast day, and the compound had a dejected feeling that seemed to imply nothing much could ever happen there. As the plane taxied down the runway, I saw only two unused passenger planes and a lone soldier clad in the standard olive-green uniform. The soldier's crumpled shirt was open at the neck, and he leaned against a tree, smoking a cheroot and gazing at the plane through lazy, half-closed eyes.

The atmosphere inside the airport terminal was no different from how it had been on previous trips I'd made. The Burmese people getting off the plane were laden down with the usual array of duty-free goods: boxes of chocolates, makeup, and whiskey. The handful of foreigners, most of whom were probably undercover journalists or aid workers slipping into the country on tourist visas, waited silently in the immigration queue, perhaps all sharing the same worry: *I hope they don't know what I really do; I hope they don't kick me out before I even get in.* Beyond the high glass walls that separated the immigration checkpoints from the greeting area, there was the familiar tight throng of people waiting eagerly for returning family and friends.

The immigration officer stamped my passport without even glancing up at me, and within minutes I had collected my suitcase and was sinking into the mildewed back seat of a battered Rangoon taxicab. The drive into the city used to be one of my favorite journeys. It was about a thirty-minute ride along tree-lined boulevards that skirted one of the city's picturesque lakes, circled roundabouts with sculpted floral centerpieces, and passed the gardens that surround the majestic golden presence of the Shwedagon Pagoda. Alongside the newer Chinese-style buildings, which had increased in number over recent years, there was still the architecture of bygone times. There were dark wooden houses half hidden behind forests of trees, ornate monastery buildings with strips of paint peeling off the domed roofs, and brick-walled colonial homes set at the end of overgrown driveways. The thick covering of greenery along the route had always given the city a hushed and secretive atmosphere.

After the skyscrapers of Bangkok, driving down the low-rise leafy streets of Rangoon felt to me like slipping back in time, which, in some senses, it was; my trips to Burma always meant relinquishing the modern-day technological gadgets I rely on at home. There is no international roaming service in Burma, and my mobile phone was useless there. Internet providers are heavily monitored by the regime to prevent anti-government material from getting into or out of the country, and access through the city's cramped and crowded Internet cafés was often irregular and infuriatingly slow. Unable to distract myself with sending SMS text messages or calling people during the cab journey into the city, there was nothing to do but sit back and watch the streets. And, always, there was the particular smell of Rangoon rushing in through the taxi's open windows—a familiar dank and musty odor, like a room that has been shut up for a long time and is in need of a good airing.

But this time, even during the short taxi ride, I could see that the cyclone had totally transformed the city. Enormous hundred-year-old trees had been uprooted and tossed aside. Telephone and electricity poles lay across the pavement, tangled up with wires and broken branches. Parts of the roofs of old houses had blown away, leaving gaping holes. Advertising billboards had been wrenched out of their moorings, though some shreds of the posters remained—among one set of twisted iron poles, a well-manicured hand held a steaming cup of coffee and a white-toothed smile fluttered in the breeze.

Before my arrival I had tried to book a hotel room, but with communication systems down after the cyclone, I had been unable to get through or even to ascertain if any hotels were still operating. Foreigners visiting Burma are not allowed to stay in Burmese homes, where all guests and overnight visitors must be registered with the neighborhood authorities, so a friend of mine had arranged for me to stay at a house temporarily vacated by an expatriate tenant. The house was a solid cement bungalow located in a well-to-do residential neighborhood and, apart from some minor damage to the overhanging roof, it had withstood the storm.

I spent my first few days in Rangoon checking on friends and delivering the supplies of cash and medicine I had brought. Though I knew the city well, I became lost a number of times, as so many landmarks had been altered; towering trees were no longer standing and buildings once obscured by greenery now stood out in the open. Having gone to the trouble of getting myself to Rangoon, I felt disoriented and useless once I was there. When I had finished dropping off the items I had brought with me, there didn't seem much for me to do. Being a foreigner, I was conspicuous, so I wasn't able to go down to the delta easily and report on events. I had few other skills applicable to a disaster zone, so, for the time being, I had to content myself with following events as best I could from within the city.

The house I was staying in was almost unbearably quiet in the evenings. Without power and phone lines, there were none of the reassuring sounds of a home—no television, no music, no ringing telephone. The house was located some distance from the main street, so even the sound of passing traffic was absent. At nighttime, the darkness was absolute. Each evening I would put on my headlamp and wander from room to room in its feeble tunnel of light.

FINDING RELIABLE SOURCES of information in Burma has always been difficult. The regime exerts control over the country in part by attempting to constrain the very reality in which people live. Everything that is published in Burma must first pass through a government censorship board. Each day censors are hunched over their desks sifting out sensitive news articles and searching for criticism of the regime that might be disguised in an allegorical short story or hidden within the rhyming couplets of a poem. To fill the gap left behind by the removal of independent news and views, the regime produces its own version of events, energetically rewriting the news in its favor and eliminating any contrary views.

The *New Light of Myanmar*, a newspaper published in both English and Burmese language editions, is the regime's de facto mouthpiece. Printed on coarse paper in cheap black ink that rubs off onto your fingers, the daily specializes in good news. Few people I know consider it to be anything other than pure propaganda, but I read it every day whenever I am in Burma, not so much as a source of news but as a window onto the point of view of the ruling generals. News as it is portrayed in the *New Light of Myanmar* does not represent how things actually are; it represents how the generals want things to be. And, in the case of Cyclone Nargis, the *New Light of Myanmar* expressed a unique take on events.

According to the official chronology of what happened after the storm, Burma's prime minister, General Thein Sein, who was appointed the chairman of the National Disaster Preparedness Central Committee, convened a meeting in the new capital city of Naypyidaw at 8.30 A.M. on May 3, while the storm was still raging in Rangoon. State media reported that Thein Sein traveled south immediately afterward to begin overseeing the national relief operation. Almost every day the general was featured on the front cover of the *New Light of Myanmar*. When he was not pictured tirelessly briefing other soldiers in a never-ending schedule of meetings, he was shown inspecting government-run camps that had been set up for storm victims. According to the *New Light of Myanmar*, the relief effort was already a laudable accomplishment. Private citizens and the military had banded together in the country's hour of need and, with the help of global goodwill, this disaster would soon be overcome. In the pages of the *New Light of Myanmar*, at least, everything was under control.

My Burmese friend Ko Ye, a publisher working in Rangoon, once taught me that if I wanted to know what was really going on in Burma, I should look for the absences; as the truth of events cannot be read in the pages of newspapers or seen on the nightly news, it is more likely to be found in what is *not* published or broadcast—the stories, or bits of stories, that are excised.

There were, for example, no disaster pictures in the *New Light of Myanmar* or in any of the many privately owned weekly publications. The images of bereft families and broken homes usually seen in the news after a major disaster were absent. Though many Burmese publications had been able to use the disorder that ensued after the cyclone to defy the censorship board, and had run stories and photographs of the destruction, by the time I arrived in Rangoon the censors had regained control of the news.

The editor of a weekly news journal showed me a recent issue in which the censors had scrawled hasty lines across all photographs considered to be "negative" (images of collapsed buildings, sunken boats, unhappy people, etc.). Out of some one hundred photographs, the censors had only approved four images. Less than two weeks after the cyclone, Burmese journalists and editors were summoned to the central censorship office, the Press Scrutiny and Registration Division, and were told that the emergency period was over. From then on, all Nargis-related stories published in Burma had to focus on rehabilitation and convey only positive messages.

It was impossible to see how the local media would be able to squeeze any positive stories out of the ongoing events. The conversations I had with friends and aid workers during my first few days revealed a reality that couldn't be more different from that described in the *New Light of Myanmar*.

Aung Thein Kyaw, a middle-aged man who runs a tour company, had temporarily shut down his business and was making repeated trips to the delta to hand out rice and medicine. The conditions he encountered were horrifying. In a tight and carefully measured voice he talked about how the boat he traveled in kept bumping against dead bodies. He described survivors with ghastly injuries. During the cyclone, flying sheets of corrugated iron had severed limbs and torn flesh from bone. While trying to stay afloat in the choppy waters of the storm surge, people had been battered by loose logs, boats, and planks of wood. Without medical attention, their gaping wounds were turning gangrenous. Survivors who had held on to trees for the ten-to-twelve-hour duration of the storm had clung on so tightly and for so long that the skin on their arms, chests, and legs had been rubbed away.

Wa Wa Myint, a doctor working in Rangoon who had been down to a delta town to treat patients, described some areas where the roads were lined with thousands of desperate and homeless people begging for food. "There are so many, many people," she said. "And they have nowhere to go. They have nothing left. Some of them were naked after the storm. They have no home left and no family—they have absolutely nothing, not even their clothes."

One evening, a friend took me to meet Chit Swe, who had just returned from traveling with a group of fellow businessmen to the southern stretches of the delta. Even before the storm, the lower regions of the delta were accessible only by boat, as no road network had ever been built there. Hardly any news had been heard from those areas, and it was believed that villages there must have taken the brunt of the storm. The businessmen had companies in the delta—fishing operations and rice-trading firms—and they had left the city soon after the storm, heading out to the villages in a large boat loaded with rice, drinking water, and tarpaulin sheets that could be used for shelter. Though the prime minister had warned members of the business community who were organizing similar donations that cameras were prohibited in the delta, Chit Swe had taken a camcorder.

To see the footage, we went to Chit Swe's house—a mansion with a sweeping teakwood staircase leading up from a high-ceilinged entrance hall. It was by far the grandest home I had ever visited in Burma, and it made me think that these men must be working closely with the regime to secure such profits. Regardless of their connections, they had gone against the prime minister's orders to collect evidence of conditions in the delta that they now wanted to show to foreigners. We gathered around a flat-screen television. It was late at night, and Chit Swe—a bulky, overweight man whose chubby fingers were being strangled by gem-studded gold rings—had cracked open a bottle of Johnnie Walker whiskey that he drank on the rocks as we watched the grim journey they had made to the delta.

Taken about a week after the cyclone struck, the images were staggeringly bleak. Most houses in the delta are built out of bamboo or wood and have palm-thatch roofs—in the event of a cyclone as powerful as Nargis, they are no better than origami huts folded out of paper. The first villages the businessmen arrived in had been completely demolished. Even the few concrete buildings in each village—often small monasteries or schools—had been reduced to heaps of rubble. Blank-faced survivors wandered aimlessly amid the wreckage, occasionally bending over to pick up a soggy scrap of cloth or a bamboo pole that might be useful for rigging up a shelter.

In one village along the Pyan Mae Law River, the businessmen came across a small group of people who had made a lopsided tent out of a ragged piece of tarpaulin and some planks. Chit Swe said somberly that at least 80 percent of the people living in the village were now dead or missing. The flooded paddy fields surrounding the makeshift shelter were littered with corpses of people and farm animals. Those who had survived had done so mostly by holding on to trees and managing to stay above the storm surge. One survivor commented that the dead were lucky compared to the living, who now found themselves trapped in a place that looked and felt like hell itself.

Chit Swe explained that they had to ration their supplies so that they could cover more ground and assess conditions in a number of villages. As they traveled farther south, the situation grew progressively worse. It was the ill-fated villages closer to the coast and those located along the banks of large rivers that appeared to have suffered the most. Wherever the boat docked, subdued groups of men would approach the vessel and quietly off-load whatever supplies the businessmen had to offer. In these areas, where the storm surge had been especially violent, there were often few women and children to be seen, because they hadn't had the physical strength needed to hold on for the duration of the storm. When the boat left, the same men would stand in a row on the riverbank. They did not wave or smile or talk. They just stood there, silhouetted against the washed-out, monsoon sky, and watched the boat sail away.

At the final village the businessmen went to before they ran out of supplies, they met a monk who showed them where the monastery had once stood. Though it had been made of concrete, only the foundations remained. The monk pointed to a large tree that was still standing and explained how thirty people had been saved by the tree as they clung to it while the water swirled around them. He directed the camera to a life-sized Buddha statue that was miraculously untouched by the storm. With its gentle half smile, the Buddha image looked incongruously serene and placid.

The camera panned out from the statue to take in a diabolical view of countless human corpses and the carcasses of farm animals that had swollen to twice their usual size. The monk said that the dead were not people from his village but had been washed up by the storm surge. Exposed to the elements for many long days, they had become unidentifiable and almost inhuman-looking. In Buddhist communities, the dead would customarily be cremated, but the land was saturated from the storm and the constant drizzle that followed it, and villagers had no wood or matches to construct funeral pyres. So the bodies remained, lying on the land and floating in the waterways.

The monk raised his arm and pointed into the gloom, across the flat, broken land. He indicated villages that were located farther south, and his voice seemed devoid of all emotion as he said, "Down there, it is even worse."

The footage Chit Swe showed us was from one short journey along a single river in the Irrawaddy Delta and represented only a tiny fraction of the overall picture. There are innumerable waterways in the delta, and the cyclone-affected parts amounted to some 9,000 square miles, a landmass over twice the size of Lebanon, that was home to more than seven million people. The townships around Rangoon were also known to be in a bad condition, as people there live in flimsy slum housing on low-lying land that is vulnerable to heavy winds and flooding. The same scenes we saw at Chit Swe's house could have been replayed over and over again just beyond the edges of Rangoon and out across the vast expanse of the delta.

During their journey, Chit Swe and his colleagues did not see any other assistance being delivered. There were no soldiers or navy boats on the water and no aid workers in the villages. Many villagers said that the help the businessmen gave them was the first they had received.

Chit Swe and his colleagues wanted to continue to help but were unsure what was needed, and the conversation in the room turned to a discussion of what they could do next. Someone in the room suggested that their footage of the delta should be taken to the U.S. embassy, as it was hard-to-get evidence of actual conditions after the storm that should be shown outside the country. Chit Swe quickly dismissed the idea; the film contained images of the businessmen delivering aid, and they did not want it to be seen beyond their own circle of trusted viewers. They wanted to help, but they didn't want to anger the authorities. In this uncertain climate it was not yet clear whether donating aid and recording suffering caused by a natural disaster would be perceived by the military junta as a crime.

DESPITE THE POSSIBLE DANGERS, everyone I knew was doing something to help. With little visible government support and restricted assistance from abroad, private citizens were stepping into the breech. Throughout the city groups of Rangoon residents banded together to collect money and deliver much-needed supplies to the delta and the outlying areas around Rangoon. Relief missions were being coordinated by traders, doctors, schoolteachers, students, writers, actors, musicians, and just about anyone who had even the slightest means. Like many celebrities, the popular comedian and former political prisoner Zargana was organizing a team of volunteers to move lifesaving supplies to people in the delta. Leading monks and abbots, such as the revered Sitagu Sayadaw, activated their countrywide donor networks to support monasteries that were sheltering survivors. The expatriate community was also pitching in, with gutsy women whose spouses worked at foreign embassies making use of the diplomatic license plates on their cars to storm through checkpoints with food and medicine.

A couple of days after I arrived in Burma, I went to deliver some cash I had brought for a friend who ran a private school in Rangoon. All classes had been put on hold as the school's teenage students were help-ing to coordinate their own small-scale emergency response. The school grounds had become the headquarters for the operation. Sacks of lentils, rice, and potatoes were piled up around the yard. Mud-splattered trucks were parked in the gateway. Students were frantically sorting through boxes of medicine and counting out sheets of tarpaulin. A map indicat-ing the path of the cyclone had been pinned to a wall and next to it was a whiteboard charting the daily movements of relief teams being sent to the outskirts of Rangoon.

On the morning I was there, a group of emergency experts had just arrived from Israel. The four-man team had traveled on tourist visas, as they would not have been allowed to enter the country in an official capacity as aid workers. Its members were well versed in the skills needed after a natural disaster, and the team leader had a PhD in disaster management. Trained to perform search-and-rescue missions and provide medical care in the field, these men had dealt with catastrophes across the globe in places as far afield as Turkey, Chad, and El Salvador. Here in Burma, however, they were rendered almost useless; their access to the disaster zone was blocked by military checkpoints, and they could not even publicly declare that they were there to try to help. If they wanted to contribute their expertise, they had to do so in a low-key, semi-secretive way.

To this end, the emergency team had come to the school as advisers, to brief the students on techniques that might be useful in the field. The team members sat on a low stage at the front of the school hall and talked to a crowd of around thirty people. It was Disaster Response 101, aimed at creating instant relief workers out of inexperienced but eager Burmese volunteers. The audience listened attentively, but the room was rustling with barely contained impatience. The speakers had to talk above a con-tinuous percussion of tapping feet and muffled conversations.

The leader of the emergency team began by asking for information from anyone who had been to the cyclone-affected areas. "Give me only descriptions, no emotions," he said. "Please try to separate your emotions."

Most of the descriptions came from the edges of Rangoon, where sprawling shantytowns were hit hard by the cyclone. In these areas, thousands of people whose homes had been destroyed by the wind and floods had sought shelter in local monasteries, but the monasteries were filled to bursting point, and there was no more space for people to sleep. Some monasteries had been stocked with food in preparation for Buddhist Lent, when resident monks remain inside the compound for three months during the rainy season, but within just a few days, these supplies had been depleted. The monasteries had run out of resources; they were feeding the hungry masses with watered-down rice gruel. In some areas, local authorities were trying to provide assistance but were overwhelmed by the sheer volume of need. A young medical student described how some seven hundred people were camped in and around a single-story school building that had only four bathrooms.

The reports were often confused and sometimes conflicting. One person described conditions in one neighborhood as under control; minutes later another person describing the same area said that the situation was deteriorating by the hour. The emergency specialists suggested that people take photographs wherever they went and mark down the time, date, and location so that they could monitor whether conditions were getting better or worse. The team leader had a reassuringly calm manner and offered plenty of easy-to-follow practical advice. Most heads in the room were bowed over notebooks as people scribbled down his five-point checklist for assessing a disaster. He explained that the quality and quantity of the following necessities (listed in order of importance) were essential to survival:

1. Drinking water
2. Food
3. Shelter
4. Sanitation
5. Medicine and medical treatment

It sounded quite simple, but it was critical knowledge for first-time aid workers volunteering in extreme circumstances and it illustrated just how inexperienced they were in dealing with an emergency situation. I jotted it all down, just in case:

- If there is no clean drinking water, carry purifying tablets or, in a worst-case scenario, use drops of iodine (five drops per quart).
- People will also need something to hold the water—make sure to have a good supply of jerricans.
- Remember that any kind of relief supplied should be complete. There is no point in giving rice if people don't have a pot to cook it in. There is no point in giving pots if they don't have matches to light a fire. Matches or a lighter are useless if people don't have access to tinder.

The morning was wearing on and the hall began to heat up. A strong smell of onions permeated the room, coming from the sacks of produce that had been stacked against the walls. The audience became ever more restless; the foot tapping had increased, and every so often someone pushed back his chair and crept out into the yard, lured by the noise of activity outside as trucks were packed with commodities and students were chosen to accompany the vehicles. By the time the emergency team broached the topic of sanitation, the crowd had dwindled to about ten people, and the noise outside had reached a distracting crescendo of urgent voices and revving truck engines.

As the audience dispersed, the Israeli team talked to individuals who approached them with specific questions. The doctor offered to look at photographs of wounds and advise young medical students present on how to treat them and what medicines would be useful to carry. I picked up snippets from disparate conversations taking place around the yard; topics under discussion included the disposal of dead bodies using powdered lime, the cooking time required for lentils, and how to diagnose the first symptoms of gangrene.

I chatted with a member of the emergency team who was morosely chain-smoking cigarettes. He explained that he was accomplished in search and rescue and could save people's lives underwater, high on mountaintops, or wherever they might be in danger. Stuck here in Rangoon far from the scene of the emergency, he was not getting his adrenaline fix.

"This is not how I like to operate," he said. "I do not want to be sitting here giving lectures. I want to be out there. I need action!" It was a sentiment that was shared by many foreigners itching to get into the field. Organizations like Médecins Sans Frontières and Save the Children were sending out teams of local staff but, because of the government's restrictions on the movement of foreigners, the more experienced international staff had to stay in Rangoon coordinating efforts from a distance. As one aid worker aptly put it, they had been forced into conducting an emergency operation by remote control.

I saw aid workers unable to get to the places where they were needed, killing time around the city. When I went to meet a friend at Monsoon, one of a handful of fancy restaurants in Rangoon, the place was packed. Monsoon is an elegant luncheon spot set in a row of renovated shophouses. Black ceiling fans swirl the air-conditioned air, and the menu offers Asian favorites made palatable for the Western palate, from *pad thai* to *nasi goreng*. At one table a group of Red Cross workers, wearing the fire-engine-red vests that identify them in the field, lingered over a lunch of many courses. At another table I recognized some UN staff clinking beer glasses. It was not exactly where I had expected to see aid workers during an emergency operation. But this, clearly, was not your average emergency.

Even before Cyclone Nargis, the UN and NGOs operated under tight constraints in Burma. In addition to curtailed movement, there were limitations on what kind of programs could be conducted, and the authorities insisted on vetting and monitoring all proposed activities. In recent years there had been clashes between the regime and various aid organizations. In 2005, the regime decided to appoint its own representatives to observe International Committee of the Red Cross meetings with Burmese prisoners. As the ICRC upholds a policy of total confidentiality during its discussions with inmates, it has therefore been prevented from monitoring Burmese prisons since the end of 2005. In the same year, the Global Fund to Fight AIDS, Tuberculosis, and Malaria pulled out after promising more than US$98 million for disease control; the fund stated that its ability to manage programs was compromised by the ever-tightening travel restraints on international aid workers.

When viewed in the light of the country's extreme poverty, these controversies were tragic. UN reports show that more than 30 percent of children under the age of five are malnourished, and that Burma is the only country in the world where beriberi, cased by vitamin deficiency, still kills infants. The government's will and ability to provide social services has been severely diminished over decades of military rule, and it has the lowest government health spending worldwide, with reportedly a meager 0.3 percent of the gross domestic product allocated to public health care.

Yet, due largely to the difficulty of working with the dictatorship, Burma receives far less international assistance than other countries in the region. The United Nations Development Programme recorded that people in Burma received just under US$3 worth of aid per year per capita—a shockingly low amount, especially when compared to the $38 per person received in Cambodia and $49 in neighboring Laos.

Aid workers responding to Cyclone Nargis who were not among the few international NGOs registered with and approved by the Burmese government had to keep a low profile and cover their tracks. At a hotel business center, I listened to a Western man talking on a long-distance telephone line about how many blankets and tents he had been able to send down to "the special place." Though he had obviously been organizing aid deliveries, he never used the words "cyclone" or "delta" and must have been concerned that the phone line was being tapped.

Back at the school, the nervous energy spinning around the yard had been ratcheted up a few more notches. Rumors were spreading that the regime's restrictions on the movement of foreigners would soon be extended to Burmese people as well. Already there were reports of trucks being stopped and soldiers at checkpoints taking down the ID numbers of anyone going to the delta. Though they had no assurance that vehicles carrying aid would even be allowed to leave the city, the students carried on loading food and supplies onto trucks as fast as they could.

THERE WERE NO soldiers on the streets of Rangoon. With four to five hundred thousand troops, the regime has a huge source of able-bodied men at its disposal; why were they not more visible in the city, clearing roads, restoring electricity and phone lines, or unclogging sewage pipes?

The first soldiers I saw involved in the post-cyclone mop-up were a ragtag band wandering around the smart Golden Valley neighborhood, where houses set in large gardens are laid out along winding lanes. The area used to be shaded by trees, but the cyclone had stripped away the greenery and left the homes bare and exposed. The air smelled of freshly hewn wood and rotting vegetation, like a damp forest floor.

I had been in the neighborhood dropping off medicine and money for Rosalind Maung, a retired teacher of English literature who had helped me research George Orwell's influence in Burma for my previous book. She was showing me the trees in her garden that had been up-rooted or snapped by the storm (a mango tree planted by her grand-mother, two hefty tamarind trees she and her brothers had played under as children). The gang of soldiers came up to her property and began banging rhythmically on the iron gate. I looked through the bars of the fence and saw that their uniforms were stained and tattered. One carried a rusty scythe and another gripped a wood-handled machete. Rosalind reluctantly walked over to the gate to speak with them. It transpired that they were mercenaries of a sort, going door-to-door offering their ser-vices for hire to chop logs and dispose of trees that had been felled by the cyclone. Rosalind declined the offer. As soon as the soldiers walked on and began rattling her neighbor's gate, she went into her house and brought out a padlock that she used to lock her gate from the inside. You can never be too sure, she explained, when Burmese soldiers are wander-ing around the city carrying weapons and offering help.

According to the state media, soldiers and policemen were being deployed throughout Rangoon and the delta to clear up the storm dam-age. But only very occasionally was there any evidence of these activities and, even then, they were never very industrious or effective. I saw a team of policemen tasked with cleaning up a park who were doing little more than leaning against piles of logs, smoking and joking. Four of the policemen were asleep on the ground, their bodies limp beneath the diminished shade offered by one of the few trees still standing. I wondered why they seemed so unconcerned about being reprimanded for their inaction, but then I realized that they had no tools. The team of twenty or so men had only one ax to chop the fallen logs and branches of an entire park.

Not long after that I saw a truck filled with soldiers driving down Bogyoke Aung San Road, one of the main streets in downtown Rangoon. The street is where the city's most famous market for dry goods is located. Built during British times, the market has a high, gracefully arched roof, and it is still encircled by cobblestone streets. The goods on sale are considered high-end commodities; stalls sell jade, jewelry, fabrics, imported cosmetics, and velvet slippers. Across the street from the market there is a row of colonial shop-houses that must once have been a prestigious place to live, but years of neglect have taken their toll. Mold has stained the stucco façades and fluted Corinthian columns, and the fretwork balconies of the upper stories are knotted with weeds. Farther along the street are two of the city's most modern structures, Traders Hotel and Sakura Tower. With twenty-plus floors, these buildings are skyscrapers by Burmese standards, and they tower above everything else in downtown Rangoon.

The soldiers were packed into an open truck and looked at their surroundings as if they were seeing them for the first time. They had probably been transported from some distant provincial outpost to do manual labor, and this may well have been their first trip to the historic city that was once the capital of Burma. They seemed excited to be in the city, about to undertake a heroic task in the wake of disaster, and many of them hung over the sides of the truck waving at pedestrians.

No one waved back. Indeed, the response was so stony it was as if there had been some prearranged agreement for all passersby to ignore the soldiers. As I watched the enthusiastic young men drive by, I felt strangely sorry for them.

In the immediate aftermath of the cyclone, it was not soldiers who were to be seen in the streets. Instead, people saw their neighbors and monks from nearby monasteries as locals rallied together to repair their own communities. Civilians had done the best they could with household tools, piling up the debris and sawing larger trees into small pieces that could be lifted off the roads. No one in Rangoon had bothered to wait for soldiers; they knew better than to expect help from the regime.

At any rate, some of the soldiers may have been occupied with other tasks. One battalion had apparently been dispatched to the Shwedagon Pagoda. Considered to be the holiest site of Buddhist pilgrimage in Burma, the Shwedagon is usually open by four in the morning so that worshippers may climb the steps to the marble platform around the golden pagoda before dawn. In the days following the storm, however, the Shwedagon was closed to the public. The shopkeepers who sell religious wares—gilded Buddha images, laminated photographs of holy sites, fresh flowers, candles, incense—from stalls along the stairwells were prevented from entering. Soldiers stood guard at each of the four entry gates around the pagoda.

This story was just another Rangoon rumor, impossible to verify, but most people were convinced it was true and speculated that it must have had something to do with the jewels. At the very top of every pagoda in Burma is a conical structure known as a *hti*, or umbrella. The *hti* is traditionally draped with gems and serves as a crown for the pagoda structure. At nearly seventeen feet high, the *hti* at the top of the Shwedagon is an elaborate construction of multiple tiers, plated with gold and silver and hung with donations of personal jewelry. The structure reportedly holds some 83,850 pieces. Among the treasures are rings embedded with clusters of sapphires and diamonds, ruby-studded earrings made of precious metals, and prayers minutely etched in antique Pali script onto paper-thin sheets of gold. At the very pinnacle of the *hti* is a golden globe encrusted with 4,351 diamonds and topped by a single 76-carat diamond the size of a mandarin orange. It is an ostentatious and seemingly careless display of devotion; imagine the crown jewels of England strung together, hoisted up the steeple of Westminster Abbey, and allowed to twirl in the breeze above London.

Gazing up at the Shwedagon, it looked—amazingly—as if the *hti* had not been affected by Cyclone Nargis. Perhaps to quell suspicions, the *New Light of Myanmar* even ran an article describing how a survey team used Japanese technology to ensure that the *hti* had not been tilted and remained intact. But the shopkeepers who work in the stairwells of the pagoda said that many jewels had been shaken loose by the cyclone and that emeralds, rubies, diamonds, and sapphires were scattered across the gardens like fallen fruit.

Along with the general public, the ruling generals had also donated valuables for the *hti*. There is immense spiritual and symbolic significance in placing personal items at the highest point of the country's most revered Buddhist site. The jewels are valuable in monetary as well as spiritual terms, and so it was said that the generals ordered their soldiers to retrieve the missing treasures. Each three-man team was composed of men from different battalions so that they would not be tempted to pocket any of their findings, as they would not know if they could trust their team members not to report them.

It was a sad but not implausible answer the question of the soldiers' whereabouts. While Rangoon struggled to overcome the battering it had received from Cyclone Nargis, and unimaginable miseries were unfolding in the delta, some of the soldiers had been sent to collect gems for the generals in the gardens of the Shwedagon Pagoda.

TWO

Over a fortnight had passed by the time the country's leader, Senior General Than Shwe, publicly acknowledged that a massive natural disaster had taken place in Burma. Than Shwe had sent felicitations to Israel for Independence Day and to King Harald V on Norway's National Day. He had also remembered to convey a message of congratulations to the newly appointed Russian president, yet he had had no words for his own countrymen during this time of crisis. He and his wife had cast their votes in public on the morning of the referendum, which was held as scheduled on May 10 in parts of the country not affected by the cyclone. But it was not until May 18, sixteen days after Cyclone Nargis, that Than Shwe found time to inspect the emergency operation.

Than Shwe is a famously reclusive leader. He is never interviewed by journalists and rarely appears in public. Even the sound of his voice is unknown to most people, as recordings are prohibited; if he makes a speech at a live gathering, it will later appear in written form in the newspapers or recited verbatim by a news anchor on television. But even these speeches are few and far between, and on the rare occasion when the senior general deigns to appear in public, the event is a carefully scripted affair.

Than Shwe's first appearance after Nargis began with him posing awkwardly at a relief camp in Dagon on the outskirts of Rangoon. The pictures were on the front page of the *New Light of Myanmar* the next day. Donations had been arranged in front of him like offerings at a pagoda; there were neatly stacked cooking pots, biscuits from China, bottles of orange soda, and platters of fresh fruit. Than Shwe walked along a row of blue tents, each one shaped like a house, complete with mock framed windows. The inhabitants of each tent stood to attention at the doorway, holding their hands together in front of their chests in a respectful position of prayer. "Senior General Than Shwe comforts storm victims," claimed the captions, but Than Shwe clearly hadn't memorized his lines or concentrated during the rehearsals, because his efforts at providing comfort looked most unconvincing. In one scene, a retinue of uniformed generals stood behind him looking on as he stretched out a stiff hand toward a baby. Most of the survivors appeared immobilized in his presence and stared straight ahead, as if they had been turned to stone.

It was hard to know what had triggered this belated and clumsy attempt at public relations. It may have been that the Chinese government provided a helpful lesson after being widely praised in the international media for its fast and efficient work in assisting victims of the Sichuan earthquake that struck on May 12, shortly after Cyclone Nargis hit Burma. One week after the earthquake a three-day period of mourning was declared in China, and the flag was flown at half-mast in memory of the tens of thousands who had been killed. The very next day the Burmese government copied the gesture by lowering flags and announcing its own three days of mourning.

I followed the Than Shwe Disaster Tour in the *New Light of Myanmar* as it unfolded across the delta throughout the rest of the week. At each stop Than Shwe provided what the newspaper referred to as "necessary guidance" for the government's rehabilitation plans. He met the minister who had been put in charge of each delta township and inspected repair work conducted by selected companies known to be cronies of the regime. When Than Shwe arrived in Kunyangon, a township south of Rangoon, the minister for energy, Brigadier General Lun Thi, briefed him on the progress being made and listed the hospitals, schools, and government buildings already being repaired (courtesy of Asia World Co.). Farther along in the delta, at Pyapon, the senior general was briefed by the minister for hotels and tourism, Major General Soe Naing, and listened to similar tales of progress and reconstruction (courtesy of Dagon International Ltd. and Yuzana Co., among others). It didn't matter where Than Shwe went in the delta, the script was always the same, and the model camps looked identical.

As I read the papers each day, I found little in the repetitive coverage that looked like anything other than theatrical performance. Nothing about the senior general's tour had the ring of truth. The tents in the camps were too well appointed and the survivors too well dressed. There was none of the deprivation I had seen in Chit Swe's film, and I was quite sure that the route the general had traveled had been cleared of any remaining corpses or people begging along the roadside. This may go some way toward explaining Than Shwe's extended absence after such a cataclysmic natural disaster. He couldn't have gone to the delta any earlier because the authorities there had been unprepared for a visit from the country's leader; in the widespread havoc caused by Nargis, it took some time to make things presentable by erecting the necessary stage set and casting the required extras.

Urgently Needed: Fifty families (preferably with young children) and fifty tents (preferably new and matching) for one-week tour of the Irrawaddy Delta.

THE MONSOONS ARRIVED early in Burma, and by mid-May it was raining heavily every day. The storms were sudden and incredibly heavy. Umbrellas buckled under the daily downpours, and the roads of downtown Rangoon were transformed into dark, sludgy canals. Some parts of the city remained persistently flooded, and stones or planks were placed in areas where the water was too deep to wade through or too wide to jump across. Even when it wasn't raining, water dripped incessantly off the plants and the eaves around the house where I was staying. Inside, the air was as hot and humid as in a greenhouse. The moisture in the atmosphere seeped into everything; the sheets on my bed felt slightly damp and the pages of my notebooks curled up at the corners.

One afternoon I was caught in a rainstorm while walking along Maha Bandula Garden Street in downtown Rangoon. The rain came down in such thick torrents that I could barely see across the narrow street and had to duck into a shop for cover. The shop was a general store on the ground floor of a colonial-era shop-house with its front wall open to the street. A single fluorescent bulb dangled from the cobweb-strewn ceiling and shed a sickly light across the interior of the shop and the goods for sale—mosquito coils, packets of roasted nuts, plastic combs. The proprietor sat in the back, obscured by shadows and engrossed in animated conversation with two other men. Though the men sat close together, they had to shout to hear one another above the roar of the storm. When I heard them mentioning the now familiar names of Dedaye, Bogale, and Pyinzalu, I knew they were talking about

Nargis. I had rarely heard these delta townships spoken of before the cyclone, but the names now had a horrible resonance, evoking images of desolation and death.

From my perch on a low wooden stool at the entrance to the shop, I gazed at the solid wall of water gushing down. The street beyond emerged in fleeting snapshots whenever the rain eased momentarily. A car drove at walking pace down the street, the top of its tires only just visible above the flood. A group of drenched pedestrians who had given up the pretense of trying to stay dry waded through the murky water as if they were fording a river. Mostly, though, the streets were deserted, as the rain had driven everyone indoors.

Not long after I sat down the shopkeeper came over to me and, yelling above the noise of the storm, asked where I was from. When he heard I was American, he expressed surprise that I had been allowed into the country at a time like this and hurried to the back of the shop to fetch a digital camera, which he handed to me excitedly. The photograph showing on the screen was of a human corpse lying facedown in a paddy field.

The man told me that he and his friends had been to Kunyangon to hand out rice and cooking oil to cyclone survivors. Pointing at the photograph, he said simply, "The dead are still waiting for peace."

I asked about the living. The shopkeeper grabbed his camera back and clicked through an alarming number of dead-body photographs before coming to a picture that showed crowds of people squatting on either side of a dirt road, holding their hands up toward the camera. "They have nothing. They have no money. They have no shirts. No shoes. Nothing. And there is no help for them. I saw no officials there to assist them. With nothing, how will they survive?" I thought it was a rhetorical question, but the shopkeeper seemed to be waiting for an answer. I couldn't think of a reassuring response; it didn't seem possible that people who had nothing left could survive without help. We sat in silence for a few moments and listened to the rain.

Photographs of dead bodies had become common in the city. Everyone I met who had been to the delta returned with at least one image of a corpse, if not many. When I was watching footage of the delta with Chit Swe and his fellow businessmen who had taken aid down there, they often paused the film on particularly gory images so that we could all take a good leisurely look. There was the body of a child protruding from beneath a dead buffalo; the toddler's tiny feet made the beast on top of it seem abnormally large. There were arms and legs emerging from piles of rubble that had been twisted into impossible positions, and corpses in various stages of decomposition. And there was one particular image that had generated much curiosity: the camera had captured the intact skin of a human hand, complete with fingernails, lying on the riverbank. After some discussion as to how the skin could become detached from flesh and bone, we eventually concluded that bodies floating for long periods in the river become so saturated that the skin must somehow loosen, thereby allowing the casing of a human hand to slip off and end up on a riverbank, like a discarded glove.

At first, I found these images and conversations deeply unsettling. But within just a week or so of arriving in Rangoon, I had seen so many pictures of dead bodies that it was hard to acknowledge each one for the individual tragedy it represented; a father who had left behind a wife and children, or a child whose parents might be praying their firstborn would still be found alive. I was disturbed to notice that I became quite comfortable discussing the details of human decay. I easily flicked through photographs of dead people in the same way I might politely look through an album of someone's holiday snapshots, asking questions and feigning interest but hoping there wouldn't be too many more. Most of my friends in Rangoon felt the same; it was a necessary coping mechanism for processing the relentless horror of the images we looked at each day. And there would be no shortage of dead-body photographs for some time to come. By May 13, eleven days after the storm, the official death toll had risen to more than 31,900, with a further 29,700 missing. There was little doubt in anyone's mind that the numbers would continue to escalate.

Bootleg DVDs featuring the destruction caused by Cyclone Nargis were available at streetside stalls and at traffic intersections, where boys walked between the vehicles stopped at red lights and held the covers up for viewing. Most of the DVDs had simple titles, sometimes written in English (*Cyclone Nargis*, *Nargis*, *Nargis Storm*), though I came across one DVD poetically entitled *Gone with the Wind*. The DVDs were poorly packaged, wrapped in cheap color photocopies of photographs taken in the delta. Almost all the cover shots featured a corpse or two, a sort of gruesome teaser for the dead-body pornography on sale.

There was no voice-over or commentary on the DVDs, and they were often little more than compilations of mismatched footage. Most were filmed from boats sailing through the delta and depicted an unrelenting vista of broken homes and floating corpses. Riddled with waterways, the delta is a low and featureless terrain, and watching these films often felt repetitive: *Haven't we been down this creek already? Wasn't that the dead body that was floating in the bend of the river the boat passed earlier?* The amateur footage was filmed anonymously, probably by people who had taken donations down to survivors. There was also aerial footage that must have been taken by cameramen working for the regime who were allowed onto military helicopters and had later decided to leak their material.

With all other media in the country vetted meticulously, these DVDs were a welcome if dismal dose of reality. There are few other ways for people to get information that hasn't first passed the censors. Many people listen to Burmese-language news broadcasts from radio channels such as the BBC and Voice of America and, in urban areas like Rangoon where there is access to the Internet, people can go to Internet cafés and use specially installed software to get past the regime's firewalls and blocks on news channels. Still, at a time when few reliable reports were emerging from the delta, nothing quite matched the visceral visual content of the DVDs, and the films served an important function by documenting the aftermath of Cyclone Nargis, providing an uncensored record of the full extent of the damage it had caused.

But it turned out that the DVDs were only available for a limited period. One day in mid-May state media announced that foreign news agencies and local "destructive elements" were trying to manipulate public opinion by broadcasting false information. It was an oblique warning, but it was enough; the very next day the DVDs were gone. The boys who sold them at traffic intersections went back to selling garlands of flowers or cigarettes. I went to the movie vendor on a busy market street where I had previously bought copies. His stall was still there, but the only DVDs on display were Chinese and Korean soap operas with Burmese subtitles. I asked if he had any Nargis DVDs left. "DVDs of Nargis?" he asked, laughing loudly. "There are no such things."

It was not at all unusual for the authorities to clamp down on these informally made films. The regime has always had an intense dislike of news outlets it cannot control. During times of political tension when events in Burma make international headlines, warnings are posted in the newspapers ordering people not to believe foreign news sources and not to listen to foreign radio channels that produce what the writers of regime propaganda refer to as a "skyful of lies."

Yet the regime's attempt to cover up the destruction wreaked by Cyclone Nargis was counterproductive. The initial images were a chronicle of nature's fury, not of the regime's misrule or brutality. By banning them and preventing the local press from running photographs deemed to be negative, the authorities were handling the disaster as if it was something that needed to be hidden from public view. As a result of this secrecy, the contraband images served a different function; images of people killed by a natural disaster became atrocity pictures that portrayed the callous neglect of an already vilified regime.

People were afraid that the decaying corpses could spread disease. This is apparently a common and enduring myth in the aftermath of large-scale disasters; though people using water sources contaminated by corpses can contract gastroenteritis, it is generally acknowledged by emergency experts that bodies, especially those killed by sudden trauma, do not cause cholera or typhoid epidemics. The greater concern is the psychological toll for survivors who must live in close proximity to the dead.

There was no widespread, concerted effort by the authorities to collect the corpses or to try to identify them. When a brigadier general was asked what should be done with all the bodies, he allegedly replied that there was no need to do anything: "The fish can eat them," he said.

Back in the store, the shopkeeper who was sitting next to me told me that he did not believe the generals could be real human beings. "How can they witness such suffering and be indifferent to it?" he demanded. His friends had joined us at the front of the shop, and one of them said, "You're right, brother. They are not human. They are devils. Only devils can ignore suffering so great."

The rain continued to pour down, and I had to raise my voice to ask them what they thought about the U.S. government's recent offer to send Navy ships to provide assistance. They were enthusiastic about the idea, and they all agreed that it would even be a good thing if the United States were to invade. Though it was a frequently expressed opinion, I was always slightly incredulous that people would welcome the idea of foreign troops in Burma. "Do you *really* want to be invaded by U.S. soldiers?" I asked. "Surely you don't want Burma to become like Iraq is now . . ."

"It would not be like that here," one of the men replied. "The *Tatmadaw* [Burmese army] are not brave like those Iraqis. They would only have to see one American soldier on Burmese soil and they would run away."

There was much laughter at the idea of Burma's cowardly soldiers being chased by hulking American GIs, and our conversation became almost jolly as we talked about the possibilities of amphibious landing craft off-loading soldiers onto the muddy delta shores and U.S. helicopters air-dropping sacks of rice to hungry villagers. The talk seemed to me to be lighthearted fantasy, but the shopkeeper's eyes had become wet with tears. "You must authorize the invasion," he said to me earnestly, as if I was the admiral of the fleet and it was within my capability to issue such a command.

We stopped speaking for a while and I turned to look at the street. A sodden rat climbed out of the water and into the stairwell of a nearby shop-house, where it sat exhausted and panting. The floodwater had turned an ugly gray color and the consistency had thickened—a sign that the city's sewage pipes were overflowing. As plastic bags and other scraps of rubbish floated past, a fetid, unhealthy smell began to rise from the waters.

THERE IS A BURMESE PHRASE that perfectly describes the contrast between the limited amount of aid being delivered after the cyclone and the enormity of the need: it was like tossing sesame seeds into the mouth of an elephant.

It took the regime almost a week to grant landing permission at

Rangoon airport for planes flying in aid supplies. The first flights that were allowed to land came from nearby Asian countries such as Thailand, China, and India, as well as cargo flights chartered by the UN. A few days later the regime began allowing U.S. Air Force planes carrying relief supplies to land each day but only under the condition that the contents of the C-130 planes were unloaded by the Burmese military and distributed through the authorities.

It was clear to everyone involved that this small number of flights was not nearly enough to ferry in the supplies and logistical support needed to set up and maintain a major emergency operation. By comparison, the relief effort launched within forty-eight hours of the Indian Ocean tsunami in December 2004 involved aid from countries around the world, with more than thirty national militaries dispatching troops and providing helicopters, aircraft, and ships. The U.S. government alone committed eighteen thousand soldiers, sailors, and Air Force personnel. Just a couple of weeks after the tsunami, a fleet of helicopters was flying over 430 sorties a day out of the airport at Banda Aceh, the capital of the worst-hit region of Aceh in Indonesia. In Burma, where it was feared the disaster could be of a comparable scale, there was hardly any activity at the airport, and the regime had so far prohibited the UN from bringing in helicopters to deliver aid.

The limitations were further exacerbated by a lack of speed. It could take an entire day to off-load the few planes able to land, as there was only one forklift available for use at the airport. Security personnel insisted on painstakingly combing through the cargo, filming and noting down exact quantities before letting it pass through customs. And some goods, such as communications and IT equipment flown in for UN agencies to use in the delta, were brazenly confiscated by customs officials.

The *New Light of Myanmar* offered a characteristically faultless version of the goings-on at the airport and documented the arrival of aid in detail. The newspaper ran numerous photographs of planes at the airport with the oft-repeated headline "International Relief Supplies Continue to Arrive." The paper also displayed cargo lists for each craft. One U.S. plane, for instance, flew in 9 tons of relief supplies (including 6,340 bottles of water, 3,150 blankets, and 4,200 mosquito nets). Most of the descriptions ended with an unconvincing final sentence stating that all goods were being "immediately sent to the storm-hit regions."

Few people were taken in by this alternative reality. Foreigners and Burmese alike had little faith that the authorities were able to conduct an adequate emergency operation or handle donated goods in a trustworthy manner. An American working at the U.S. Embassy in Rangoon told me that even the embassy's staff were unsure where the supplies were being taken. "Five C-130s landed yesterday," he said. "Their contents should be loaded onto big trucks, taken down to delta towns, transshipped into smaller trucks or boats, and headed to villages. Instead, they are being loaded onto Burmese military vehicles, and we have no idea where they're going. No one is telling us anything. We're bringing in all this stuff and it's all going into a big black hole."

Theories as to where the aid was ending up abounded. Some thought the goods were being repackaged and sold off as regular commodities at distant markets in places like Mandalay, a day's journey north of Rangoon. Many believed the regime was letting soldiers hand out the aid so that the military could take credit for the donations. It was also suggested that the wives of the ruling generals were out at the airport laying claim to the imported goods, though it was hard to picture the well-heeled women standing on the tarmac picking over stiff blankets and vitamin-fortified biscuits.

Once aid supplies made it past overzealous customs officials and covetous wives, it was still a long and convoluted process to reach survivors. My friend Ko Ye, who had an encyclopedia of stories to share each time I met him, told me about a gem company owner who had raised 40 million *kyat* (around US$40,000) for donations but had been forced to give K10 million to the Rangoon regional commander. The commander promised him that the money would be turned into aid. ("Yeah," smirked Ko Ye. "Aid for his own family.") On his way down to the delta, the donor had to hand over sacks of rice at military checkpoints in order to be allowed past. Disgusted by the soldiers' greed, he eventually gave up and returned to Rangoon.

Donors who did persevere were careful not to channel any donations in cash or kind through the authorities, preferring instead to work with monks and monasteries. Aung Thein Kyaw, the man who had closed down his tour agency to help with the relief effort, described how he had gone to a delta hospital to donate medicines and was told by the nurses to come back at night, because during the day soldiers were often sniffing around for commodities they could sequester. To avoid having large amounts of food snatched by the authorities, one crafty restaurant owner in Rangoon divided her donation of rice and curries into five thousand small bags to hand out to individual recipients.

In addition to hurdles set up by the government, aid agencies also had to deal with the formidable logistical challenges of delivering supplies across a vast flooded area where much of the infrastructure had been damaged or totally destroyed. As there were no roads in the southern stretches of the delta, a significant portion of the deliveries had to be made by boat, but many boats had been sunk or rendered useless during the cyclone. The daily storms also conspired to make water routes dangerous, and there were frequent reports of smaller vessels capsizing due to waves or unpredictable currents. The roads and bridges that did exist before the storm were deteriorating rapidly under the traffic of aid convoys and the constant rain.

I kept thinking back to the shopkeeper's question: *With nothing, how will they survive?*

———

AT A WET MARKET somewhere in Rangoon, a fishmonger reached into a bucket of still-writhing fish. His expert hand moved patiently through the mass of bodies, stroking scales and caressing wriggling bellies. When he found a fish the size and weight he was looking for, he slid his fingers tightly around the tail and lifted it out of the bucket, slapping it onto a wooden chopping block that was already slippery with fish gut and varnished pinkish red with blood.

With well-practiced delicacy and speed, the fishmonger slipped the sharp point of his knife into the fish and cut a fine slit along the silvery underbelly. A fist-sized tangle of innards plopped out onto the chopping block. As he swiped his knife over the pile to scrape the unwanted parts into a waiting bin, he discovered something that should not have been there. Amid the quivering mound of steaming fish gut, he saw a human finger.

This being Rangoon, word spread quickly. *A finger has been found inside a fish.* The fish, people said, was a freshwater fish. It was assumed that it must have come from one of the many waterways coursing through the delta. The fish had probably been swimming along the creeks where thousands of dead bodies were still floating. The bodies were disintegrating in their watery graves, and fish were beginning to nibble on the loosened appendages.

As this story of the human finger found inside the belly of a fish was passed on, it was rapidly transformed from rumor into fact. People stopped buying fish. In restaurants there was uncomfortable laughter when someone suggested ordering fish; most people shook their heads emphatically. People also abstained from eating crabs, lobsters, or prawns—it became another much-touted fact, a fact that everyone seemed to have always known, that crustaceans feast on the flesh of the dead.

And the dead were now everywhere. They had found their way out of the delta and into the city.

AS THE STRANGLEHOLD on news was drawn ever tighter, it became increasingly tricky to sort fact from fiction. Every day I heard unverifiable tales that began, in my mind, to take on the elements of myth.

In the hard-hit township of Kunyangon, just a few hours from the city, thousands of angry women had surrounded a police station demanding that the officers cowering inside release food and shelter supplies they had stolen from donors.

A relief boat carrying cyclone survivors from their destroyed village to the safety of a larger town was caught in a monsoon storm. The boat sank and five hundred people drowned, or fifty, or five—depending on which version was being told.

A Bengal tiger was captured prowling along the banks of Kandawgyi Lake in Rangoon, searching for prey. Animal cages at Rangoon's zoo had been ripped apart when the cyclone raged through the city, and some of the animals had escaped. People kept spotting monkeys scampering across the road or dangling playfully from lampposts.

Perhaps none of these stories was true; perhaps all of them were. In the hothouse environment of Rangoon, where the truth was malleable and facts and figures could be plucked out of thin air, anything seemed possible. As there are so few reliable sources of news in Burma, rumors take on an added significance and act as a barometer of people's hopes and fears. What becomes important in this context is not whether they are true but whether people believe them to be true.

During the chaos immediately after the storm, a handful of gung-ho foreign correspondents were able to get to the delta and file news reports. The authorities, however, had been quick to muster their resources and blockade road and river access. For a short while, a few journalists still managed to slip past them, hidden beneath rice sacks or wrapped in tarpaulin sheets. Some Asian journalists donned Burmese dress and traveled freely past the checkpoints. But within only a week or so, the restrictions on movement were, like the restrictions on news and information, firmly in place.

I met a British journalist in Rangoon filing for the *Daily Telegraph* who told me he had tried every way possible to get down to the delta and had been rebuffed at every turn. He was halted at roadblocks and prevented from boarding passenger ferries. And he had not been able to hire a Burmese fixer to arrange transport for him no matter how much money he offered—the job had become too dangerous. Traveling to the cyclone-torn areas with an aid organization was also out of the question, as aid groups were not willing to risk what little access they had negotiated for themselves. In the end, the journalist had resorted to reporting on Cyclone Nargis from his hotel. He was staying at a prominent business hotel in Rangoon where some UN agencies are headquartered. "There's a lot of aid agencies working out of the hotel, so I can pretty much cover the story from there, and in considerable comfort," he cheerfully admitted.

A number of foreign journalists had been caught by the authorities and deported. Teza Oo, a Burmese writer who also acted as a fixer for visiting foreign correspondents and was used to working undercover, had a close call while assisting some French reporters. Leaving Rangoon at

3:00 A.M. to avoid checkpoints, he had taken the reporters to the delta town of Bogale but was stopped by a soldier as soon as they reached the town. The soldier took the Frenchmen's names and passport details and ordered them to return to the city. When Teza Oo went to meet the reporters at their hotel that same evening, he saw them in the lobby being questioned by a group of Burmese men he did not recognize; though they wore plain clothes, he knew instinctively that they were government spies. The soldier in Bogale must have filed the newsmen's details with his commanding officers, and from there it was a simple step for the authorities to check hotel registration lists and confirm where they were staying. Luckily for Teza Oo, the soldier had been focused on the foreigners and had neglected to note down his identity. To avoid seeming suspicious to any curious onlookers in the lobby, he went up to the front desk and made a mundane inquiry about room rates before quickly leaving the hotel.

"It's of absolute importance to me that this story stays in the international news, so that we can keep the pressure up on the generals," Teza Oo said, clearly frustrated that he was no longer able to play his part in making that happen. "I feel it's my duty to help document these events and get the information out of the country but, at the end of the day, I must also think of my family and keep them safe."

Without being able to go to the delta, foreign journalists had to rely on secondary sources. A friend from Bangkok, who was in Rangoon filing for a daily in Europe, regularly did the rounds at NGO offices and UN agencies, but she still wasn't able to gather many concrete answers. I accompanied her one day when she went to meet a spokeswoman for ECHO, the European Commission's Humanitarian Aid office. The European Commission has a small office in the unlikely setting of the Kandawgyi Palace Hotel, a fanciful construction of intricately carved teak roofs set in a small jungle alongside the lake. The offices are located in several hotel guest rooms where the beds have been removed and replaced with office furniture. We were ushered into a guest-room-turned-meeting-room by a spokeswoman who seemed harried and overloaded. "To be quite frank, we haven't been able to get an overview of the situation and assess what the needs are," she told us. "It is becoming more and more difficult for our staff to get down to the delta. We have the staff here [in Rangoon]. We have a rapid response coordinator, a water sanitation expert, a doctor, but we can't get them down there."

The only way to accumulate information was to collate impressions from, say, a private donor who had traveled to Dedaye, a doctor returning from helping out at a clinic in Myaungmya, or an aid worker who had been able to travel south of Laputta and conduct an informal assessment. "It is like a jigsaw puzzle," said the ECHO spokeswoman. "We are just trying to put the pieces together."

Survivors in the delta had been moving away from devastated hamlets and villages and into larger towns, migrating to places where food and shelter might be available. In the towns, people were crowding into monasteries, schools, or camps set up by the Burmese government. There, they were being assisted by the local authorities, UN agencies, and NGOs, all trying to provide enough aid for a population that appeared to be growing larger each day.

It was still not possible to accurately gauge how many people were in need of assistance. In front of Save the Children's headquarters, I saw a whiteboard that was regularly updated with the latest estimates. Over two weeks after the storm, the following figures were scrawled on the board:

Affected: High 2.5 million—Low 1.5 million
Dead, Missing: High 182,000—Low 60,000

Estimates of how many people had been reached by then with some kind of assistance averaged out at around one-third of those in need, but I never met anyone who could explain how this fraction was calculated (especially when the variable was as high as one million people) or, indeed, what "reached" actually meant. And I continued to hear that there were areas, particularly in the southernmost parts of the delta, that had not been reached at all—places from which no news had yet been received.

I began to wonder if there was anyone in Burma who had any real idea as to what was happening beyond Rangoon. Everyone, it seemed, was lost in the fog of a mass unknowing.

Everyone, that is, except for the regime.

The authorities churned out statistics that were suspiciously precise. On May 17, the *New Light of Myanmar* ran a small article tucked away at the bottom of page six, entitled "Latest Casualty Figures." The article listed the official death toll to date, stating that 77,738 people had died, 55,917 people were missing, and 19,359 people had been injured. It was another staggering leap in the official number of casualties; the dead and missing combined now amounted to more than 133,600.

No one seemed to know how these figures were being sourced. A Burmese researcher, who was experienced at sifting through dubious government sources in search of concrete information, explained that the numbers were probably an estimate drawn from existing government population figures for each village and township that had been in the path of the cyclone. As the last census was conducted in 1983, the numbers were out-of-date and the resulting figure was likely to be grossly inaccurate.

A few days later, diplomats and aid agency representatives were invited to a presentation on the government's relief and rehabilitation program. They were told that 76.28 percent of telephone lines had been restored in Rangoon and that running water was now being supplied to 98.5 percent of the municipal area. The authorities had also put together a PowerPoint presentation detailing losses incurred due to the cyclone and cataloging with remarkable precision the number of farm animals killed (the casualties reportedly included 136,804 buffalo and 1,250,194 chickens).

Though these numbers may have been estimates based on farm animals registered before the cyclone, they were obviously fictitious—no one could have possibly been around the entire delta counting and confirming the death of each missing chicken. While the rest of us patched together disparate eyewitness reports and scrambled around after intangible facts, the generals were producing solid answers. The image they were trying to portray seemed to be one of omniscience and supreme power: the regime knows *everything*, even that which is, ultimately, unknowable.

OUT ON THE ANDAMAN SEA, not far off the coast of Burma, the warships were gathering. The U.S. government had mobilized four ships from the USS *Essex* Amphibious Ready Group that had been in the region for Cobra Gold joint task force exercises with the Thai military. Since May 13, these huge vessels had been positioned offshore in preparation to assist the relief effort. Though they were there on a humanitarian mission, they were equipped for combat. One of the ships, the USS *Mustin*, was a guided missile destroyer. According to a Navy press release, the fleet boasted four amphibious landing craft that could operate in areas inaccessible by road, twenty-two helicopters, and more than five thousand U.S. military personnel.

The United Kingdom and France had also redirected craft toward

Burma. The UK had sent the British frigate HMS *Westminster*, and France was moving the amphibious assault ship the *Mistral*. Moored in international waters, this impressive fleet of ships was not visible from land, but there could be little doubt that they were out there. The U.S. Navy released photographs of exercises being conducted on the Andaman Sea. One photo showed a Seahawk helicopter, part of the Helicopter Sea Combat Squadron 25, transporting pallets of supplies between ships. In another photo, a landing craft shot out from the well deck of the USS *Harpers Ferry* in a burst of sea spray.

From the perspective of Burma's ruling generals, the display of benevolent force assumed a somewhat less benevolent air in the light of debates taking place in the international arena. Though France's foreign minister, Bernard Kouchner, had not been able to convince the UN Security Council to adopt the principle of responsibility to protect and deliver aid to Burma by force, the idea lingered in mainstream debate. The responsibility to protect was reduced to a jaunty acronym, R2P, which seemed somehow out of sync with the enormity of the action itself. "Is It Time to Invade Burma?" asked an article in *Time* magazine. A former United Nations emergency relief coordinator, Jan Egeland, was quoted in the piece as saying, "We're in 2008, not 1908. A lot is at stake here. If we let them get away with murder we may set a very dangerous precedent."

Egeland went on to recommend options other than armed force, such as freezing the assets of the generals and issuing warrants for their arrest that would come into effect if they left Burma. But the bellicose tone of Kouchner's initial call for a moral crusade that would storm the shores of Burma and rescue the people from their own government continued to resonate.

The idea that an invasion could be imminent took hold in Rangoon. In addition to the tea-shop chatter about the pros and cons of such an eventuality, a leaflet circulated advising people what to do if they encountered enemy forces. Beneath a picture of a tank with civilians standing nearby was a large red X and a caption that read, "Do Not Go Near." In the next picture the figures were standing at a safe distance from the tank, and beneath them was a blue check mark with the caption, "Stay Far Away." This commonsense message was probably borrowed from old combat pamphlets but was now being sent around anonymously.

The barely contained sense of panic that was ever present in Rangoon during the first few weeks following the storm was rising. As I was leaving the house of a Burmese friend one afternoon, an elderly man approached me. A dirty bandage was wrapped around a wound on his arm, and he looked disoriented, lurching around as if he had forgotten how to walk. He stretched his wounded arm toward me and croaked, "Nargis! Nargis!" My friend stepped between us and shooed him away angrily. "He's not real," she said in quirky English. "You must not trust anyone in these days."

There were reports of looting, murder, and violence. A man killed a noodle vendor who made *monhinga*, the popular Burmese noodle soup, for the thin gold chain around her neck. To protect against looters, a friend's family buried what valuables they had in their garden and armed themselves with machetes. In Hlaingtharya, a poor neighborhood on the outskirts of the city, a group of women stabbed a township officer with their kitchen knives when he tried to stop donors from handing out food. At Pyapon in the delta, a laborer who was helping to unload donations off a truck was trampled to death by a hungry mob. In some parts of the delta, donors were afraid to stop their cars for fear of being attacked, so they were throwing food and donations out of the car windows.

It was thought that mass riots would break out soon as tempers rose toward a boiling point. Driving past the Ministry of Mines one afternoon, I noticed truckloads of the dreaded *Lon-Htein* riot police parked in the compound, in readiness for any upheavals on the streets.

Back at the house, I took to double-checking the locks each night. Sometimes I would get up in the middle of the night to make sure the catches on the windows had been secured. I wasn't afraid of anything specific; it was more a vague foreboding that lurked just beyond the reaches of my comprehension. "Don't you think something is going to explode soon?" asked an American expatriate friend who had lived in Rangoon for some years. "I can't sleep at night because I lie in bed waiting for it to happen."

My friend was right. The violence, the pamphlets, the ships moored out on the Andaman Sea, it all seemed to add to an inescapable feeling that something was about to happen. It was like the high pressure that builds up in the atmosphere before a monsoon storm, when the air becomes too thick to breathe and everyone waits impatiently for the first drops of rain to alleviate the tension. People in the city were over-excitable and agitated, myself included; we were talking too fast and fidgeting compulsively as we waited for the storm to break above our heads.

THREE

I was at the office of a Burmese weekly journal when the big breakthrough
was announced. The offices had access to CNN via a satellite dish,
and as soon as Burma was mentioned with a "Breaking News" tagline
flashing across the bottom of the screen, the journalists gathered around
the small television. The news item concerned a landmark meeting
between United Nations Secretary-General Ban Ki-moon and Burma's
Senior General Than Shwe. Having repeatedly ignored the secretary-
general's overtures since Cyclone Nargis, Than Shwe had unexpectedly
acquiesced to granting him an audience.

When Ban Ki-moon arrived in Burma on May 22, it was a historic
moment: he was the first UN secretary-general to visit the country in
forty-four years (the last one being U Thant, who was Burmese). But
few people in Burma had high hopes for the visit. All previous attempts
by the UN to mediate with the generals of Burma on various issues had
failed miserably.

The first UN special rapporteur on human rights, Yozo Yokota, resigned in 1996, stating that he did not have the resources to fulfill his mandate of conducting fact-finding missions and making recommendations on the situation in Burma. Three years later, Alvaro de Soto, a UN special envoy to Burma charged with facilitating dialogue between the regime and other political organizations, also resigned, having been unable to bring about any positive development. The second special rapporteur, Rajsoomer Lallah, quit in 2000—he was never even allowed into the country. And, in 2006, Razali Ismail, a special envoy of the secretary-general, also resigned after being refused entry to Burma for nearly two years.

The next appointed special rapporteur, Paulo Sérgio Pinheiro, cut short a visit to Burma when he found a listening device taped under the table while he was conducting a government-arranged interview with a political prisoner. Most recently, the Nigerian UN undersecretary-general, Ibrahim Gambari, who made numerous trips to Burma, consistently failed in his attempts to convince the generals to start a dialogue with Aung San Suu Kyi—she remained under house arrest, forcibly isolated from politics and prohibited from communicating with her party members and the general public.

In the light of Burma's flagrant disregard for the values of the United Nations as well as its envoys, it was doubtful that the meeting would result in any significant achievement.

Ban Ki-moon flew to the new capital of Naypyidaw to meet Than Shwe on the morning of May 23. Burmese state media showed the two men seated stiffly in a spacious reception hall, both dwarfed by their splendidly carved oversized chairs. A Burmese interpreter was hunched over on a low stool between them. The UN representatives sat in a row on one side of the hall, with thick files and notebooks perched on their laps and leather satchels at their feet. Opposite them, across a wide expanse of highly polished parquet flooring, sat Burma's top-ranking generals, dressed in full uniform and bedecked with medals. It hardly seemed a setting conducive to honest negotiation and compromise.

So I was amazed to watch the CNN news anchor announce that the meeting had resulted in a concession from the junta to allow "all aid workers" into the country, regardless of nationality. The announcement was billed as a "major breakthrough," but no one standing around the television with me seemed at all excited. The assembled journalists shuffled back to their desks without comment when the next news segment came on. Min Lwin, the editor of the weekly, with whom I had been discussing events, was skeptical of the announcement but grateful to the UN and foreign governments for trying. He saw the continued presence of the U.S., French, and British navy ships, and the arrival of Ban Ki-moon, as part of a connected strategy. "It seems they may be using a stick and carrot approach," he said. "The ships offshore are the stick and Ban Ki-moon, well, I guess he's the carrot."

The announcement was ambiguous to say the least. What exactly did it mean to "allow all aid workers" in? Allow them to go where? And to do what? There were optimists who interpreted it as the beginning of something much bigger; the hermetic regime's first tentative steps to open up to the outside world. But most people treated it with suspicion, or even downright contempt. "The announcement was a lie," said a Burmese businessman who had frequent transactions with the regime. "Our senior general, he is lying all the time, every day, so it is not a big thing for him to lie to the secretary-general of the United Nations."

After the announcement I visited a Christian preacher who was rallying his Rangoon congregation for cyclone relief activities in the delta. He gave me his judgment in a slow, sermonizing manner, his voice growing louder with each sentence. "Before the Second World War, the British prime minister went to see Hitler and came back saying he was a man that spoke of peace," he began. "This is the same situation we see before us now. At worst this is a program of extermination. At best, it is absolute incompetence conducted under the banner of evil." His voice was operatic in volume when he spoke of the promises being made by the generals: "Their words are sweet as butter, but war is in their hearts."

Included in Ban Ki-moon's trip to Burma was a whistle-stop tour of the delta; he and his entourage were flown across the affected areas in two Mi-17 helicopters. He visited a camp of cyclone survivors who lived in the same blue tents featured on Than Shwe's Disaster Tour. Some said the tents were actually empty before the secretary-general arrived; people could not stay in the camp all the time, as it had to be kept clean and tidy for VIP viewings. Whenever a high-ranking general or foreign diplomat was scheduled to visit, survivors were brought in to sit in the tents and put under strict instructions to say they had received more than enough aid and assistance, thank you very much.

While there was no way to prove exactly how these show camps functioned, there was much evidence to suggest that this was not far from the truth. Ko Ye, the Rangoon publisher, had been talking to an abbot who had five hundred people sheltering at his monastery on the outskirts of Rangoon. Soldiers came to the monastery one day, herded the people onto trucks, and drove off to an unknown destination. "And you know where they turned up?" asked Ko Ye, unable to conceal his dismayed delight with the answer: "Standing in front of a row of little blue tents just in time for a visit from a VIP!" According to Ko Ye, the camp was later emptied, but the survivors were not allowed to return to the monastery where they had been sheltering.

Also tagged onto Ban Ki-moon's itinerary was a visit to the Shwedagon Pagoda and the nearby tomb of the late UN secretary-general U Thant. The latter is a forlorn and neglected memorial that is usually padlocked shut. A few days earlier I had seen a team of municipal cleaners hurriedly raking the cyclone debris of rubbish, leaves, and broken branches from around the tomb to spruce it up in time for the secretary-general to pay respects to his predecessor.

Events over the next few days indicated that the agreement Ban Ki-moon had elicited from Than Shwe wasn't much of a breakthrough after all. On May 24, the final stage of the referendum was held in the cyclone-affected regions of Rangoon and the delta. When Ban Ki-moon and the UN had called on the regime to concentrate on the relief effort rather than the referendum back in early May, the plea had gone unheeded. It was yet another diplomatic snub that the regime chose to conduct the final stages of the much criticized referendum while Ban Ki-moon was visiting the country.

Few people I knew in Burma took the referendum seriously. It was ostensibly being held so that citizens could accept or reject the recently completed constitution—a process that had begun in 1993 and taken fourteen long years to finish. During that time, the constitution had earned little credibility. The 702 delegates responsible for drafting it were mostly handpicked by the regime, and Aung San Suu Kyi's party, the National League for Democracy, which had won the 1990 elections, walked out of the proceedings early on. Written into the final draft were a number of foolproof mechanisms for the military to maintain power: 25 percent of the seats in Parliament, for instance, are guaranteed to military officers, and any amendments will require a parliamentary majority of more than 75 percent, thereby ensuring that the military contingent can veto any proposed changes.

Most people voting in the referendum had not even seen the draft constitution (published as a 194-page book available for purchase) and probably had very little interest in, or understanding of, its contents. Everyone knew they were supposed to vote yes. The authorities issued an edict forbidding criticism of the new constitution and government media ran encouraging slogans: "To approve the State Constitution is a national duty of the entire people today. Let us all cast 'Yes' vote[s] in the national interest."

Though all my Burmese friends recognized the futility of the process, they were divided on whether to vote. "My wife and I will vote no," said the editor of the news weekly, Min Lwin. "We understand that it won't make any difference, of course, but it is our right, and we feel we must exercise that right." Others did not want to draw attention to themselves by voting no. A young teacher who gave private tutorial classes from his cramped downtown apartment told me he didn't see the point in voting against the constitution: "They've already won. If I vote no they can find out who I am—I'm not going to risk that for no purpose."

By the time the second part of the referendum was held, the rest of the vote had already been counted, resulting in a landslide affirmation; according to state media, 92.4 percent had voted in favor of the new constitution. Even so, the authorities were determined to garner the same positive results from the remainder of the population.

People in the delta were afraid to vote no as they were worried that further aid would be withheld. Survivors staying at one monastery were told by local authorities that if they voted yes they would be allowed to stay on, but if their vote was negative they would be sent back to their villages.

In Rangoon, various tactics were used to ensure the referendum endorsed the regime. In some neighborhoods, votes were collected in advance. I was introduced to a young musician in his early twenties who was keen to cast his no ballot, as it would have been his first ever vote. He told me that local officials visited his house while he was out and collected yes votes from his mother and sister. And while they were there they bullied his mother into ticking yes on his ballot as well. The authorities also found creative ways to coax positive votes out of those who managed to get to the ballot stations. A young woman I met who worked as a cleaner for a friend was warned that she would have to pay K160,000 (around US$160—an unaffordable amount for most ordinary Burmese) if she chose to vote against the constitution. You're free to tick the no box if you want to, they told her. We'll just come to your house later to collect the money. But if you decide to vote yes, you won't have to pay anything—it's up to you.

Meanwhile, aid workers waiting in Bangkok for entry visas to Burma planned to test Ban Ki-moon's big breakthrough the following Monday morning. But the Burmese embassy turned out to be closed that Monday after a fire broke out in the compound. That a fire should close the embassy right after the announcement was made seemed an extraordinary coincidence, and many people thought it had been started on purpose. Though there was no proof of these accusations, the mystery of the fire was never solved. When Thai police offered their assistance in finding out what caused the fire and who was responsible, they were apparently told that it was an internal matter that could be handled by embassy staff.

As if to confirm its belligerent stance, the regime announced that the second part of the referendum had resulted in an even higher yes vote than the first, with 92.93 percent of votes counted in favor of the new constitution. A few days later, the constitution was duly ratified and promulgated—an act that the regime claims renders the 1990 election victory of the National League for Democracy null and void, thus confirming the generals as the country's legitimate rulers.

Around that time, Aung San Suu Kyi received a visit from a government official informing her that her detention would be extended for another year. Her latest period under continued house arrest had begun in 2003 under the State Protection Act, a law to "safeguard the State against the dangers of those desiring to cause subversive acts." As the law allows for a maximum detention period of five years, keeping her under house arrest was patently illegal. No reason was given for the extension, and it was viewed as yet another sign that there was no softening behind the scenes in Naypyidaw.

The endgame was playing out just as the preacher had suggested; the words uttered by the generals implied one thing, but their intentions were turning out to be something else entirely.

SHORTLY AFTER THE CYCLONE, the United Nations and international NGOs working in Burma had instigated a "cluster" approach of pooling information to oversee the emergency operation. The cluster system, a relatively new tool in the humanitarian-response kit box, allows organizations working in similar fields to have regular meetings to discuss and coordinate their approaches. There are clusters for each of the various sectors involved, such as food, shelter, logistics, and water and sanitation. In Rangoon, cluster meetings were held at the Chatrium, a hotel located just a short walk from the main UN compound. Every so often, when I tired of traipsing in circles around the city, I would pick a random cluster meeting and slip in as unobtrusively as possible to soak up the air-conditioning and glean an inside perspective on how the relief effort was progressing.

The first cluster I attended was an agricultural one held toward the end of May, which, unexpectedly, turned out to be rather a lively and heated affair. The cluster was led by the UN's Food and Agriculture Organization, and the meeting I went to was chaired by two men from FAO: a burly South African and a German wearing aviator glasses and a neatly pressed slate-gray safari suit. The aim of the meeting was to co-ordinate the operation of all the groups involved in agriculture. The FAO began by introducing its team of imported experts, who were qualified in the various fields of farming, fisheries, livestock rearing, and veterinary science. The rest of the participants, seated around a satin-skirted meeting table, were representatives of other UN agencies and international NGOs, who were either already working in Burma or were among the limited number of aid workers able to obtain visas after Cyclone Nargis.

First on the agenda: the availability of seed for planting rice in the delta. Stocks from the first crop of the year had been rendered inedible, as rice warehouses were flooded or had collapsed during the cyclone. Farmers in the region generally plant two rice crops a year and, to avoid longer-term repercussions and possible famine, it was essential that they should be able to plant the year's second and final crop. As seed stocks and much of the equipment used for planting and harvesting were destroyed by the cyclone, the job of those assisting in the agriculture sector was to make sure that farmers had what they needed to begin replanting. The FAO spokesmen said they had been working on finding out precisely what kind of seed was available. While they expressed satisfaction that there was enough seed in-country, there was some confusion as to how to assess the exact quantity and quality of the seed and how to get it to farmers in the delta. Unable to provide any finer details, they resorted to a much repeated phrase: "At the moment, it is still unclear."

There were sighs of frustration around the table. A few people rolled their eyes with undisguised impatience. A man sitting next to me began doodling compulsively on his program sheet.

Representatives at the meeting quickly agreed that whatever the condition of the seed, time was of the essence and tried to establish what date the seeds needed to be planted by and how long the window of opportunity would last. Again, there were no straightforward answers. No one, at least no one in the room, had been able to establish the cutoff date for planting a second crop. I wondered why they didn't just ask a farmer, but I must have been oversimplifying the matter, as the conundrum generated considerable debate around the table and the German FAO representative often began his sentences with phrases that implied only a seasoned expert could ever get to the bottom of the matter: "Looking at the problem agri-ecologically . . ." he would say ponderously.

The issue of seed and replanting totally unresolved, the meeting moved on to another item on the agenda: the emergency Flash Appeal. A flash appeal is an overview of immediate needs and requirements compiled by the UN and NGOs to justify the release of funds for use during the first six months of an emergency operation. The FAO was responsible for compiling the agricultural sector's overview for the flash appeal and asked participants at the meeting for any useful information that should be included. The meeting coordinators explained that they had been severely hampered, as they were not allowed to do the kind of assessments they would normally do and were working with inaccurate secondhand information. At the very least, they seemed to know what they *didn't* know. "We have a clear view of areas we have *not* assessed," said the German in the aviator glasses, going on to list the townships from which he had no data: Kunyangon, Dedeye, Wakema, Maw-lamyainggyun (shortened by the cluster participants to the more easily pronounced *Maw-gyun*), Bogale, south Laputta . . . Bewildered looks were cast across the meeting table—the list seemed to encompass almost the entire delta.

My neighbor's doodling picked up pace. Though I had no other clusters to compare it to then, it looked as if the meeting was not going to be a roaring success, and the conversation implied that even those employed to conduct the emergency operation were clueless as to what was happening in the delta.

At one point, however, someone from the United Nations Development Programme listed UNDP agricultural activities being undertaken in cyclone-hit areas, such as the provision of seed, pesticide, basic equipment, and livestock. As soon as he began speaking, it became clear that he had in his possession some actual facts about the delta. The FAO reps were visibly irritated on learning of this hitherto withheld data. "We need all the information you have," snapped the German coordinator. "This is not for FAO or for UNDP. This is for the country!"

Still rattled when he made his closing remarks reiterating the need for data for the flash appeal, the coordinator concluded with a curt command: "We need information in detail. You have until the end of the week. I don't want any surprises."

Like a naughty schoolboy, the doodling man next to me had scribbled on his notepad, in large letters, "WOOHOO," and was busying himself with adding a constellation of exclamation marks.

One of the key aims of the cluster meetings following Cyclone Nargis was to establish which areas had been reached with assistance and which had not, thereby preventing any gaps or overlaps in the delivery of food, shelter, and other relief materials. The system had met with varied results and, especially outside the UN, the effectiveness of the cluster system was hotly debated. There was tension between the UN and international NGOs, as NGO staff complained that UN agencies used the clusters to exert control over the entire humanitarian community. Some NGOs refused to attend on principle. An American woman, who runs her own charity in Burma, was vociferous about the "five-hundred-dollar-a-day so-called experts who have never set foot in Southeast Asia, let alone Burma" and said that attending cluster meetings was a waste of her taxi money. Another American succinctly referred to them as "clusterfucks."

Local Burmese NGOs initially were left out of the cluster equation; many did not attend because they were not contacted or because of the language barrier. Representatives of the Burmese government were also absent. It is usually expected that government staff attend the clusters in order to help extend coordination efforts. During the first few weeks after the cyclone, no one from the Burmese government came regularly to the cluster meetings, at least not in an official capacity.

"Oh, god, those meetings are so depressing!" sighed a European doctor who had been working for a charitable organization in Burma for many years. "They are all so concerned about 'overlap.' Let me tell you, in this country, this is not a problem. Just start walking from here and go north, go south, go east, go west. I don't care which direction you go, you will not find any overlap." We were chatting over beers one evening at an outdoor bar, and he puffed on a cigar-sized cheroot, reflective for a moment, before bursting out with a final thought on the matter: "And you know what? If you *do* find overlap, then you're happy! You're shit happy! Because it's almost impossible to find anyone getting any kind of help here!"

From the doctor's perspective, the hours spent debating the pros and cons of various approaches and mapping out areas of overlap and underlap could be better spent just getting things done. "It's not rocket science," he said, leaning in close, as if divulging a great secret. "These people in the delta have been through a major natural disaster. What do they need? They need food, water, and shelter. So just give them that!"

The agriculture cluster I attended closed on what seemed like a sour note as the coordinators asked, "Any other business?"

A woman from Save the Children introduced herself, saying that she was in Burma for the first time, had just arrived the previous day, and was seeking sources of information. "I really need some stats on livelihoods in the delta," she said. "Does anyone here know where can I access the data?"

The meeting participants turned to the top of the table, looking to the FAO reps to answer the question. Being well-established in Burma, the organization must have had the information but, if it did exist, the file on delta farmers and fishermen appeared to have been marked classified.

One of the FAO men said that they were not able to release any data on the topic yet, as they were obliged to have it cleared by HQ in Rome and their regional office in Bangkok.

More sighs rippled around the table, and I got the sense that everyone left the meeting feeling a bit flat. Luckily, the hotel staff had organized a little pick-me-up out in the marble-floored foyer. As the attendees sipped warm cups of tea or coffee and munched their way through a buffet of finger sandwiches and cream cakes, the mood appeared to lift slightly.

THERE IS AN archaic type of prophecy in Burma known as *dabaung*. Passed on by word of mouth and spoken in poetic form, *dabaung* are said to arise spontaneously from the population. One that surfaced after Cyclone Nargis gave an accurate reading of commonly felt but otherwise unexpressed emotions. The *dabaung* was easy to recite, even in my stilted Burmese, and I found myself repeating it often, like a nursery rhyme I couldn't shake out of my head:

> *Mandalay pya pone,*
> *Yangon thit pone,*
> *Naypyidaw ayo pone.*

Or, in English:

> *In Mandalay, a pile of ashes*

[frequent fires have razed whole neighborhoods in the parched city],

> *In Rangoon, a pile of wood*

[the cyclone uprooted hundreds of trees],

In Naypyidaw, a pile of bones

[the prophecy that the new capital will one day be filled with bones, presumably those of the ruling generals].

When I happened to recite the *dabaung* to a Burmese academic connected to Rangoon University who often helped me with my research, he told me that there could be some truth in the prediction. His colleagues had been involved in a seismological survey conducted together with Chinese specialists and had found that there was a fault line running directly through Naypyidaw.

Whatever the seismological readings, the *dabaung* was also like an expression of collective wishful thinking; with no public outlet for frustration against the regime, dissent was manifesting itself in whispered rhymes.

A WEEK HAD PASSED since Ban Ki-moon's announcement and the atmosphere in Burma was darkening.

The U.S. ships left the coast during the first few days of June, having waited there for three weeks. The commander of the U.S. Pacific Command, Admiral Timothy J. Keating, said in a press release, "We have made at least 15 attempts to convince the Burmese government to allow our ships, helicopters, and landing craft to provide additional disaster relief for the people of Burma, but they have refused us each and every time. It is time for the USS *Essex* group to move on to its next mission." The British and French ships left too. The *Mistral* had sailed to Phuket in Thailand to off-load its cargo of humanitarian relief goods for transshipment to Burma, where UN agencies would take responsibility for getting it to the cyclone zone.

While there had been some improvement, concessions made by the regime were niggardly and not at all in keeping with the expansive promise that "all aid workers" would be allowed into the country. Visas were being granted, but the process was slow and the visas were for ridiculously short periods of time, with many aid workers arriving in Burma on three-, five-, or seven-day visas. Only a very small number of aid agency staff in Rangoon had been able to get to the delta, and the access they achieved initially was severely limited. Once they had gone through the laborious process of applying for travel permission to leave Rangoon, many were only allowed to make one-day trips and had to be back in the city by nightfall. Each foreign aid worker who went to the delta at that time had to be accompanied by a government liaison officer, who, as one Italian UN worker told me, wrote down *everything*: "I swear he even marked down in his little notebook each time I smoked a cigarette!"

With the majority of international aid workers trapped in Rangoon, the rumors that travel restrictions would be extended to Burmese people were validated by various actions taken by the authorities in the delta. Soldiers at checkpoints started handing out a leaflet stating that it was time to wrap up efforts to help storm victims, as the relief phase of the operation was over and rehabilitation had begun. The text told donors to stop giving aid to people sitting by the road, claiming that they were not real storm victims and had only gathered at the roadside to receive free handouts. From now on, those who wanted to help should contact the Disaster Management Committee in the relevant townships. It seemed a polite enough note, but it was accompanied by increasingly harsh vigilance. Cars and trucks carrying aid were frequently impounded and their contents confiscated. In one instance, a convoy of twenty trucks was stopped on its way back to Rangoon; the drivers were arrested and kept in jail overnight.

In the last week of May it came to light that the government was resettling people in the delta. Camps set up in and around the main delta towns were closed down. Schools and monasteries where storm survivors had taken shelter were forcibly emptied. Survivors were loaded onto boats and ferried back to the destroyed villages they had recently escaped from. In some areas the clearances happened quickly; as the emergency phase was now officially over, the authorities wanted people back in their villages by June 2, when the next school term was scheduled to begin. But survivors had no idea what they were returning to; was there even anything left at the places they had once called home? And how would they get food and water there?

In Rangoon, four hundred Christian villagers from the ethnic Karen group in the delta who had been sheltering in a Baptist church compound at Insein in the northern part of the city were unceremoniously evicted in the middle of the night. Only a few sick people and one heavily pregnant woman were allowed to stay on at the church.

Unable to prevent these forced resettlements, aid organizations operational in the delta assembled supplies, so that returnees would have at least a few days' worth of food and water, and some materials with which to build a shelter.

The students at the private school I had visited, who were still energetically delivering aid, went to a camp where they had been making regular deliveries only to find that it no longer existed. The camp, located by a road on the outskirts of Rangoon, had vanished, along with the two hundred families who had been sheltering there. After making discreet inquiries, the students learned that township authorities had ordered the people to return home. But their homes had been ruined by the cyclone and they had nowhere to go. The students found a small group hiding out in a nearby grove of trees and gave them tarpaulin so they could construct new shelters, but when they returned the next day with additional supplies, they discovered that the authorities had taken the tarpaulin. "What are we supposed to do?" asked the enraged teacher who had been supervising the students. "Do we give them more? If we do, won't they just take it again? We may as well just give it directly to the township officers!"

One of the students had dared to ask a township officer why the relief camps were being disbanded so soon. The officer replied that staying in a camp was like living in a hotel, as the people had breakfast, lunch, and dinner served to them. He explained that the authorities were concerned that people would grow used to this decadent lifestyle and become too lazy to work for a living.

This sentiment was echoed in the *New Light of Myanmar*, which ran an article about how storm victims were surviving perfectly well without help from the outside world. "Myanmar people are capable enough of rising from such natural disasters even if they are not provided with international assistance," the article stated. "Maybe they need temporarily instant noodle and biscuit packets. However, [they] can easily get fish for dishes by just fishing in the fields and ditches. . . . In the early monsoon, large edible frogs are abundant." The article concluded that people in the Irrawaddy Delta could survive "even if they are not given chocolate bars from the international community."

On June 4, the popular comedian Zargana was arrested. Since the cyclone, Zargana had managed to build up a team of over four hundred volunteers to deliver aid to scores of villages across the delta. He had talked openly with the international media, criticizing both the government for its negligence and the United Nations for pandering to the generals and not taking a more hard-line approach with the regime. When asked whether people in the delta were surviving without chocolate by catching fish and frogs to eat as suggested by the *New Light of Myanmar*, he replied, "We renamed the Irrawaddy River and Bogale River by the color of the water. The rivers are a chalky white color. We call it the Nargis color. There are many dead bodies and cadavers of cattle floating in the rivers. We call that the Nargis odor. The odor sticks with us when we come back from the villages. Nobody can stand it, and [it] causes some people to vomit. How could people find edible fish and frogs in that environment?"

While it was unclear what crime Zargana would be charged with, his arrest, combined with the random impounding of vehicles at delta checkpoints, was enough to make other donors nervous, and the number of private citizens taking supplies down to the delta began to dwindle. Rangoon took on the feeling of a city under siege. It was as if an invisible wall had been built around the city and we were all trapped within its boundaries, unable to get over it or see beyond it.

Each morning I woke up to the sound of crows cawing in the garden. With so many trees felled by the cyclone, the crows could find nowhere to settle, and they flitted restlessly around the cloudy skies, perching for a precarious moment or two on the battered branches of the few remaining trees. Their insistent cries were maddening to listen to, and I often went out to feed them the remains of my breakfast. When I threw slices of mango and crumbled toast onto the grass, the crows swarmed around me, forming a panicky black cloud of flapping wings and snapping beaks.

MY BURMESE VISA was about to expire. Almost four weeks had passed since I had arrived, and I would soon have to leave the country. It would be just over a month before I was able to return and gain access to the delta, but at the time, tired of chasing information that wasn't available and asking questions that had no satisfactory answers, I was ready to leave.

By then, most of the international media attention had died away. Headlines that once featured Burma had been replaced by other more topical events elsewhere around the globe. The outrage expressed by world leaders, United Nations officials, and NGO representatives had been quelled or simply run out of steam. Either way, it seemed to me that righteous moral indignation had been traded in for a shoddy compromise with the regime. The generals, I decided, were smarter than they were given credit for. They had pacified angry and powerful critics across the world with an empty promise and were staving off further criticism from aid agencies in Burma with continued assurances of a few more entry visas and a little more access. It was a tried-and-tested method that the generals had used before in times of crisis, and it boiled down to a simple strategy: toss out some concessionary crumbs to appease foreign detractors, hunker down, and wait for the storm to blow over. As a U.S. diplomat I spoke with said, "They know they have a six-to-nine-month window after they've promised something for the international community to realize that they didn't deliver."

Meanwile the emergency operation was limping along at a snail's pace. The UN's Office for the Coordination of Humanitarian Affairs stated, "[P]reliminary estimates indicate that 1.3 million beneficiaries, out of the estimated 2.4 million people affected [by Cyclone Nargis], have been reached with some assistance." In other words, one long month after the cyclone, help had gotten to only just over half the people who needed it. OCHA went on to clarify that most of those 1.3 million had "received very basic assistance, which is inadequate and below minimum requirements" and that "a large number of villages have not received any support from the UN, international NGOs, or the Red Cross."

The Burmese state media stuck doggedly to its version of the truth. Highlights from the relief effort could be seen on television accompanied by a soundtrack of rousing martial music. Bottles of drinking water were handed along a human chain of strong-armed soldiers. Cooked rice was scooped out of steaming vats by motherly women and ladled with generous helpings of curry. Doctors operated in well-equipped, tented theaters. Nurses bandaged scrapes and administered pills. Men in smart business suits handed checks worth millions of *kyat* to smiling generals. The mood conveyed was one of happy and productive activity, of hard times overcome thanks to the government's heroic contributions.

In the never-never land of the regime's imagination, survivors of the storm suffered no trauma and felt no grief at having lost family members, homes, and livelihoods. Relieved to be so warmly looked after by their benevolent leaders, they sat smiling obediently amid mountains of Mama noodles and brightly colored plastic buckets.

A FEW DAYS BEFORE I departed from Rangoon, I dropped in on an emergency-shelter cluster meeting By then the cluster system had expanded and become more official, with microphones for participants and government representatives in attendance. The aim of the meeting was to ensure that shelter materials were being properly and comprehensively distributed, and the meeting opened with a short speech delivered by the deputy director of the international relations department of the Ministry of Social Welfare, Relief and Resettlement. He expressed his pleasure that coordination among all the agencies and the government was going so well and said that, due to the rainy season, shelter was of the utmost importance. "My specific data is that shelter is not enough," he said in hesitant English. "We would like to request the need for shelter. Today it is a priority."

A staff member of the International Federation of Red Cross and Red Crescent Societies was chairing the meeting, and he said he needed answers to the following questions: Who has done what? Where are the gaps? Who should be doing what? The IFRC handed out basic forms to the agencies involved in delivering shelter, so that they could list what resources they had available and how much they were planning to supply. There was a distinct weariness in the IFRC man's voice as he reiterated, "Please try to be exact. Write down the number of shelter kits you have delivered and what is in those kits."

Shelter kits distributed during emergencies, I had learned, were available in varying calibers. At the top of the range were those supplied by the UK charity ShelterBox. The ShelterBox concept is to supply survivors with a fully stocked box containing everything a person trying to survive after a disaster might require. Typical contents include: a ten-man tent (plus blankets or mosquito netting), a multi-fuel stove (complete with pans and utensils), working tools (such as a hammer, an ax, and a saw), and even a few treats for children (drawing books and crayons). But, with just over two thousand ShelterBox kits delivered in Burma, it was really only the luckiest survivors in the delta who received one. Standard kits were more economical and provided only the bare essentials: a sheet of tarpaulin, a rope, and a leaflet on how to tie tarpaulin to bamboo poles.

The IFRC lead also tried to establish geographical areas of operation—who was working where? "The longer you delay in giving us information on where you are working, the more we will end up with overlaps and areas without [shelter]," he said. "If you're planning to work in an area, you need to tell us." Few people responded, and it seemed that most attendees had come to the meeting to gather information rather than share it. Or it may have been that the unnerving presence of the government representative contributed to their laconic attitude.

There were, however, some offerings of information. Smaller clusters were being organized in delta towns where aid agencies had been able to set up delivery hubs and temporary offices operated by Burmese staff, and focal points were established for each town. Two organizations announced their involvement in body collection with a recently arrived Australian specialist offering his chilling expertise to anyone who might need it: "I personally have extensive experience on body collection and mass disposal."

"AOB?" asked the tired lead.

A man from the World Society for the Protection of Animals piped up with a winning grin, "This really is *Any Other Business*, but . . ." There were sniggers around the room in expectation, perhaps, of a pitch to supply cyclone-affected poodles with an adequate supply of chew toys and flea powder. The WSPA representative asked if anyone had heard of people bringing companion animals with them to the camps, as had happened after Hurricane Katrina in the United States, and whether any support was required for livestock in the delta.

The meeting coordinator, keen to wrap things up, directed him to the UN's Food and Agriculture Organization and offered a slight variant on the usual response to any requests for information: "We are not at the stage where we have a view on that."

The meeting ended with the same sense of dissatisfaction that tainted most of the cluster meetings I had attended. Nothing much seemed to have changed; critical questions remained unanswered; and, though progress was being made, it was still nebulous and agonizingly slow.

After his opening words, the deputy director from the Ministry of Social Welfare had remained mostly silent throughout the meeting. He didn't stick around for the finger sandwiches and tea that were on offer outside the meeting room but strode off in a hurry, swinging his brief-case manically, as if he was late, very late, for another very important meeting. As I watched him rush away, I noticed that the briefcase looked incredibly light and wondered idly if it might actually be empty.

PART TWO

NO BAD NEWS FOR
THE KING

NOVEMBER 2005

It is just before midnight and the Shwedagon Pagoda has been surrounded by heavily armed soldiers. A military convoy is approaching the southern entrance. At the center of the cavalcade is a black limousine with darkened windows. When the limousine pulls up in front of the giant stone lions that stand guard at the pagoda's entrance, an aide rushes up to open the passenger door. A short, elderly woman steps out of the vehicle and the soldiers salute smartly, clicking their heels together in unison.

The woman is dressed in rich attire, with a traditional Burmese sarong of shimmering silk and a jade-green chiffon scarf floating lightly upon her sloping shoulders. She wears emerald earrings, as large as sugar cubes, that shine with an otherworldly, iridescent glow.

As the woman waits at the foot of the stairwell leading up to the pagoda, a group of soldiers brings forward two big cages, each cloaked with a velvet cloth. The woman starts to climb the stairs and motions wordlessly for the soldiers to follow her.

The stairway is long and empty, and the woman tires frequently. A soldier walks ahead of her carrying a cushioned chair so that she can sit down to rest. Whenever she pauses in her ascent, a younger woman waves a fan around her face and dabs her sweat-damp forehead with a white lace handkerchief. Every so often the humid silence of the stairwell is broken by a loud grunt and the sound of hurried, heavy breathing coming from beneath the velvet cover of one of the cages.

At the top of the stairs the pagoda is ringed with a battalion of soldiers standing as motionless as statues amid the myriad shrines on the outer edges of the platform. In the shadows beneath the multi-tiered roofs of the meditation chambers and prayer halls, it is just possible to make out sculptures of miniature wizards, writhing serpents, and mythical beasts that are half lion, half man.

Here, before the pagoda, the two cages are uncovered and opened. A handsome white dog bounds out of one cage and is sharply restrained by a soldier. More grunts issue from the other cage, and it takes some time for the soldiers to drag out a very large, very reluctant pig. A gold cord is tied around each animal's neck and handed to the woman.

Leading the dog by one hand and the pig by the other, the woman begins to walk counterclockwise around the Shwedagon Pagoda. The platform is still slick from the afternoon rains and the old woman walks unsteadily. Spot-lit in the floodlights that illuminate the great golden pagoda, her thickly powdered face looks pale and worn. She appears to be mumbling to herself, praying perhaps. The night is almost impossibly still, and the only other audible sound is the rhythmic click-clack of the pig's trotters on the marble tiles of the pagoda platform.

FOUR

The Burmese regime has always been inscrutable. Outsiders are not welcomed within its ranks. Its archives are closed to the public, and few bona fide biographical details about its members have ever been released. Years of isolation have kept the generals obscured behind a smoke screen of propaganda, artifice, and rumor.

Ever since I first began traveling to Burma in the mid-1990s, I have been intrigued by the elusive military junta. The confused attempts to negotiate with the generals in the wake of Cyclone Nargis were proof that few people in the international community had any real understanding of Burma's rulers or indeed any idea of how best to communicate with them. Some years before the cyclone I met a Burmese man whose family was closely connected with the military and asked him how best to learn more about the country's ruling generals. He quickly corrected me. "First of all, it's not general*s*," he said, turning the final s into a remonstrative hiss. "It's just one general. To understand the regime, you need to understand only one man—Senior General Than Shwe.

What we have here in Burma is a classic textbook case of totalitarian dictatorship."

It was an opinion I had heard repeated in many of the conversations I had had with Burmese people about the regime—that the man who has ruled Burma for almost two decades has become the sole source of power within the military's increasingly centralized command structure, in the same way as his predecessor, the late dictator general Ne Win, had done. Unlike dictators such as Mao, Stalin, or Kim Il Sung, who headed personality cults that projected their godlike status, Than Shwe has stayed mostly behind the scenes and prefers to manipulate events in the style of a Machiavellian puppet master who remains—for the duration of the show—hidden from view.

As nothing about Than Shwe can be published independently in Burma, his life story is only told there orally and can only be chronicled by media outside the country. In these forums, Than Shwe is mostly portrayed as the quintessential mad dictator—secretive, superstitious, temperamental, vehemently xenophobic, and possibly mentally unhinged. He flies into a rage at the mere mention of Aung San Suu Kyi's name and is dependent on fortune-tellers and black-magic practitioners for advice on matters of state. A football fan and Manchester United supporter, he stays up late into the night watching matches broadcast live from England. It is also said that he fosters a fanatical obsession with Chinese martial-arts dramas—the kind set in ancient dynastic kingdoms that feature valiant heroes and fiendish villains able to fly through the air and knock down their foes with a well-aimed kung-fu chop.

But these details are all hearsay, and may be overblown. A foreign politician who met Than Shwe during a regional meeting of Asian leaders told me that Burma's feared and tenacious strongman was distinctly *un*charismatic in person. At the meeting, Than Shwe came across as an insipid man who spoke in a monotone, showed no emotion, and made no eye contact with other participants.

With only a handful of unsubstantiated facts available in the public realm, it is almost impossible to say anything for certain about Than Shwe. The senior general is a myth partly of his own making; by revealing only carefully chosen aspects of his life and character, he leaves the rest to guesswork and repeatedly confounds analysis.

In 2005, Than Shwe surprised the entire population of Burma, as well as Burma watchers abroad, when he suddenly moved the country's capital city from Rangoon to an undeveloped plot some two hundred miles to the north. The relocation, which began at 6:37 A.M. on November 6 (a time probably deemed auspicious by regime astrologers), was alarmingly unanticipated. Plans to relocate the capital had been kept well under wraps, and it was not until the day *after* the move had begun that the regime held one of its rare press conferences to explain what had happened. Even then, government representatives were tight-lipped. The minister of information, Brigadier General Kyaw Hsan, had little information to offer other than the fact that certain government ministries were moving to a new administrative center. The only reason given for the apparently sudden decision was that government operations would run more smoothly if some ministries were moved to a more strategic location.

News of the move came as a shock even to the civil servants involved. The moving date was set for a Sunday, and government employees from the first group of ministries scheduled for relocation were informed about their imminent departure on the Friday, just two days before it happened. They were ordered to leave their families behind in Rangoon, as the new administrative center was still poorly equipped for habitation. Basic amenities such as electricity and running water were not yet functioning properly. And, upon arrival, most government staff had to sleep in their ministry offices as the residential quarters were still being built; senior staff slept on desks while their subordinates camped out on the floor.

Some months later, when civil servants were given permission to bring their families to join them, few leaped at the chance. Schools had yet to be built and there were no fully operational hospitals or clinics. There were also no opportunities to make the extra money they needed to support their families. Salaries in the civil service are so low that many take on extra work: running a video rental library from home; managing a food stall or a tea shop; or selling their government employee gasoline rations on the black market. In the bleak and unfinished city they had moved to there was little hope of earning the necessary funds, as there was not yet any streetside commerce, and there were no shops, markets, or restaurants.

Than Shwe named his new capital "Naypyidaw," or the Royal City (sometimes more poetically translated as the "Abode of Kings"). For the few years after its founding, it remained enshrouded in mystery, and the authorities made it clear that the capital was off-limits. In December 2005, two Burmese journalists were arrested for taking photographs of Naypyidaw while traveling on a bus in the city. They were charged with violating Article 32 (a) of the Television and Video Act, which prohibits filming communication footage without an official license, and sentenced to three years in prison.

I visited Burma around that time and tried to gather impressions of Naypyidaw. The new city was described as a military bunker built on a grand scale. The capital was said to have been constructed for maximum protection, with an extensive system of tunnels driven through the surrounding mountains that could house entire regiments of soldiers. No one was able to say what was hidden behind the walled compounds being constructed around the city; they could have been mansions for the generals or the sites of nuclear reactors.

Though photographing the capital was forbidden, pictures did occasionally circulate. They were mostly blurred images taken surreptitiously from the windows of moving cars. There was an air of unreality about them, as they often included images reflected by the car window—a camera lens, a bottle of water, a human arm. I saw photographs of construction sites above which human fingers grasped at clouds in the sky and uninhabited buildings bore the ghostly imprint of a wristwatch.

While friends in Rangoon told their usual dark jokes, laughing at the irrational and inexplicable relocation of the capital city, there was a nervous edge to their good humor: *Has the government abandoned Rangoon for good? Who can know for sure what they will do when there are no more civil servants or military personnel resident in the former capital? They could cut off all the electricity, sever the phone lines, or maybe they are planning to poison the water supply . . .*

Most people saw the founding of Naypyidaw as a worrying sign that an already isolated regime was choosing to quarantine itself even further. Government staff working and living at least a day's journey away from Rangoon, where embassies and UN missions were based, would have even less contact with representatives of the international community. During the first few days after the move, bewildered foreign diplomats expressed their concern about maintaining contact with members of the Burmese government. The regime's response was to provide them with a single fax number. Sequestered in their newly constructed fortress, Than Shwe and his government were obviously not in the slightest bit concerned about staying in touch.

DURING A TRIP to Rangoon not long after the government relocated to Naypyidaw, I visited the one place in Burma where the regime puts itself on display. Located in central Rangoon, the Defense Services

Museum is a hulking four-story structure designed to glorify the might and absolute power of Burma's rulers, or the *Tatmadaw*, as the armed forces are known in Burmese. Anyone can go there, even foreigners, provided they write down their name and passport number in a ledger, relinquish their camera, and pay the three-dollar entrance fee.

Though I went to the museum on a Saturday afternoon, I had the dubious privilege of being the only visitor. No one had bothered to turn on the lights in many of the cavernous rooms, and the museum felt half closed. The soldiers in charge of the exhibitions were dressed casually, with most wearing just a green army singlet and a well-worn *longyi*. It was a hot and muggy day, and they lazed around in the gloom of their unvisited exhibits, dozing or gazing listlessly at the ceiling. The empty hallways were so quiet that whenever one of them coughed, the sound seemed to echo through the entire complex.

The museum boasted separate wings for the army, navy, and air force, with exhibition rooms for individual units such as the signal corps or the armory. Each government ministry was represented, as were many municipal divisions and cultural assets. But, for all its efforts to impress with size and scope, the museum's displays had the show-and-tell feel of a school classroom. Store mannequins were lined up in a static fashion show of army uniforms. Miniature battlefields had been clumsily replicated from sheets of felt and plastic toy trees. The progress of the mighty *Tatmadaw* was detailed with pie charts and graphs made from colored sticky tape and painted cardboard cutouts.

Amid all the bric-a-brac there was, however, one unifying image: that of the commander in chief of the *Tatmadaw* and the country's leader, Senior General Than Shwe. The general's face is not so ubiquitous elsewhere in Burma; he does not appear on billboards or banknotes and his portrait generally hangs only in schools and other government buildings. Yet, inside the military's museum, his surly mug shot was everywhere.

High on the wall of the lofty entrance, Than Shwe's photograph crowned the pyramid of ruling generals. Throughout the museum there were posters with his larger-than-life form superimposed onto collages of newly constructed dams, airports, and schools. There was even a formal painted portrait of the senior general in full ceremonial dress. The artist had been kind to the aging general; his face was not quite so jowly as it is in photographs and his stocky frame seemed a tad leaner. The pale uniform he wore was studded with medals and topped off by five golden stars on each shoulder, identifying him as the commander in chief of the army and the country's absolute ruler.

According to official sources, Than Shwe was born in 1933, when Burma was still under British colonial rule. His family lived in the village of Myinzu near Kyaukse town on the arid central plains just south of the old royal capital of Mandalay. He was not yet ten years old when Burma became a bloody battleground during World War II. The young Than Shwe would have witnessed the clumsy British retreat from invading Japanese forces. As the remnants of the colonial government fled overland to India, they practiced a "scorched earth" policy aimed at burning and destroying anything that might be useful to Japanese troops. The fleeing British Raj left in its wake a smoldering trail of burned bridges, buildings, and oil refineries.

To many Burmese, the triumphant Japanese troops were seen as liberators. The Japanese were fellow Asians and Buddhists, and they brought with them promises of freedom from the white colonial master. When Japanese soldiers marched into Burmese villages they were often welcomed with songs and platters of fresh fruit.

Along with these soldiers came Burma's own homebred heroes in the form of the Burma Independence Army, the first incarnation of today's *Tatmadaw*. The BIA was founded by the intense and determined student leader Aung San (later to become the father of Aung San Suu Kyi) together with twenty-nine other young men who left Burma in 1941 to train with the Japanese military. On Hainan Island in the South China Sea, they studied military and guerrilla tactics designed to enable a core nucleus of men to lead an armed uprising against the British rulers. Known as the "Thirty Comrades," this small band of freedom fighters would become national heroes of their time. After they returned to Burma with the Japanese troops at the end of 1941, their ranks swelled into a ragtag army that numbered in the thousands.

It was a pivotal moment in Burma's history for a young boy to witness. During the final years of the war, the fate of the entire world appeared to rest on the outcome of epic battles being waged on Burmese soil between two imperial armies. Children listened to head-spinning tales of the courage and derring-do of the Thirty Comrades. There were stories about the secret training on a faraway island and about how the comrades had drunk each other's blood while in Siam to pledge undying loyalty to their cause and to one another. The most popular tales were those that told of the many and varied ways in which they vanquished the once invincible British soldiers. I read accounts of the time in which Burmese men of Than Shwe's generation recalled the excitement they felt as they ran out to greet the conquering soldiers. A BIA comrade later wrote about the electrifying effect of seeing Burmese men in military uniforms after long years of humiliating colonial rule: "We ate the food that the villagers offered us, wooed their daughters, brought danger to their doors and [then] took their sons with us."

But the euphoria of freedom was short-lived. The Japanese administration soon took on the traits of an occupying force. While soldiers requisitioned crops and cattle from farmers and slapped people in the face for perceived disrespect and minor misdemeanors, the Kempeitai, the Japanese military police, hunted down British sympathizers. The Thirty Comrades became frustrated. Realizing that the Japanese were not going to grant Burma anything more than a sham independence, they switched allegiance and, by 1944, had joined the underground resistance movement being coordinated by Allied forces. The general population, weary from hunger and humiliation at the hands of Japanese soldiers, enthusiastically supported the resistance. Clandestine meetings were held in safe houses in towns and villages across the country, and leaflets were distributed urging people to "Rise and attack the Fascist Dacoits [armed bandits]!"

When the Allied forces began their campaign to retake Burma in 1944, the country once again became a blood-soaked battleground. Cities were bombed and fierce hand-to-hand combat forced the Japanese southward out of the country. By the time the British government had reestablished its colonial administration in Rangoon in May 1945, the country was in ruins. Roads, railway lines, and bridges had been destroyed by the scorched-earth policy and aggressive bombing campaigns. The population was starving and disease was spreading. In the face of this mass destruction, and after its ignominious defeat by the Japanese, the British government lacked the will to hold on to its Burmese colony. Aung San took the lead role in the negotiations for independence, traveling to London to sign the agreements with Prime Minister Clement Attlee. Final details were ironed out, a date was set, and the country eagerly awaited the day on which it would regain its sovereignty.

But, on July 19, 1947, there was a startling and tragic turn of events. Aung San and most of his newly formed cabinet were gunned down by a rival politician while attending a morning meeting at the Secretariat, the seat of the British government in Rangoon. It was just months before Independence Day, and the man who had been the principal architect of that longed-for freedom was dead at the age of thirty-two. Aung San had attracted a widespread following; ecstatic crowds attended his speeches; and poems and songs were composed in his honor. In death,

he was instantly immortalized, and his framed photograph—often showing the iconic image of him dressed in the broad-collared greatcoat and
peaked cap he wore while visiting chilly London—hung in homes and
government buildings throughout Burma. Reeling from the aftermath
of World War II and the death of Aung San, Burma faced a precarious
future.

In a dimly lit upper story of the Defense Services Museum I came
across two cabinets that contained relics of that period. In the first was
the British flag that was lowered in the early morning of Independence
Day, January 4, 1948. In the second was the red-and-blue Burmese flag
proudly hoisted into the air that same day. The once bold colors of the
flags had faded to pale pink and watery blue. Hanging limply in the
dusty cabinets, they failed to capture anything of the exhilaration or
terror of those times.

Than Shwe was a teenager during the early years of Burma's independence and would have been fully aware of the tumultuous events he and
his family were living through. The departure of the British administration left behind a power vacuum that was filled with nationwide chaos,
which one historian described as an "orgy of violence." A series of armed
rebellions broke out around the country. The central region of Burma,
where the Burmese ethnic majority live, is surrounded by mountainous
areas that are home to seven major ethnic groups who were given varying
degrees of autonomy when governed by the British. In 1949, the Karen
ethnic group launched an armed struggle against Burmese rule. In the far
south, Mon nationalists took up arms, and in Arakan State, in the northwestern part of the country, an Islamic insurgency was brewing. Meanwhile, the Communist Party of Burma marched off into the forested
mountains and began to wage war against the central government. The
Union of Burma, its borders determined by the departed British government, looked as if it was about to splinter apart.

The nascent Burmese army was tasked with restoring peace. From a military standpoint, the democratic government was proving to be ineffectual. Politicians quarreled among themselves and added to the proliferation of armed and angry young men by supporting militia groups to safeguard their territories. Rangoon was often paralyzed by labor strikes, as civil servants demonstrated for better working conditions. The countryside was lawless, and people were scared to leave urban areas for fear of bandits who held up trains and preyed on lone travelers.

It was against this backdrop of shattered national unity that Than Shwe decided to join the army in the early 1950s, when he was twenty years old. It must have been a difficult decision; the army did not hold the promise of a long and stable career, and enlisting during a time when the country was wracked by civil war was a dangerous choice. Perhaps the upheavals of Than Shwe's childhood—the extreme violence of World War II and the patriotic bravado of the BIA soldiers—had inspired him with heroism. Or perhaps, as most of my Burmese friends suggested, he simply didn't have the skills to do anything else.

The official record states that Than Shwe completed high school but did not attend university, and was working in a post office before he enlisted. I came across a description of what drove young men to join the army in a collection of profiles written by the late Burmese journalist Ludu U Hla. In the 1950s, U Hla recorded an interview with a soldier who had enlisted in the same year as Than Shwe. The soldier had signed up at the suggestion of his friends after they saw a recruitment poster that was part of the army's drive to scour the country for able-bodied men. The poster listed the salary and monetary value of rations, uniform, and equipment that would be issued to each new recruit: "The total seemed an enormous sum to me," the soldier told U Hla. He also spoke of the duty he felt to defend his country. The army attracted young men with the lure of money and the chance to become one of the gun-toting heroes they had seen and heard of during their childhoods.

By the time Than Shwe became a soldier, the Burmese army had wrested back large chunks of territory from the ethnic rebel forces, but there was another even more difficult battle to fight. Of grave concern to the Burmese government was the growing presence of the Kuomintang, Chiang Kai-shek's nationalist army, which had been driven out of China when Mao Tse-tung seized control in 1949. What had started with a few deserters escaping into Burma had grown into an entrenched force of some twelve thousand troops that held sway over substantial areas of Shan State along Burma's northeastern border with China. Fearing a possible Chinese invasion, the government requested help from the United Nations, but the assistance it received was inconsequential, and the *Tatmadaw* had to continue fighting against the encroachers.

The first decade of Than Shwe's military career was one of great growth and change for the army. Having gained in strength and battle experience, the *Tatmadaw* now set about organizing itself into a sustainable military institution. On the orders of the army's commander in chief and former member of the Thirty Comrades, General Ne Win, better training facilities and specialized units were established to train soldiers in areas that ranged from counterinsurgency tactics to intelligence gathering. Officers traveled the world in search of reliable military models, borrowing ideas from the great military academies of Sandhurst in the United Kingdom, West Point in the United States, and Dehradun in India.

Than Shwe soon joined one of these newly established units, the Directorate of Psychological Warfare, or "Psywar," the aim of which was to enable the military to adopt political tactics. Psywar operations involved the production and dispersal of propaganda. Pamphlets and magazines praising the good work of the *Tatmadaw* were published for public consumption, and in-house journals covered military science and kept soldiers up-to-date on technological developments. Among Psywar's more sinister tasks was the compilation of lists of subversive elements considered to be a potential threat to the country's stability.

In 1962, a military coup ousted the civilian government and established a revolutionary council led by General Ne Win. It was a decisive moment for Burma: the regime that seized power then has ended up ruling the country in one guise or another up to the present day. Under Ne Win's rule, Than Shwe rose steadily through the ranks. He was only a captain when the coup took place, but within ten years he had become a lieutenant colonel, and ten years after that he held the powerful position of regional commander in the southwest division. Ne Win was a capricious and hotheaded leader, but he prized loyalty above all else, and Than Shwe's rise within the *Tatmadaw* probably had his tacit approval if not direct involvement.

Burma's years under Ne Win were disastrous for the country. Ne Win closed Burma off from the rest of the world. He expelled foreign residents, nationalized all business and industry, and launched the "Burmese Way to Socialism," a political system that blended Marxism, Buddhism, and authoritarian rule. More ethnic groups took up arms against the central Burmese government. With the Kachin in the north, the Shan to the east, and the Karen and Mon to the south, among others, the Burmese government was surrounded by enemies, and the country was locked in perpetual civil war. After twenty-five years with Ne Win at the helm, the economy had become so deflated that the United Nations declared Burma one of the world's least developed countries. The nationwide uprising against military rule that gripped the country in 1988 was the result of this financial deprivation. Though the demonstrations were brutally quashed by the army, they did trigger significant changes in the ruling strata. Ne Win resigned, his faux socialist policies were dismantled, and the country opened its doors to foreign investment and tourism.

Just a few years later, Than Shwe snagged the top job. By 1992, he was chairman of the new ruling body, the State Law and Order Restoration Council (SLORC). He also took on the role of commander in chief of the armed forces and minister of defense. It was a spectacular rise from uneducated village boy to the country's ultimate leader. Than Shwe had joined the army when it was still an undeveloped fighting force numbering just a few thousand men. By the time he became army chief, he had around two hundred thousand troops under his command.

My favorite exhibit at the Defense Services Museum was a section showcasing the *Tatmadaw*'s productivity. Since its early days in the 1950s, the army has had to raise revenue from businesses set up and run by soldiers. Looking around the exhibit, I had the sense that the regime could easily survive the longest of sieges—it seemed to make everything.

Apart from the obvious military tools such as bombs, grenades, antipersonnel mines, artillery, and ammunition, the *Tatmadaw* also ran factories that produced paint, metal, leather, textiles, waterproofing chemicals, shoes, and—curiously—balls (on display were one sample football, one volleyball, and a tube containing three *Tatmadaw* tennis balls). What I liked most were the oversized models of a soldier's kit that had been placed in the center of the crowded room. The models were of an enormous army-issue water bottle, a floppy terai hat the size of a bed, and a pair of leather boots big enough for a grown man to stand inside. The items were crafted so realistically that it was easy to imagine they could belong to a giant *Tatmadaw* soldier who might actually exist.

With Than Shwe as commander in chief, the army continued to grow. Throughout the 1990s an energetic recruitment effort expanded its troops from two hundred thousand in 1988 to an estimated four hundred thousand over a decade later. The army also stocked up on weapons and ammunition. Helicopters came from Russia, machine guns and mortar rounds were purchased from Pakistan, and China was a source for rocket launchers, anti-aircraft gun systems, and armored personnel carriers. The expansion made little sense in military terms; Burma has no external enemies, and many of the ethnic armies, unable to stand up to the increased might of the Burmese army, had agreed to ceasefires. Perhaps in acknowledgment of this uncertain peace, the SLORC changed its name in 1997; having restored "Law and Order," it became the State Peace and Development Council (SPDC).

The Defense Services Museum was a window onto how the regime views itself and its place in Burmese history. While the rest of the world sees a military that runs amok, the *Tatmadaw* believes it has repeatedly rescued the country from the brink of disaster. During my museum visit, I put together a simplified synopsis of the *Tatmadaw*'s take on history:

> In 1948, after World War II, the military saved the country from disintegrating by bravely fighting off insurgents and invaders.
>
> In 1962, the army took control of the government because the ruling politicians didn't have the strength to hold the country together and prevent ethnic groups from seceding.
>
> In 1988, the army yet again had to protect the people from mass anarchy when a wave of panic that was instigated by bogus students and communist agitators swept through the country.

This perspective is further heightened by the fact that many soldiers have sacrificed their lives fighting for the *Tatmadaw*, and most of today's leaders, including Than Shwe, had comrades who were killed in action. One of the special envoys of the United Nations, Razali Ismail, who met Than Shwe a number of times, was once quoted in the *New York Times* as saying of the senior general, "He believes he's a true nationalist. The first time I met him he said: 'People think we are doing this for power. No, this is for the sake of the nation. I have fought for the country. I have scars on my body'—he pointed to himself—'bullet wounds.'"

On anniversaries of significant dates, the state media publishes poems and overwrought articles in praise of its heroes in green. The following is a sample from one Independence Day edition of the *New Light of Myanmar*:

> *Glorious and shining*
> *Myanmar* Tatmadaw
> *Was formed and it grew*
> *Sacrificing lives, blood, sweat*
> *Saving nation from enslavement*
> *Regaining independence*
> *With patriotism*
> *And nationalistic fervor*
> *Independence safeguarded*
> *With blood, sweat, lives*
> *Throughout history*
> *With pride, we firmly vow*
> *To safeguard Independence*
> *For its perpetuation.*

On the ground floor of the Defense Services Museum, I wandered into the large room devoted to the *Tatmadaw* armory. As I walked among land mines and grenades laid out in tidy rows, the soldier who was manning the exhibit walked slowly and deliberately behind me, seeming to mirror my footsteps with his heavy, boot-clad feet. Determined not to be intimidated, I pushed on past a row of rocket launchers until I came to a large tank and found that I had reached a dead end. When I stopped walking, the sound of the soldier's boots came to an ominous standstill. I studied the rocket launchers for a moment or two, and then, from somewhere in the darkness behind me, I heard a soft click. I spun around to find that the soldier had switched on the lights in a glass display box. The lights illuminated a collection of miniature model tanks, each one just about the right size for an Action Man doll. The soldier beamed at me, a proud and friendly smile, and I pretended to admire the tiny tanks for a polite while before leaving. When I left the room, I heard the same click as he turned the lights out on the display.

TALES OF FEARSOME warrior kings are the stuff of popular legend in Burma. Books, poetry, and theatrical performances tell of the patriotism and martial achievements of the noble men who ruled the country until the late nineteenth century. Though the kings are often lauded for their valor and wisdom, they exercised absolute control over their subjects. They were considered to be the rightful owners of everything contained within the kingdom, from the fish swimming in the waters to all the human beings and animals walking upon the land. Known as Lords of Life and Death, it was forbidden for commoners even to look upon these deified rulers.

The omnipotence of the Burmese kings came to an abrupt end in 1885, when the British completed their colonial conquest of Burma by taking over the capital of Mandalay and dismantling a tradition of royal rule that had been in place for almost a thousand years. Within just one day of the British takeover, King Thibaw and his family had been bundled into two bullock carts and driven to the port, where they were put aboard a ship and exiled to India. It was an ignominious end for Burma's proud royal dynasties. In British-ruled India, the government placed Thibaw under effective house arrest in the town of Ratnagiri, where he lived out the rest of his years on a meager British allowance. When Thibaw died in 1916, his family did not have enough money to bury him. Unlike previous kings, who had extensive funeral rites appropriate for the valediction of a semi-divine being, the last king of Burma was buried in a casket in the yard of his house, and his remains were later moved by the local authorities to a nondescript setting in the nearby forest.

The institution of monarchy is now in the distant past, but the memory of it lives on. It is commonly thought that Than Shwe believes himself to be the reincarnation of a Burmese monarch. Though there is no general consensus on which king has manifested himself in the portly form of the senior general, some say Than Shwe thinks he is the brave king Kyansittha from the eleventh century. Others say he claims to be Bodawpaya, the eighteenth-century monarch who had 53 wives and 120 children, and who ruled over Burma at the peak of its strength; during his reign, the Burmese army conquered the territory of Arakan, bringing about the country's first clashes with British colonial forces in India. It is said that visitors to Than Shwe's home must crawl on the floor, kneeling before him like humble subjects, and that his family members speak to one another in the royal dialect once reserved exclusively for the king and his court.

Throughout their rule, Than Shwe and other members of the junta have appropriated the behavior of monarchs. In 1994, just a couple of years after he had taken over the reins, and with the divisive memory of the bloodshed of 1988 still fresh in everyone's minds, the generals arranged for a sacred tooth relic of the Buddha to be brought to Burma from China for a six-week tour of the country. When the tooth relic arrived at Rangoon airport, an elephant-drawn carriage transported it through the city. More than five thousand people, including actors dressed as celestial beings, were involved in the parade, and many thousands more lined the streets to watch. The generals were assuming the religious duties of past kings—some of whom had tried to bring tooth relics to Burma. It was a popular move; in Mandalay alone, over 775,000 people went to pay homage to the relic.

The generals and their wives have taken on plenty of other regal airs and graces. They regularly hoist the *hti*, the crownlike finial, on significant pagodas, including the Shwedagon. They have also claimed ownership of all white elephants found within Burma. White elephants discovered in the wild were traditionally brought to the palace and offered to the king. The discovery of a white elephant was considered a good omen that only occurred during the time of a devout and just ruler. During the reign of Than Shwe, at least three white elephants have emerged from the jungles of Burma to be dressed in golden capes and embroidered harnesses, so that they can play their role as sacred beasts in choreographed episodes of mock-royal theater.

I once met King Thibaw's eldest grandson, who was living a relatively humble existence in a colonial cottage in the former British hill station of Maymyo. He told me how the monarchy and memories of it still had a hold on the Burmese psyche. The previous regime, under General Ne Win, had occasionally made use of him, he said, rolling him out as a sort of royal talisman. In the villages, women knelt down and drew their waist-length hair over their heads to form a carpet for the rightful heir to the Burmese throne to walk upon. For a society robbed of its traditional ruling hierarchy, it is potent symbolism to evoke the time of kings.

In Naypyidaw, three gigantic statues of legendary monarchs stand guard over the new capital. The three kings were chosen for a reason: each one was the founder of a new dynasty, and each was credited with being able to unify Burma's divided territories. King Anawrahta founded the first Burmese kingdom, with Pagan as its citadel, in the eleventh century. King Bayintnaung started the second Burmese Empire in the sixteenth century and expanded the realm of his territory to such an extent that his reign was described by one historian as "the greatest explosion of human energy ever seen in Burma." King Alaungpaya, who ruled during the eighteenth century and launched the final Konbaung dynasty, was believed to have supernatural powers. He could fling his sword across great distances to sever a man's head. Vultures perched on the homes of his enemies, while around his own palace there fluttered a rainbow array of butterflies and dazzling birds of paradise.

Though the statues are located in an area that is off-limits to the public, they are often seen in photographs and footage shown by state media. They tower like giants over the Naypyidaw parade ground, each carrying a colossal dagger, sword, or spear. Some twenty thousand troops marched in unison beneath the stony gaze of this majestic triumvirate when Armed Forces Day, the annual holiday that commemorates the formation of the *Tatmadaw*, was held in Naypyidaw for the first time in 2006. In his speech on that day, Than Shwe hinted at the idea of a military dynasty when he said, "Our *Tatmadaw* should be a worthy heir to the traditions of the capable *Tatmadaws* established by noble kings Anawrahta, Bayintnaung, and Alaungpaya."

If Than Shwe is enacting his karmic role as king or consciously employing regal attributes to justify his rule, then the founding of a new capital is in keeping with Burma's historical trajectory. Burmese kings often moved their citadels to new locations, and the landscape is littered with abandoned capitals. Seen in this context, it is not so difficult to understand why Than Shwe might have wanted to leave Rangoon. The city was the only capital of Burma that was not founded by a Burmese ruler. Since the British seized Rangoon during the second Anglo-Burmese War in 1852 and later made it the capital of British Burma, it has been a reminder of defeat. It is a city built by invaders, men who were of a different ethnic and religious background. Even today, the legacy of British architecture and engineers is still visible; before the move to Naypyidaw, most government offices were housed in once-grand Victorian-style buildings, with colonnades and cupola roofs constructed in the image of London.

In his new capital, Than Shwe likes to receive visitors in front of a mural of Pagan, the center of the first Burmese Empire. Bordered with gold and mother-of-pearl inlay, the floor-to-ceiling mural depicts Pagan's pagodas glittering golden and resplendent in a forested, prelapsarian landscape. This idyllic vista forms a backdrop to the senior general as he holds court on his throne-like chair and discusses affairs of state with the very few guests who are welcome at his citadel.

When I first visited Pagan some fifteen years ago, I was moved by the emotive allure of these crumbling ruins. I filled my diary with elaborate descriptions of the nearly three thousand monuments built between the eleventh and thirteenth centuries. I wrote about the black-green moss that had spread like bruises across the aged bricks, the way the pagodas cast rose-red shadows in the late afternoon light, and the particular silence that can be found in the weed-strewn courtyards of Pagan's empty monasteries.

But Pagan as I saw it then no longer exists. In the 1990s, Than Shwe's government had begun an extensive "beautification" program to restore the ruins and by the time I returned in 2006, the restoration was nearly complete. Tumbledown mounds had been transformed into brand-new temples built in a simulation of the Pagan style. Almost every pagoda had been topped off with a new pinnacle. Rust-orange pagodas built of brick boasted pale cement cones that sat on top of the old monuments as incongruously as dollops of fresh cream. The broken dome of the Dhammayazika, formerly a neglected and overgrown pagoda, had been totally re-created, gilded and crowned with a new *hti*. The whispering cornfields that once surrounded it had become manicured parkland with paved walkways and pink bougainvillea.

Leaving aesthetic incongruities aside, archaeologists and art historians around the world have bemoaned the lack of historical authenticity. As there are no surviving plans for Pagan's buildings, the shape and decoration of the upper parts of the monuments are based on pure speculation. "Sadly, it has to be said that the recent work done in Pagan has not been very accurate," a Burmese archaeologist working there told me. "In many cases, we cannot call it restoration or renovation. We have to call it what it is: rebuilding."

The archaeologist explained to me how the ruins were rebuilt: "We simply look at the base mound. Is it round, square, or pentagonal? Based on this information, we construct one of three models." With a total of 2,834 recorded monuments, the sheer variety of buildings at Pagan was once staggering. As the ruins are remodeled, this diversity has been turned into uniformity. These heavy-handed restoration efforts have effectively disqualified Pagan as a potential UNESCO World Heritage site, and the late Burmese historian Than Tun succinctly dubbed the methods used as "blitzkrieg archaeology."

Efforts to resurrect the glory of the past did not stop there. The regime has also reconstructed the palaces of the country's long-dead kings. Mandalay palace, the seat of the last Burmese monarch, which was destroyed during bombing raids in World War II, has been rebuilt. As have palaces for each of the three kings whose statues loom above Naypyidaw. The regime claims that King Anawrahta's palace in Pagan is a simulacrum constructed in accordance with archaeological findings, but the archaeologist I spoke with there said that the immense and gaudy structure was a figment of historical imagination—the minister of culture simply chose the biggest and most grandiose design from a selection shown to him by architects.

There is an innate arrogance in these re-enactments and reconstructions. It is as if Than Shwe and his generals are trying to channel the unrivaled powers of Burma's monarchs by creating their likenesses, re-furbishing their pagodas, and building replicas of their palaces.

IN THE FIRST FEW YEARS of Naypyidaw's existence, foreigners were prohibited from entering the Abode of Kings, and it would be some years before I was able to get there. In the meantime, I kept an eye out for any-thing that might offer some insight into Burma's elusive ruler. One such event was the marriage of Than Shwe's daughter to an army major in 2006.

Though the wedding was supposed to be a private affair, a video was leaked a few months after the ceremony. For the first time, the general public was able to witness the extravagant private lives of Than Shwe and the country's elite. The images caused quite a stir and attracted world-wide attention as outtakes were broadcast on international news pro-grams and the full-length version was made available on YouTube.

The bride was, without doubt, the star of the show. Before the ceremony began, the film captured her as she underwent final adjustments to her face and outfit. She closed her eyes so that the makeup artist could sweep a generous layer of green shadow across her lids and pouted patiently as a fine brush painted her lips the color of a maraschino cherry. Friends and older women fussed over the bride, fixing her diamond tiara and tweaking the diamond pins in her bouffant. A collar made of diamonds was fastened around the bride's neck, and additional strands of diamonds were draped across her chest. Around each wrist she wore three diamond-studded cuffs, and the rings on her fingers were set with gems the size of gobstoppers.

The venue for the wedding party was similarly opulent. Guests walked in on a red carpet lined with fresh flowers. In the entrance hall, a series of life-sized portraits in gilded frames portrayed the bride in her wedding gown. Inside the reception room, a colonnaded palace façade had been erected to showcase the bride and groom. As the guests filtered into the room, waiters and waitresses bustled around the hall making last-minute adjustments to the table settings.

The guest list could have been ripped straight out of the pages of a *Who's Who* of Burma's ruling hierarchy. The generals and their wives appeared in lavish attire. The women wore lace blouses, richly embroidered *tamein* (the sarong worn by Burmese women), and sequined chiffon scarves. Together, their ensembles were a riot of color: candy-floss pink, electric lime green, and volcanic orange. The men who accompanied them, many of them high-ranking officers or business cronies of the regime, were dressed more soberly in silk *longyi* with traditional white or cream jackets. Once ushered to their tables, most of the guests sat stiffly, waiting for the ceremony to begin. A few women leaned toward each other and whispered, perhaps complimenting one another on their outfits or comparing notes on who had and had not been invited to the wedding of the senior general's daughter.

Than Shwe, who is seldom seen in public out of uniform, was dressed for the event in a golden silk *longyi*. The cameraman seemed to delight in filming him as he polished off a plate of delicate layer cakes and then reached for an extra helping of what looked like trifle, tucking in with steely relish. Than Shwe's wife, Kyaing Kyaing, sat silently by his side. Despite the richness of her attire, she gave off an air of weariness; her spectacles were gold-rimmed but grandmotherly, and her earlobes sagged slightly under the weight of heavy diamond earrings.

These images of unabashed wealth highlighted the dichotomy between the life of the ruling classes and that of the average Burmese citizen. While most of Burma is mired in poverty, the regime's coffers—and the generals' private piggy banks—are illicitly filled through a variety of exports. Burma is rich in natural resources, and the generals profit from the sale of gems, jade, and teak. Most of the regime's gains, however, are now made by auctioning off concessions to Burma's plentiful reserves of oil and natural gas.

A report by EarthRights International states that between 2000 and 2009 the junta earned US$4.83 billion from a controversial gas pipeline operated by the French company Total and the U.S.-owned Chevron—hardly any of these earnings were declared in the national budget, but were stashed away in offshore bank accounts instead. With explorations still being conducted, and Burma situated next to energy-hungry countries such as Thailand and China, there will be no shortage of investments. Though the generals get rich from these megadeals, the wealth does not trickle downward, and the rest of Burma has become ever more impoverished by the regime's financial misappropriations.

For most of the population, unaccustomed to such displays of wealth, the wedding of the senior general's daughter must have looked like a party fit for a real-life princess. When the ceremony began, the lights in the reception hall were dimmed. A spotlight was trained on the bride and groom as they walked down the aisle. A row of bridesmaids preceded them, scattering jasmine flowers beneath their feet. Three female attendants crouched behind the bride, carefully maneuvering the long lace train of her dress. The bride gripped the groom's arm tightly, and her expression was serious. Only very occasionally did her glossy red lips stretch into a tense smile. Close-ups of the couple were beamed onto wide-screen televisions positioned around the room. Reflected in the spotlight, the diamonds worn by the bride seemed to flash like lightning across the audience.

FIVE

One Tuesday in the middle of August 2007, an order from Naypyidaw was put into effect that triggered a calamitous chain of events. Issued by the Ministry of Energy, the order resulted in the price of gas rising by 60 percent, diesel by 100 percent, and compressed natural gas by 500 percent. Overnight, the cost of bus and train tickets doubled. By the end of the week, necessities such as rice, cooking oil, and salt had become more expensive due to increased transport charges. At some tea shops, a cup of tea that previously cost K200 (around US$.20) suddenly cost K300.

In a country where much of the population survives day-to-day on meager wages, the order represented economic disaster. A United Nations household survey conducted in Burma a couple of years earlier had found that more than 30 percent of the population eked out a living below the poverty line and did not always have enough money to cover their daily requirements. The unexpected escalation in the cost of living threatened to make life untenable.

On August 19, four days after the announcement, an estimated five hundred people demonstrated in Rangoon to demand that the government lower fuel costs. It was an incredibly rare act of mass protest and the largest demonstration the country had seen in years. The event was organized and led by the 88 Generation Students, a group of student leaders who had been prominent in the 1988 uprising. Though most of them had been arrested for their roles in organizing the 1988 demonstrations and had spent the past decade or more in prison, they had served their sentences and been released some years earlier. Since their release, they had established informal networks for social work and low-key political projects. In response to the August price hikes, they instigated a series of protests.

I was at home in Bangkok at the time and followed news of the protests on Web sites run by exiled Burmese media groups. It was always with a faint sense of dread that I clicked on the sites. I felt certain that the regime's response would be harsh; the demonstrations were destined to be short-lived, quickly quashed, and just as soon forgotten. Or so I thought. There is a Burmese saying that warns that predicting the outcome of political events is like trying to guess the color of a chick's feathers by looking at the egg, or like proclaiming what shape a cloud will take. As had happened to me many times before in my attempts to foresee the future of Burma, I was proven wrong. Though there was a government crackdown against the 88 Generation protests, something much larger and even more explosive was taking shape.

Within just a few days, the government had arrested scores of people. Protest leaders who were able to escape went underground and continued to organize demonstrations, but the number of protesters diminished rapidly and the groups that gathered in different areas of Rangoon grew smaller each day. On August 23, thirty protesters walking to the office of the National League for Democracy were arrested, as was

Ohn Than, a lone protester holding up a handwritten placard outside the U.S. embassy. The next day, twenty people demonstrating outside city hall were detained. Four days later, some fifty people led by female NLD members with black-and-white photographs of General Aung San pinned to their chests marched through the busy Hledan intersection in the northern part of the city shouting, "Lower fuel prices!" They quickly dispersed after another twenty people were arrested. With key organizers either in prison or on the run, the voices of dissent were temporarily silenced.

As I had thought, the regime's response was fast and cruelly efficient. In almost all of these instances, the authorities made use of the *Swan Ah Shin* (literally, the Masters of Force). A sinister addition to the regime's manpower in recent years, the *Swan Ah Shin* is an informal and non-uniformed army of hired thugs. Given basic military training, they are used to patrol neighborhoods and contain public disturbances. They are often large, strong men who have a prior police record or were recruited from prisons, and they are much feared by the civilian population.

Burmese journalists were able to secretly film some of the arrests made by the *Swan Ah Shin* in August 2007. The footage, which sometimes lasts no more than a few minutes, shows men who could be ordinary passersby grabbing protesters and bundling them into unmarked vans or waiting cars. The unobtrusive, lightning-quick maneuvers certainly don't look like arrests conducted in the name of the state; they look more like anonymous abductions.

Though sporadic demonstrations continued to break out across the country in the early days of September, it might all have fizzled out had several hundred monks not decided to march through the streets of Pakokku, a town in central Burma renowned for its teaching monasteries and scholar monks. Soldiers were quickly sent to the scene and fired warning shots into the air. When the monks carried on marching, the soldiers started to beat them. Two monks were tied to a lamppost and publicly flayed with bamboo sticks and rifle butts. It was believed that one monk was killed.

Monks are so revered in Burma that many laypeople are reluctant even to step in the shadows they cast for fear of giving offense. To physically attack a member of the Buddhist clergy was a horrifying act in predominately Buddhist Burma. The following day, when a government delegation visited one of the major monasteries in Pakokku to order an end to the protests, the complex was surrounded by monks and town residents. A riot broke out, and cars that had carried the delegation to the monastery were torched. Trapped inside the compound, the government officials had to wait six hours before they were able to escape through a back entrance.

To punish the soldiers, members of the monastic community threatened to invoke an ancient rite known in Pali as *patam nikkujjana kamma*, colloquially referred to as *thabeik hmauk*, or the overturning of the alms bowl. The act is a monk's most hard-hitting spiritual weapon. Buddhist monks and laypeople live in mutual dependence; laypeople donate food, robes, and other necessities to monks, and monks provide them with a conduit for making merit through this act of giving. The overturning of the alms bowl severs the cycle of practical and spiritual interdependency. For monks to hold *thabeik hmauk* against the military would mean that soldiers and their families could no longer make merit. It also would mean that military families could not participate in religious ceremonies performed by monks and would be denied any religious rites of passage, from birth to death. In spiritual terms the *thabeik hmauk* is a long-lasting condemnation, as it robs those who have been excommunicated of the ability to accumulate merit for future lifetimes.

The decision to overturn the alms bowl is not taken lightly. According to Buddhist scriptures, the rite can be enacted only against those who harm the *Sangha*, or monastic community, in eight distinct ways (these include denying a monk robes, food, or medicine; endangering the lives of monks or reducing their numbers; and using ten kinds of abusive language against them). Once enacted, the boycott can be lifted only if the person or organization targeted apologizes with sincerity. After the incident at Pakokku, a hitherto underground group of monks called the All Burma Monks' Alliance released a public statement announcing that the *thabeik hmauk* would be instigated if the regime did not make amends by September 17, 2007.

The regime issued no official comment. The minister of religious affairs, a brigadier general, allegedly organized a meeting with senior monks in Pakokku to offer them compensation of K30,000 (just under US$30) for each injured monk; the offer was not accepted. In the state newspapers and on television, the usual images of high-ranking generals kneeling before abbots to make donations seemed especially disingenuous.

Presumably in the interests of discouraging any would-be demonstrators, the *New Light of Myanmar* ran a convoluted article informing readers that "protests are no longer fashionable." The article reasoned that even the United States and Britain—countries "said to be democracy pioneers"—do not give in to demands no matter how many thousands of people are on the streets, and it cited the anti-war demonstrations against the Vietnam War and the invasion of Iraq as examples.

By that point, I had given up trying to predict the color of the chick or the shape of the cloud; events had taken an unexpected twist with the involvement of the monks and the regime's violent response against them. As *New Light* scribes penned their turgid think pieces and various members of the regime knelt on ornamental carpets in monasteries to pose for the cameras with offerings of cooking oil, rice, and hard cash, an uneasy calm descended upon the country.

OVER A WEEK PASSED, and the regime offered no official apology for its maltreatment of monks at Pakokku. The *thabeik hmauk* was duly set in place. Secret meetings were held at monasteries in Rangoon and Mandalay to conduct the necessary rites for the overturning of the alms bowl.

A recording of one such meeting, held at midday on September 18 at an unnamed monastery in Rangoon, opened with the hypnotic, gravelly sound of monks chanting in Pali. One of the monks began to speak, slowly reciting the age-old words that would invoke a religious boycott against the military and their families:

"Reverend clergy, may you listen to my words. The violent, mean, cruel, ruthless, pitiless soldier kings—the great thieves who live by stealing from the national treasury—have murdered a monk at Pakokku, and also apprehended clergymen by trussing them up with rope. They beat and tortured, verbally abused and terrorized them. Clergy replete with the Four Attributes—boycott the violent, mean, cruel, ruthless, pitiless kings."

The speaker went on to ask of the monks who had gathered for the ritual: "If the reverends consent and are pleased at the boycott and refusal of donations and preaching, please keep silent; if not, please voice objections."

There were no objections, and the speaker concluded: "The clergy boycotts the violent, mean, cruel, ruthless, pitiless kings—the great thieves who are stealing from the national treasury."

And so the monks began to march. At 1:00 P.M. that day some three hundred monks gathered beneath the Shwedagon Pagoda and walked through the streets of Rangoon. Traffic stopped as they strode across the busy roundabout next to city hall, where the Sule Pagoda is located, and on to the Botahtaung Pagoda at the riverside, where they knelt and prayed. The march lasted just under two hours, and, afterward, the monks calmly returned to their monasteries.

Over the days that followed, monks continued to gather at the Shwedagon Pagoda to begin their daily marches. Laypeople started to join in; some offered drinking water to the monks, others held hands to form a human cordon on either side of the column of monks to protect them from harm. Each day, the marches grew larger and lasted longer. Soon multiple columns of monks were charting different trails across the city. They had no planned route and seemed to be mapping a spontaneous path from pagoda to pagoda, linking the holy sites of Rangoon and drawing a living mandala through the city's streets.

A cautious euphoria took hold. Onlookers hung out of windows and balconies to clap and cheer. Flags carried by the monks fluttered above the marchers, flying the colors of the Buddha's aura: blue, yellow, red, white, and pink. The columns of monks moved like unfurling banners that rippled with the shades of the robes they wore: deep maroon, dark rust orange, and blood red. The leading monks often held their glossy black alms bowls above their heads, symbolically turned upside down. Others held up posters bearing the serene face of the Buddha. The marches even continued through monsoon rainstorms. At times, the barefoot monks walked along streets knee-deep in floods and their steady strides churned the water into a choppy sea.

Similar marches were taking place elsewhere in Burma. Monks marched in the coastal city of Sittwe, on the Bay of Bengal. They marched down from hilltop pagodas at Sagaing, the center for the country's renowned Buddhist universities. They marched in thousands in Mandalay. And, as they marched, they chanted in unison, reciting verses from the *Metta Sutta*, the Buddhist discourse on loving-kindness. The words of the *Metta Sutta* are intended to spread peace to all sentient beings in all directions across the universe, and to quell the forces of evil.

> *May all be well and secure,*
> *May all beings be happy!*
> *Whatever living creatures there be,*
> *Without exception, weak or strong,*
> *Long, huge, or middle-sized,*
> *Or short, minute, or bulky,*
> *Whether visible or invisible,*
> *And those living far or near,*
> *The born and those seeking birth,*
> *May all beings be happy!*

In Rangoon one day, a column of monks went to Aung San Suu Kyi's house and chanted the *Metta Sutta*. To everyone's surprise, a door in the gate opened and Aung San Suu Kyi appeared at the entrance with her hands folded in prayer. A photograph taken at the time shows her standing behind a row of police with riot shields. She looks tiny and out of focus in the picture, half obscured by one of the aluminum shields, but it was a moving image, especially since she had not been seen in public for so many years. Aung San Suu Kyi herself had tears in her eyes as she stood at her gate praying.

The crowds became bigger and bolder. Some said there were as many as a hundred thousand people on the streets of Rangoon each day. Members of the NLD joined the marches. Prominent movie stars and public figures donated food to the monks. The marchers began to shout demands: "Free all political prisoners! Free Aung San Suu Kyi!" Some protesters defiantly held up a bright red flag emblazoned with a yellow fighting peacock—the flag of the student movement, banned since the 1988 uprising.

When thousands of monks knelt around the Shwedagon Pagoda to pray, there were so many of them that the black-and-white tiles were completely obscured from view. All that could be seen were the shaved heads of the monks and the varied maroon shades of their robes. Buddhist nuns in their pastel pink gowns sat around the outer edges of the circle, wrapping a final ring of pale color around the band of monks. When I gazed at photographs of the scene long enough, I began to see a hazy aura around the gold of the pagoda that faded from blood red to a pale, almost translucent pink. There, at the pagoda, the *Metta Sutta* was chanted again.

> *Let none deceive or decry*
> *His fellow anywhere;*
> *Let none wish others harm*
> *In resentment or in hate.*

I was incredulous that the regime had stood aside and allowed the marches to grow so big. The ever-present surveillance and iron-fisted tactics normally used by the authorities could easily have stifled the marches. Why, I wondered, was the regime not doing anything? Or, more ominously, what was it waiting for?

By then the marches were making headlines around the world. The fact that up-to-the-minute news was getting out of the country was also incredible. Due to the regime's restrictions on foreign journalists, news organizations such as the BBC or CNN cannot easily send a camera crew to Burma, and reporters who are able to sneak in must operate under the constant threat of deportation. During the events of September 2007, news was mostly sent out via the Internet. Though the Internet had been available in Burma for only a few years, and access was limited by government firewalls, users were able to get around the constraints. Burmese journalists e-mailed information and photographs to news organizations abroad, while pseudonymous Burmese bloggers broadcast events on their Web sites almost as soon as they happened on the ground.

In media terms it was a compelling story. An epic clash was taking place between the two strongest elements in Burmese society. On one side: the morality, wisdom, and nonviolent principles of over 2,500 years of Buddhist tradition. On the other: the heavily armed might of the military honed over forty-five years of authoritarian rule and jungle warfare. In terms of numbers, it was an even match; with some four hundred thousand monks in Burma and an estimated minimum of four hundred thousand soldiers, there was at least one monk for every soldier. Would the forces of good triumph over evil? Would the monks be able to pacify the armed men with their call for loving-kindness? Or would the military fall back on its brute instinct to pull the trigger?

The answer came on the evening of September 24, almost a week after the marches had begun. The minister of religious affairs appeared on state television to say that the protests were instigated by "internal and external destructionists, who are jealous of national development and stability" and who want to "harm all the government's endeavors." He also blamed the international media for fanning the flames of unrest. The ruling council of monks, known as the Sangha Maha Nayaka—a government-appointed body—was ordered to bring the clergy in line and curtail their involvement in non-religious affairs.

That evening and the following evening, trucks rigged with loudspeakers drove through the city announcing a nighttime curfew. People were told not to march with the monks and were reminded of relevant articles in the Penal Code, which state that joining unlawful assemblies can result in a prison sentence and that gatherings of more than five people are illegal. In the middle of the night, residents who lived near the main roads were woken by convoys of army trucks driving into the city. Light Infantry Division 66 and Light Infantry Division 77 had been deployed to Rangoon.

The crackdown began in earnest the next day. Photographs and footage of excited and joyous people supporting the peaceful marchers were suddenly replaced by images of soldiers and riot police beating up monks and herding protesters into trucks. When monks tried to gather at the daily rallying point of the Shwedagon Pagoda, they found the holy site ringed with soldiers and barbed-wire barricades. The monks tried to negotiate with the authorities, but soldiers responded to their entreaties by hitting them with truncheons. Witnesses saw monks being beaten unconscious and tossed into trucks.

The demonstrators and their supporters were immediately whipped into a fearful chaos. As people tried to regroup at various points around the city, the *Swan Ah Shin* roamed the streets carrying bamboo sticks and metal rods. Soldiers fired their guns above the crowds but then received orders to shoot directly at people; first with rubber bullets and then with real bullets.

In downtown Rangoon, a Japanese photographer was shot and killed. The point-blank shooting was captured on film. A photograph taken of the scene by Reuters photographer Adrees Latif, who was positioned above the street on a pedestrian overpass, won the Pulitzer Prize. The photo shows the Japanese man, who was later identified as Kenji Nagai, falling onto his back in front of the soldier who shot him. To one side of the dying man, frantic people are scrambling over one another as they try to get away. Behind them, a riot policeman has his truncheon poised in mid-air, ready to strike. The road is littered with discarded sandals and plastic water bottles. The moment after the picture was taken, the soldier leveled his gun and continued to run after the retreating crowd.

Zaw Thu, a Burmese artist in his twenties who had taken part in the protests, later gave me his impressions of the crackdown. He spoke in a breathless manner, confusing the chronology of events and jumping back and forth between days in his haste to cover all the details. This is how he told his story:

At around one o'clock on Wednesday, I think it was Wednesday, we were at the Sule Pagoda. The soldiers stood in a row. The monks and nuns sat in front of them and meditated. The soldiers came toward them and grabbed the monks sitting in the first row and started beating them with sticks and the butts of their guns. And the nuns, too, they tore their tops off and beat them as well. People began to run away—we had to.

Then there was the day when the soldiers shot protesters. They used rubber bullets first, and, when the crowd still wouldn't go away, they used real bullets. And they had snipers to pick off the leaders. I saw a flag holder get shot, and a student holding up a portrait of Aung San. I saw at least ten people get shot that day. I think they are dead. There is no way to know. We had to keep running.

And they kept beating people. They herded them into trucks. They went into the tea shops and picked up people who were just drinking tea and they beat them. They grabbed people at the bus stops who were not involved, who were just trying to get home, and they beat them. And I saw them beat a young girl. She was really young. Too young. And the nuns, they beat them, too. They tore off their tops and they beat them.

I heard plenty of descriptions like this, their incoherence indicative of the panic and mayhem that had been unleashed. A magazine editor vaulted over a wall that was ten feet high while running away from the *Swan Ah Shin*; when he looked at the wall some days later he had no idea how he had been able to jump that high. A terrified teenage girl lay facedown on a rough tarmac road and waited her turn as soldiers searched protesters one by one, confiscating cameras and randomly kicking people. Others ran down the city's narrow alleyways, clambering up the dark, steep stairwells that lead into colonial-era shop-houses or ducking behind the buildings and sinking into the sewage-choked gutters. Zaw Thu, the young artist, had peered down from his hiding place on the upper floor of one of the shop-houses and watched as soldiers locked down the streets in the same way they would secure a battlefield. After the soldiers took control of each block, fire engines drove along the streets to hose down the tarmac and wash away the blood.

It took three days for the military to put an end to the protests. At night soldiers raided monasteries. In some cases they used trucks to batter down the gates, storming the sacrosanct premises with tear gas and gunshots, as if they were entering an enemy encampment. Hundreds of monks were arrested and soldiers were placed on guard at the emptied monastic compounds. Along with the monks, hundreds of laypeople were also arrested and taken to impromptu detention centers set up in the buildings of a technical college and at Kyaikkasan, an old British racecourse.

The flow of information coming out of Burma was stopped abruptly as the authorities shut down the Internet and blocked phone lines and mobile phone signals. With few new images or timely reports emerging from Burma, the events of September dropped from international headlines. For most of the outside world, the story ended there. The face-off between the military and the monastic order had resulted in the forces of evil vanquishing the forces of good. The men with guns did not hear, or did not care to hear, the plea for peace within the *Metta Sutta* that had been chanted on the city's streets.

"WELCOME TO MY wonderful country, where nothing has just happened," said my friend Ko Ye when I arrived in Rangoon a few days after the crackdown began. Ko Ye was often my first point of contact on landing in Burma. As a publisher, he was in daily contact with local journalists and writers. Though he collected most of his information by word of mouth, he always seemed to be ahead of the wire services when it came to news of what was, or was not, happening inside the country. I rang him shortly after checking into a hotel and he immediately chastised me for being late.

I certainly hadn't planned to arrive during a crackdown. When I applied for a visa to Burma, the monks were still out in full force, and I had half imagined I might be swept away on the cusp of a revolution. Instead, by the time I arrived, the regime had regained control. As the junta's foreign minister told the United Nations General Assembly at the time: "Normalcy has now returned to Myanmar [Burma]."

Rangoon did look astonishingly normal after the grim scenes of the previous week. There were hardly any soldiers in the streets, and the downtown area was lively with traffic and streetside commerce. In the tea shops, groups of men sat on low wooden stools with their *longyi* tucked around their knees, smoking cheroots and chatting. Market stalls on the pavements sold the usual array of goods: pirated DVDs of Korean soap operas and *Mr Bean* episodes; cheap Chinese sandals; charcoal-baked poppy-seed cakes wrapped in newspaper. Even away from the hustle and bustle of the city center, life seemed to be going on as normal.

At dusk on the day I arrived, I watched local residents stroll along the forested banks of Kandawgyi Lake as a languid sunset transformed the still waters into a molten pool of gold and pink.

The appearance of normality was, of course, deceptive. Thousands of people were still being held in the makeshift detention centers, and the authorities were hunting down not just protest organizers and ring-leaders, but also anyone who had been seen taking photographs or film-ing during the demonstrations. They were reportedly comparing footage used by international news organizations with that filmed by their own intelligence personnel in order to identify culpable individuals. Stills from the footage were circulated around township offices to be cross-checked against local registration lists and ID photographs and matched up with names and addresses. Detainees were also being interrogated to establish links between protesters. Telephone numbers from confiscated mobile phones were traced. Seized digital cameras were searched for incriminating images. In their efforts to chase up all these leads, the authorities were ransacking offices and scouring private homes. It was as if they were cleaning up a massive crime scene by attempting to erase any evidence and eliminate all possible witnesses.

It took me a while to notice that there was one very significant differ-ence in the city; I didn't notice it at first because it was an absence. Buddhist monks are usually a common sight throughout Burma. At dawn, they walk through the streets in single file to collect alms. During the day they can be seen moving between the city's many monastic com-pounds. But by the end of September that year, there were hardly any monks on the streets of Rangoon. The few I did see were mostly elderly monks walking alone or grubby boy novices out collecting spare change. While many monks were locked away in the detention camps, it was thought that many others were hiding in safe houses or had fled to the Thailand–Burma border to seek asylum or shelter amid the refugee camps there. The rest had probably gone home; during the raids, monks were forcibly disrobed and told to return to their home villages—a tactic aimed at dispersing the monastic community and preventing it from reassembling in large numbers.

Burmese journalists in Rangoon were busy trying to verify the whereabouts of the monks. They had to do it stealthily, talking to trusted contacts who lived near monasteries and might be able to provide snippets of information. When I unfolded a map of Rangoon in front of Nya Na, a journalist who worked in the city secretly sending information to international media outside Burma, he began circling monasteries with a red pen. He pointed out Ngwe Kya Yan monastery in the north of the city and told me it had been emptied of monks after a nighttime raid by the army. The following day local residents found the monastery littered with broken glass and spent bullet casings. They saw blood pooled on the floor and splattered across the walls. As many as one hundred monks had been arrested; the rest were thought to have fled. Patiently, Nya Na worked his way across my map, scrawling heavy red rings around each monastery that had been raided and was now devoid of monks.

It was immensely disturbing, Nya Na said, to be charting the disappearance of monks. The monastery in his own neighborhood had been emptied and was now home to just a handful of young novices who were too nervous to speak to anyone in the community. Every day of their lives, for as long as Nya Na and his parents could remember, the members of their household had woken at dawn to place food in alms bowls carried by passing monks. Without this fundamental daily ritual, the shape and meaning of their days were lost, and they worried for the monks. How would they survive without donations, Nya Na's family wondered: *If we are not feeding them, how are they getting food?*

It was, at that point in time, impossible to know anything for sure about the fate of the monks and other protesters who had been detained.

Wa Wa Myint, my doctor friend, had been trying to find out about injured protesters through her medical network, but the authorities were going to considerable lengths to cover their tracks. She learned that hospitals and private clinics were prohibited from admitting any injured people during the crackdown. Soldiers had picked up the wounded off the streets and taken them to the government-run Rangoon General Hospital. There, additional soldiers had been placed at the gates and at the entrance to the trauma wards. The few doctors and nurses on duty in the guarded wards had been strictly vetted and were afraid to leak any information in case the authorities found them out. Wa Wa Myint said that many wounded people were treating themselves at home and believed that those with serious injuries were dying because they could not seek medical assistance for fear of arrest.

Wherever I went in Rangoon, I took to trying to spot the security forces who were hidden around the city, ready for instant mobilization. As I picked my way past fruit sellers who sat behind small mountains of lime, papaya, and watermelon on one of the crowded streets near the Sule Pagoda, I glimpsed a platoon of alert soldiers tucked away inside a disused shop-house. When I peered through the wire mesh that covers the windows of city hall, I could just make out a long row of olive-green canvas bags, red scarves, and bamboo truncheons—evidence that troops were stationed inside. I also saw truckloads of riot police sequestered in a derelict British railway building and in the leafy compound of an abandoned government ministry.

The nightly curfew was in place from 10:00 P.M. to 4:00 A.M., and the downtown streets, usually laid out each evening with pavement tea shops and beer stalls, began to empty around 9:00 P.M. as people hurried home.

Confined to my hotel room, I made a habit of turning off the lights and sitting by the window. At first there was nothing to see, and I sat and listened to the amplified sounds of Rangoon under curfew. When bats swooped out from the belfry of an old church tower next to my hotel, I could hear the leaves rustling as they settled into the branches of a nearby banyan tree. Rats scuttled around a pile of garbage on the ground, six stories below. A bottle was knocked over and its bell-like ring echoed along the deserted street. Then, I heard a deep rumbling noise that I couldn't identify. Suddenly, an army truck appeared out of the darkness. The truck was followed by two police vans that were headed downtown. As they passed beneath my hotel window, the sound of their engines was deafeningly loud in the otherwise silent city.

Later, after I had fallen asleep, I was woken by the noise of the truck and vans driving back in the opposite direction and realized that they must have been returning from a nighttime raid in the downtown area. After that I took to waiting for them, and each night I watched the sinister cavalcades drive back and forth beneath my hotel window. Sometimes, just before they passed, the city's stray dogs would become jittery and start to howl at one another like wolves.

In the mornings, I was always somewhat astonished to see that the scenes of everyday normality had returned.

When news emerged that some of the detainees were being released, a friend told me about Soe Thiha, a young man he knew, aged twenty-two, who had spent a week in the detention center set up at the Government Technical Institute. Soe Thiha had not participated in the protests and had only followed along out of curiosity, but the soldiers had arrested him anyway. He was held in a large room with around one hundred men and women. They were given no food or water for the first twenty-four hours and were kept in total darkness. As the detainees were not allowed access to toilet facilities, and the roof was leaking due to the rains, Soe Thiha had to sleep on a filthy, wet cement floor. Some of his

fellow inmates had bad wounds from being beaten during the crackdown or interrogations and, on the third day, he woke up to discover
that three people had died in the night and that their corpses were still
lying in the room.

To secure his release, Soe Thiha's parents signed a form promising that
he would not take part in any political activities. He arrived home in a
pitiful state. His back was covered with oozing welts from the regular
beatings he received during his interrogations. He had also become afraid
of the dark and insisted on sleeping with the lights on in his bedroom.
Soe Thiha's parents were enraged by what had been done to their son,
and I was told they might be willing to speak to me about it.

We went to their home one afternoon and were greeted at the door
by Soe Thiha's mother. She offered me a seat on a faux-leather settee
in the front room and went to the kitchen to prepare coffee. It was a
typical Rangoon apartment, low-ceilinged and cluttered with family
artifacts—graduation and wedding photographs, school sporting tro-
phies, and examination certificates. Coffee was served on a flowery
melamine tray, and Soe Thiha's mother and father sat down opposite me.
We exchanged a few pleasantries, and then his mother disappeared back
into the kitchen. A few moments later, her husband got up and excused
himself.

We waited awkwardly for them to return, but they never did. After a
while, a voice called out to us from the kitchen, "Sit! Sit! Stay, and enjoy
your coffee." We sat and tried to enjoy our coffee, but it eventually became clear that they were not prepared to risk speaking to me, and that
it was time for us to leave.

Beneath the veneer of normality, the city was seething with untold
stories. Like those indefinable movements you catch out of the corner of
your eye, they seemed to tremble and sputter just beyond reach. While

sitting in a taxi near the eastern gate of the Shwedagon Pagoda, a place that had been a rallying spot during the demonstrations, I caught sight of an army truck parked in the gateway of a decrepit redbrick apartment block. I glanced up at the building and saw a soldier standing at the third-floor entrance to one of the apartments. There was a woman standing beside him, and the door to the apartment was open. They were both watching whatever was taking place inside. With a sudden jerky movement, the woman collapsed at the soldier's feet. From a distance, I couldn't tell whether she was fainting or falling on her knees to plead with him. Then the taxi I was in rounded a corner and the scene disappeared from view.

MONKS IN MANDALAY were said to be holding out against the soldiers. Whenever soldiers approached the monasteries there, the temple bells were rung and monks would mass together to form a barricade and prevent them from entering. At one monastery, where soldiers made placatory offerings of food to the monks, the supplies had been rejected and thrown back over the monastery walls. Sacks of rice and dry noodles had piled up on the street outside the compound.

There was good reason to believe that the monks of Mandalay might be able to stave off the men with guns. The city is home to some forty thousand monks. Mandalay's monasteries are vast complexes, with the biggest ones, such as Ma Soe Yein, housing up to eight thousand. The city was also the site of the last major overturning of the alms bowl, in 1990. Then, when monks had congregated on August 8 to remember the 1988 uprising, soldiers had attacked the crowd, wounding some monks and provoking them to instate a religious boycott against the military. During the subsequent crackdown scores of monks were arrested, and orders were issued to dissolve all independent Buddhist organizations and outlining the correct behavior for monks. Since then, individual members of the regime had made frequent public displays of piety to demonstrate that they were in fact decent and respectful Buddhists. The result was an unspoken truce between the generals and the *Sangha* that would remain in place as long as the religious community stayed within the bounds of the new orders and did not become involved with non-religious matters.

It is not the traditional role of monks to take on political issues, but throughout Burma's history they have intervened on behalf of the population. When monks marched in Pakokku in September 2007, they pledged an oath in poetic form that explains their reasons. The poem, written in Pali, expresses solidarity with the laypeople from whom monks receive the support they need to survive, and it states that it is their duty to repay this kindness by cautioning those who have taken excessive actions. It ends with the following declaration:

We march,
It is our obligation, and
It is our gratitude for the alms that the people have offered to us.

The All Burma Monks Alliance, which came to the fore in September, added a strong political slant. The four demands they issued were very specific: they wanted the government to apologize for harming monks, to rescind fuel price hikes, to release all political prisoners (including Aung San Suu Kyi), and to enter into a dialogue with the opposition that would lead to national reconciliation. With Rangoon's monks in prison or in hiding, reports of the situation in Mandalay suggested that there was still hope that these demands might yet be addressed.

Though tourists usually visit Mandalay's famed monasteries, I doubted that it would be possible for me to do so during such tense times. Together with a Western friend, I planned a tour of the city that was intended to look as innocent as possible. In Mandalay, we met up with Aung Moe, a Burmese friend who worked as a tour guide. Aung Moe had an endearingly mellow manner and was always calm and collected, even in the sweltering heat of Mandalay. He agreed to take us to one of the monasteries as long as we promised to act like tourists and not ask any tricky questions; the monasteries were already rife with informers, he warned. The distrust and fear spreading through the lay population was equally virulent behind the monastery walls, perhaps even more so. There were "new" monks with recently shaved heads—military spies infiltrating the monastic order to weed out protest organizers and check for warning signs of future demonstrations. As a result, monks were no longer talking openly within the monasteries.

Aung Moe took us to a renowned teaching monastery, where several thousand young monks studied and memorized the Buddhist scriptures. A popular stop on the tourist trail, the monastery presented a peaceful idyll with airy hostels and learning halls set around leafy courtyards. I wandered around with my camera trying to look like a good tourist by taking photos of the picturesque scenes before me. In the open-air kitchen, a monk preparing the morning meal stood amid a cloud of smoke and steam as he stirred a humongous cauldron of *daal* over a wood fire. Two young monks sat under a frangipani tree with their heads bowed over palm-leaf manuscripts, the tree's pungent white flowers scattered around them.

As we wandered through the grounds, a solitary monk unexpectedly approached us and mentioned that some seven hundred student monks had left the monastery in the previous days. Cautiously, we asked why they had left, and the monk replied that their parents were worried and had summoned them home. It was the rainy season and, according to monastic code, monks were supposed to remain in their monasteries and refrain from traveling during that time. When Aung Moe translated this, the monk gave a wry smile and explained that monastic discipline allows monks to break their retreat during the reign of a bad or evil king.

The monk ended up speaking quite frankly with us and went on to say that monks from the monastery who had organized protests were now on the run. It was difficult to contact them for guidance, because almost all the monastery's phone lines had been cut, and those that remained in use were being tapped.

Finally Aung Moe asked a question of his own. "I feel as if we have lost," he said. "Is this true?" The monk shook his head vigorously. "It's not true, and it's still possible that this will continue," he replied. "At the moment the monks here are considering what to do next. It is not an easy decision, because if we take action we know now that we will be arrested or killed. So we must think hard about the next step."

Our conversation was short by necessity as we spoke in a public place, and the monk seemed intensely agitated throughout. When we said our good-byes, he expressed his frustration. "We have nothing to fight with," he said. "We cannot fight with weapons. All we have is *Metta* [loving-kindness]."

The same emotion reverberated through almost all the conversations I had during that trip, the great sense of injustice that being on the side that holds the moral high ground is not enough when the other side has guns and brute force. It was once said that a monk could fan his robes across a criminal and protect the wrongdoer from the wrath of a king. Now the monasteries were unable to offer any kind of sanctuary.

The hopeful rumors that Mandalay monks were holding out against the army turned out to be just that: rumors. We visited other monasteries and pagodas, but many had soldiers posted at the gates and no other monks were willing to speak openly with us. By the end of our short tour, Aung Moe was despondent. "It's over for us," he said. "There is talk that the people will rise up again, but how? They [the regime] know well how to keep the people down. They have a lot of practice in doing this."

Around that time a protest poster was being pasted anonymously on monastery walls that seemed to sum up conditions, not just in Mandalay but throughout the country. The poster showed an image of the Buddha wrapped in chains and preaching to his disciple monks. "Run now, my sons," says the Buddha. "I cannot protect you anymore, for I, too, am in chains."

IT WAS A curious coincidence that a film telling the story of Angulimala, a murderous villain of Buddhist legend, was showing in Rangoon throughout the month of September. A prominent movie billboard in the downtown area featured a gigantic image of the ferocious killer wearing a gory necklace of human fingers, each one still dripping with blood.

According to legend, Angulimala begins life as a young boy called Ahimsaka who is born into a wealthy family of high-caste Brahmins during the time of the Buddha. Ahimsaka is a clever and talented boy. At school, he outshines the other pupils, and they soon become jealous of him and plot his downfall. The pupils manage to turn the teacher against Ahimsaka and persuade him to set the boy a task that he will never be able to complete. The teacher gives Ahimsaka an outrageous mission; he tells the boy that he must kill one thousand people. The boy trusts his teacher and assumes that he has no choice but to fulfill the command. He begins to roam the forest and waylay unwary travelers. Each kill poisons his mind with hatred, and he grows up to become a diabolical and dangerous creature. To keep count of his victims, he chops a finger from each corpse and hangs it around his neck, taking on the moniker "Angulimala" (literally, "garland of fingers" in Pali).

As the crimes of Angulimala become known throughout the land, people live in fear that they may be his next victim. The king finally decides to capture Angulimala and put an end to all the killings so that travelers can pass safely across the land. As the king organizes his troops to raid the lair of the beast, Angulimala's mother comes to realize that her son is the target of the king's soldiers. Though he has become barbaric and cruel, her motherly instinct drives her into the forest to warn him of the impending ambush.

By that time, Angulimala has 999 fingers hanging around his neck and needs only one more digit to prove that he has completed the gruesome task he has worked so long on and sacrificed so much for. Angulimala waits eagerly in the forest for his next victim. When his mother arrives, Angulimala's bloodlust is so great that he does not recognize her. As he charges toward his mother to kill her, the Buddha miraculously appears between mother and son. Angulimala turns his rage on the Buddha and starts to chase him. The Buddha walks at a sedate pace, but Angulimala is not able to catch him, even though he is running as fast as he can. Exhausted and maddened, he roars at the Buddha to stop. The Buddha replies calmly, I *have* stopped—it is *you* who has not stopped. The Buddha explains that he has stopped killing and harming other beings and that the time has come for Angulimala to do the same. Stunned by the Buddha's words and the phenomenon he has just witnessed, the weary villain drops his weapons and bows down before the Buddha, renouncing his wicked ways.

Later, the king arrives at the monastery where the Buddha was residing, and the Buddha asks him what he would think if he was told that Angulimala had become a monk. Unable to imagine the slathering beast who wore human fingers around his neck transformed into a monk, the king says that if it were indeed true, he would pardon Angulimala of all his crimes. The Buddha then points to the meek form of Angulimala dressed in the robes of a monk. The astounded king marvels that such a task could have been accomplished with neither weapons nor force, and he kneels to pay his respects to the newly ordained monk.

And so Angulimala lives out his days in the monastic order. Villagers, remembering the fear and bloodshed he caused, throw stones at him as he goes about his daily alms round. Angulimala tolerates these attacks in silence, knowing that it is karmic penance for his sins.

THE SAME QUESTION was being repeated over and over again: How could soldiers abuse and kill monks? How could Buddhists commit such unthinkable acts against their own clergy?

Most people reasoned that the soldiers could not have been Buddhists; they must have been Christian soldiers recruited from Chin State in the northwest who did not have the same reverence toward Buddhist monks. Some said the soldiers were high on amphetamines—witnesses who had seen them at close range noted that their eyes were bloodshot. One man was convinced that the soldiers had recently been released from a military lockup and told that if they followed orders during the operation they would be freed. Another had a source in the military who informed him that they were part of an orphan brigade the generals had been grooming for just such an occasion—a ruthless band of killers raised from childhood with no ties to family or community.

For Buddhist soldiers, the order to attack a monk must have gone against every grain of their spiritual upbringing. The *Tatmadaw*, however, trains its soldiers to follow orders without question or hesitation. The willingness expected of a soldier is encapsulated in the Burmese saying that a cup must be filled with water even if it is cracked and leaking. As a Burmese man explained it to me, "If a commanding officer says, 'Get me a cup of water,' the soldier must fulfill the order, whether or not the cup is broken. There are no excuses."

The *New Light of Myanmar* printed its own creative explanation for the attack on monks; according to the state newspaper, they weren't real monks. The "unrest" was blamed on rogue monks who had been manipulated by student leaders from 1988, the National League for Democracy, and others. One article listed the evidence found during a monastery raid in Rangoon. It was a long list that attempted to cover every offense a monk could possibly commit against the religious order. Among the incriminating artifacts were the following: four pornographic photographs and ten condoms (sex); eighteen swords, thirteen catapults, six wooden rods, and one ax (violence); thirty booklets featuring football match fixtures (gambling); and transcripts of NLD speeches and one book of anti-government poetry (political involvement). Included at the end of the list, presumably for good measure, were one Nazi headband and two U.S. headbands.

I discussed the article with a Buddhist scholar who spent much of his life in monastery libraries deciphering the Pali scriptures. He scoffed at this clumsy attempt to discredit the monks and pointed out that one of the five greatest sins a Buddhist can commit is to attempt to destroy the monastic order. "The penalty for this sin is to suffer in the eighth chamber of hell for a period that will last eons and eons," said the scholar, going on to describe what Burmese Buddhists believe to be the lowest and most frightening layer of the cosmos. "There are many tortures that those condemned to the eighth chamber must endure. They will be fried alive in hot oil like fritters. They will be eaten bite by bite by dogs and bees. They will have no food and so will have to eat each other."

The authorities, apparently undeterred by the miserable end that awaited them, busied themselves with organizing mass rallies across the country in support of the regime. They were huge gatherings that, in some cases, boasted an attendance of over a hundred thousand people. Such large crowds were nothing new in Burma; just the usual rent-a-crowd, who had been bribed or bullied into attendance. Aung Moe, who had helped me in Mandalay, described how local authorities and policemen had come to his house a few days before one such rally to demand that two members of his household attend the event. If they didn't show up, the family would have to pay a fine of K3,000 (just under US$3.00 and considerably more than an average daily wage in Burma). Aung Moe could afford to buy his freedom, but there were thousands of people around Burma who couldn't. Like puppets, they marched through the streets and assembled at sports stadiums to raise their fists and wave placards that read, "Don't Destroy Peaceful Conditions," "Support the Government's Measures," and "Oppose External Interference."

As the regime wrenched the narrative of events into a plot that better suited the generals, I noticed that the people I met were closing in on themselves. I visited a poet who told me he rarely left his apartment. Most of his fellow writers were lying low, he said, afraid to convene in tea shops and talk and debate as they used to, because government spies were being extra vigilant. Trapped and isolated inside his own home, he had no outlet for the anger he felt. "We just have to put it away inside, and we end up feeling constricted here," he said, thumping his chest to indicate his heart. "On the outside, we have no choice but to keep talking, making jokes, and laughing."

Unable to express himself in any other way, he wrote poems and distributed them anonymously among trusted colleagues. The poems were bleak streams of consciousness that held no offers of hope, as the following verse shows:

Imagination, dead lost, dead imagination.
Depression, dead depression.
Core, dead core.
Meditation on death.
Buddha, dead Buddha.

Alice, a Burmese friend who works as a translator, expressed similar feelings. She was having trouble sleeping and had become very nervous. One day she heard a helicopter fly overhead and was convinced that the generals had decided to bomb Rangoon. "I know such thoughts can't possibly be true," she said, "but I still feel afraid." She had stopped going to pagodas and was only comfortable praying in private, in front of the family shrine that most Burmese Buddhists keep in their homes. Recordings of monks chanting and preaching were only played at low volume so as not to arouse the suspicions of the authorities. "At least they can't see what we are doing inside our homes," said Alice. "They can't see us light candles or hear us when we pray inside."

Despite the hopelessness and helplessness that had engulfed so many people, there were still those who refused to believe it was over. I heard tales of monks arming themselves on the Thailand-Burma border and marching toward Rangoon to retake the city. Though the holy army never materialized, the rumor took some time to fade and was even bolstered by new details with each retelling (the United States had covertly provided the monks with guns and grenades; the monks were recruiting in monasteries along the way and had formed a force that was seven hundred strong). In Mandalay and Rangoon there were predictions of new protests set for various dates. But the dates came and went without event.

More subtle methods of demonstration were also being employed. A few people wore yellow (the color of the NLD) or black (to signify mourning for the dead). Wreaths of red flowers were placed around the city at locations where people had been killed. Though I never saw any, Ko Ye explained that it was considered a dangerous activity to distribute the flowers, and that each wreath was laid in what he called "a hit-and-run operation." Some men had shaved their heads in solidarity with the monks, but when they went out in public they wore baseball caps to hide their baldness.

One evening in Rangoon, I went for a drink with Ko Ye, who tried to convince me that the pause was simply the lull between battles. Ko Ye argued that the protests would continue sooner or later, because they were not predominately about democracy or religious ideals; they were about desperation. Monks and laypeople have become interdependent in ways that go beyond the daily alms round, he said. With few social services factored into the government infrastructure, many monasteries provide care for people in need, such as orphans and AIDS patients. As the economy worsens, people are less able to donate money and goods, and the monasteries have become overburdened and under-resourced.

"The root cause is economics," said Ko Ye. "The people will continue to get poorer, and they will continue to go out on the streets to protest, and the government will continue to shoot them. This will happen again and again until the underlying economic problem is properly addressed."

At the end of the evening, having filled up an ashtray with cigarette butts and emptied a few bottles of beer, Ko Ye made a toast. I couldn't tell if he was being facetious or sincere when we clinked our glasses together and he said, "Here's to the revolution!"

I stayed in Burma for a few weeks before returning home to Bangkok, but nothing more happened. I left with the disorientating feeling that I had watched history being rewritten before my eyes. At the end of the year the UN released a report that estimated at least thirty-one people had been killed during the crackdown and that a further seventy-four were missing. But the regime had done such a thorough job of cleaning up its crime scene that the full details of what happened during those heady days in September would probably never be known.

SIX

By the time I was able to get to Naypyidaw, the events of September 2007 had been subsumed by the tragedy of Cyclone Nargis. People in Burma had said to me that what the regime did to the monks that September was the worst act that could possibly have been committed, a hostile attack on the country's religion that struck at the soul of each individual Buddhist. But, just over half a year later, the regime blocked international efforts to deliver aid after the cyclone in May 2008, leaving hundreds of thousands of people destitute in the wake of a natural disaster. More than ever, I wanted to visit Than Shwe's citadel. Having seen the aftermath of the regime's cruel decisions and unconscionable policies, I wanted to go to the centrifugal point of the regime's malignant power and see what kind of brave new world the senior general had created for himself.

In early 2009, I made inquiries about traveling to Naypyidaw. Though no official announcement was ever made, the prohibitions on foreign visitors appeared to have been lifted. By then, Than Shwe's city was being

billed as a tourist destination in publications that listed the country's
must-see sites. One glossy guide even ran advertisements for the city's
fancy hotels and numerous golf courses.

Yet it still wasn't particularly easy to get to Burma's capital city. Buses
left Rangoon every night, but at the bus station there was confusion as
to whether it was permitted for bus companies to take foreigners to
Naypyidaw. A Rangoon travel agent informed me that there were only
three flights a week to the capital, and that all flights were fully booked
for the few weeks I was able to travel. In the end, I hired a car and driver
from a tour company willing to take me after first checking that there
were indeed no travel restrictions for foreigners.

It was raining as we drove out of Rangoon in the late afternoon, and
the crowded downtown streets rolled past in a blur of brightly colored
umbrellas and *longyi* as people hurried to escape the rain. We soon left
the city behind and began traveling northward along a busy highway,
past pagodas, tea shops, and wooden rest stops set up along the roadside.
After about an hour, the car turned off the main road and pulled up at
a shiny new tollbooth. The modern construction seemed out of place
against the dusty, old-world landscape. This, the driver explained, was
where the road to Naypyidaw began.

The road was an empty and eerie thoroughfare that cut an almost
unswerving line through desolate countryside. For most of the journey,
the car I was in was the only vehicle on the road; the purpose-built
eight-lane highway to the capital was supporting the traffic of a tiny
country lane. There were few road signs and no streetlights. It was
nighttime when we stopped to stretch our legs, and I stepped out into
a blackness so complete that it seemed to swallow up the car's headlights. Wild elephants reportedly roam the shrublands and sometimes
amble across the highway, but all I saw was one small, unidentifiable
animal. Caught in the diminishing beam of the car headlights, its eyes

glowed green and its black body looked hunched and worried as it scurried across the road.

We arrived at Naypyidaw around midnight, and at first glance the city was a welcoming spectacle. The wide streets were, like the road we had just come along, devoid of any life, but they were at least well lit, with orderly rows of bright streetlights—a public amenity seldom available in other Burmese cities. The driver drove directly to the hotel zone, the only place where foreigners were allowed to stay. The zone comprised a number of luxury hotels, all designed in a similar style, with villas dotted across a man-made landscape of rolling green hillocks. Built and run by companies belonging to cronies of the regime—such as Max Myanmar, Asia World, Htoo Trading—the hotels were well-appointed affairs with tennis courts, swimming pools, and spa services.

Despite the late hour of my arrival, the manager and six eager staff were waiting for me at the hotel where I had made a booking. I was ushered into a plush entrance hall and presented with a cocktail glass of fruit juice by a waiter wearing maroon silk pantaloons. Once my guest registration forms were filled in, another pantaloon-clad bellboy loaded my luggage onto a golf cart and drove me to my villa. The room was elegantly decked out with teak flooring, moody watercolors of traditional Burmese scenes on the walls, and a pair of gold satin slippers at the foot of the bed. CNN was available on the television and there was a Yellow Pages directory for Naypyidaw on the desk. Having read cloak-and-dagger accounts written by foreign journalists who had snuck into this forbidden city, this pleasant welcome was not at all what I had expected.

At the hotel restaurant the following morning, a smiling waiter brought me food from the breakfast buffet, cheerfully toasting bread and serving up slices of crisp honeydew melon and Chinese pear. The other diners appeared to be preparing for their morning meetings with the government. There was a table of Singaporean businessmen deep in discussion with their Burmese colleagues, a Western representative of the United Nations Office on Drugs and Crime studiously leafing through a report, and a few smartly dressed men typing at their laptops. It felt a little like sitting in a roomful of courtiers who, while preparing to petition the king, were dining in splendor in the outer reaches of the palace.

NAYPYIDAW IS NOT the sort of place you can stroll around. It is a vast and sprawling city built on a grand scale. Wide boulevards feed into landscaped roundabouts decorated with immaculate arrangements of palms and flowering plants. The buildings are huge and set far apart on large plots of land. City hall is a palatial structure with a long, sweeping driveway. At the fire station, three lollipop-red fire engines are parked in a spacious lot beneath a high-roofed garage. There are few cars on the roads, and the only people I saw on my first day there were workers tending the young saplings planted alongside the thoroughfares and at the expansive roundabouts. Wearing long-sleeved shirts and conical straw hats to protect themselves against the blistering sun, they seemed tiny and insignificant against the monumental backdrop of Naypyidaw.

Though it is often assumed that relocating the capital was done on a whim of the senior general—inspired by a portentous dream he had had or a prediction by one of his astrologers—there may also have been practical considerations. Naypyidaw is more defensible in the event of an invasion by foreign powers, as it is inland and backs onto a protective mountain range. Rangoon, by contrast, is located by a major waterway and is vulnerable to an attack from the sea. It was earlier in 2005, the year the regime began shifting the capital, that the United States included Burma on a list of "outposts of tyranny" around the world, along with Cuba, North Korea, Iran, Zimbabwe, and Belarus. Having watched the United States invade Afghanistan and Iraq, Burma's generals—who come from a generation of men born while their country was under the rule of foreign invaders—may well have felt the need to fortify themselves against possible attacks.

According to the traditional model of Asian states, power emanates outward from the citadel, and Naypyidaw's central location in the heartland of the country also makes it a more functional headquarters. Moving the seat of government away from Rangoon provided the generals with the added benefit of being able to maintain control in the event of civil unrest. When civil servants joined in the protests during the 1988 uprising, numbers on the streets swelled and the government came to a standstill, as there were few employees left to manage day-to-day affairs. In Naypyidaw, civil servants are housed in a special zone cut off from the mainstream population, thereby lessening the likelihood of a similar scenario.

Than Shwe was apparently lauded for his foresight, as the move to Naypyidaw came just in time for the ruling administration. During September 2007, civil servants and government offices were safely located a couple of hundred miles away from the upheavals and were therefore unable to join in or be influenced by the protesters. The move also saved government offices and military personnel from the destruction and disruption caused by Cyclone Nargis. One government minister is said to have stood up during a meeting and thanked the senior general for having the wisdom to lead the government to a safe haven.

When I arrived in Naypyidaw, Than Shwe's vision was still very much a work in progress. At various points around the city, foundations were being excavated and pyramids of timber and brick were piled alongside the road. There were areas of unused land enclosed in fancy gold-tipped fencing and barren stretches where nothing had been built yet. But the city had come a long way from what I had seen in the early photographs and was beginning to display the trappings of a proper metropolis. The hospital and school had been completed. The authorities were aiming to create unrivaled centers of health and learning in Naypyidaw by poaching the best doctors and teachers from institutions around the country (when the regime summons you, it's hard to say no).

Though there was a covered market surrounded by a few small shops and a handful of restaurants, there was still much that was missing. In an upmarket shopping zone with identical rows of empty shops linked by chirpy pink pavements, there was nothing for sale. And the city had few cultural attractions; there were no historical sites, no cinema or theater, and only one museum (showcasing gems). It was rumored that the national museum would be transferred from Rangoon, and plans had been set in place to shift the national library to Naypyidaw (much to the dismay of students and academics in Rangoon). In this made-to-order city, Naypyidaw's urban planners seemed to be working against a checklist that detailed the necessary requisites of a capital:

A reputable hospital, check.
Some good schools, check.
Markets and restaurants, check.

For lack of anything else to do while in Naypyidaw, I went to visit the Water Fountain Garden. It was one of the city's touted attractions, but I must have arrived on the wrong day or at the wrong time, as all the fountains had been turned off and the gardens were mostly deserted.

The park had lots of hopeful features, but they had all been poorly or cheaply constructed. In the gardens there was a pond with stone dolphins leaping out of the water in neat formation, but the sculptures were already beginning to crack and the tail of one of the dolphins had fallen off into the water. A flowering vine had been trained into the shape of a heart so that couples could sit inside it and have their photographs taken, but the heart was scrappily rendered and the grass around it was parched and brown. I later read in a local publication that a "third phase of construction" on the Water Fountain Garden was about to begin, and that the gardens were to be extended with additional features. An army colonel was quoted as saying that the gardens were an important attraction for local people, government employees, and visitors.

Water Fountain Garden, check.

Over the few days I stayed there, I saw plenty of fissures in the showpiece of Naypyidaw. In stark contrast to the imposing buildings were the hidden shantytowns where the laborers who were building the city lived. At the foot of a hill behind air-conditioned restaurants catering to well-to-do diners, I saw a cluster of huts cobbled together from scraps of leftover building material. The flimsy shelters looked as if they could be blown away by the slightest of breezes. While automatic sprinklers soaked the landscaped greenery of the roundabouts in Naypyidaw, the surrounding area struggled for water. In the old town of Pyinmana, which is connected to Naypyidaw, running water was not always available and horse-drawn carts went from house to house delivering water in wooden barrels.

Many people I have spoken to, both in Burma and outside, think that Than Shwe may not even realize the full extent of the country's woes. Surrounded by yes-men, he makes few forays around the country and, when he does travel, his trips are planned meticulously. Some years previously, when I traveled through the north of the delta region, I noticed that the road had been recently upgraded. The potholes had been filled in with still-sticky tarmac and neat yellow lines painted down the center of the road. There were shiny new street signs and intersections decorated with potted trees and flowering plants. I later learned that the road was given a makeover because the senior general would be using the route on his way to Ngwe Saung Beach for a holiday. Though I didn't have a chance to see the road after the general had driven down it, I could easily imagine that the trees and street signs had been packed away and driven off to the general's next destination, where they would be laid out again, courtesy of the Department of Pleasant Scenery for the Esteemed Commander in Chief.

Bad news does not filter upward in Burma. Government staff afraid of punishment or dismissal find ways to omit unpleasant information from their reports and opt instead to put the best possible spin on what facts they do include. On paper, crime is negligible in Burma, and theft is reported to be a rare occurrence. Pupils pass their exams with flying colors and the country's literacy rate is ludicrously high (94.83 percent). As news and statistics progress up the hierarchy, they are said to gain more and more distance from the actual truth. By the time a report or newspaper is placed on the senior general's desk or an officer reads him a brief, it may bear little, if any, resemblance to reality. It is a phenomenon that a friend of mine lyrically refers to as "no bad news for the king."

With hardly any people walking along its broad streets and none of the lively street life of Rangoon, Naypyidaw had a quiet, almost ghostly atmosphere. At the time of the relocation, political analysts expressed concern that the already ostracized regime would become more isolated. Naypyidaw definitely felt cut off. There were no international companies or organizations based there. Though foreign governments had been allotted land to build new embassies in Naypyidaw, none of them had taken up the offer and they had all kept their embassies in Rangoon. At the time of my trip, there was only one representative of the outside world planning to establish an embassy in Naypyidaw, and that was North Korea.

The city's star attraction, listed in the Yellow Pages and mentioned in the glossy tourist guide, was the Naypyidaw Zoological Gardens. I had heard a lot about this zoo. Many animals had been moved there from the old zoo in Rangoon, built over a century ago by the British. In a scene reminiscent of Noah's ark, leopards, lions, hippos, vultures, snakes, deer, elephants, monkeys, bears, zebras, turtles, and crocodiles were loaded onto trucks and transported to new enclosures at Naypyidaw. Additional animals were also acquired. The Bengal tigers were left to prowl restlessly around their mildewed Carnivora house at the Rangoon zoo as two infinitely more exotic Siberian white tigers were purchased from China for Naypyidaw's menagerie.

According to the leaflet, the Naypyidaw zoo is home to eighty-one different species. The complex is built in the style of an open zoo with few cages. Lazy, long-armed gibbons live on their own private islands. Eagles and vultures swoop beneath the almost invisible net of an aviary set around a picturesque lake. The white tigers pace within an enclosure that boasts a waterfall and mini mountains. The baboon and his fiery harem rage along a clifflike outcrop of rocks. But the zoo's greatest success by far has to be the much talked about penguin house, home to the country's first and only colony of penguins.

Keeping penguins alive in the scalding hot plains of central Burma requires prodigious amounts of air-conditioning, and the penguin house was icy cool. It was built in the rough shape of an igloo from cement frosted to emulate a block of ice. The walls of the interior were painted to look like the endless skies of the Pacific Ocean and the room was bathed in a luminous blue light. The aquarium-style enclosure allowed visitors to marvel at the flightless birds both on land and under the water.

The twenty-five African black-footed and Humboldt penguins seemed a merry bunch as they waddled inelegantly on the fake ice and chased each other through the water. The penguin house was surely the most crowded place in the city as a steady stream of visitors—families of civil servants and the odd day-tripper from nearby Pyinmana—filed through. A young girl stood with her face pressed against the glass, mesmerized by the underwater antics. A group of monks sat for a long time on the benches that lined the wall and gazed in silence at the cavorting penguins. One of the monks told me he liked the penguins so much that he was on his third visit. The penguins were definitely a success.

As I was leaving, I examined a miniature model of the zoo on display in the entrance and noticed that there had been no penguin house in the original plan. I pictured Than Shwe solemnly walking around the model before construction began. As he leaned over the tiny plastic trees and matchbox-sized animal shelters, the senior general may have said that the kangaroo run should be a little longer and the hippo pond a tad wider. These details were easy to fix, but consternation and kerfuffle undoubtedly ensued when the senior general asked where the penguin house was. Every *proper* zoo possesses a few crowd-pleasing penguins to show off to its visitors—the omission was an unforgivable oversight. And so, I imagined, it was at the last minute that space had to be found for a penguin house at the Naypyidaw zoo, as staff set about acquiring air-conditioning units and frantically looking for an available colony of penguins.

Penguins, check.

THERE ARE NO HAPPY endings for military rulers in Burma. The country's history is littered with untimely demises and surprise betrayals. Once dead and gone, the hapless leaders are often erased from the history books. Their photographs and portraits disappear and their names are expunged from the public record.

The army's own founding father, Aung San, died a sudden and violent death at the hands of a rival politician. Once revered in the chronicles and pageantry of the *Tatmadaw*, the historical importance of this legendary hero has been whittled away over the past few decades, ever since his daughter, Aung San Suu Kyi, came to prominence as a strong opponent of the ruling junta during the pro-democracy movement of 1988. Aung San's image no longer hangs in public offices. His picture was once featured on Burmese currency notes but has been replaced by a mythical lion known as the *chinthe*—an image that contains no political innuendo.

The gradual disappearance of Aung San, nicely termed "Aung San Amnesia" by one scholar, extends to architectural reminders of his existence. Take, for poignant example, the Bogyoke (General) Aung San Museum, set in the house where Aung San and his family were living when he was killed. Located down one of the winding shady lanes that lead north of Kandawgyi Lake, the colonial home had lovely light-filled rooms and a turreted tower with a view of the Shwedagon Pagoda. Though the house itself must once have been quite grand, the museum displays I first saw on one of my earliest trips to Burma were rather pitiful. The museum received few visitors and those who did go often had to seek out the caretaker to gain entrance. The rooms were sparsely furnished, with the same furniture that was in place during Aung San's time. The family dining table had a plastic replica of Aung San's favored breakfast—a basic meal of beans and *naan* bread. Some of his books were placed in a glass cabinet along with the iconic greatcoat he wore in London. Aside from these few items, the rooms were mostly empty.

This neglected memorial to Burma's greatest hero seems destined to fade even further into insignificance. When I next visited, the gates at the bottom of the hill were padlocked shut. People in the neighborhood said the museum was closed for renovation and would be opened soon but, whenever I returned over the following months, it was still closed. "Ah," said a Burmese friend knowingly when I told him about the museum's closure: "It must be under *permanent* renovation."

The infamous dictator Ne Win, who fought alongside Aung San for Burma's independence, came to a miserable end in 2002, when his family was charged with plotting to overthrow the government. Though the aged ruler had officially retired, his son-in-law and three grandsons were imprisoned, and he and his favorite daughter were placed under house arrest. When Ne Win died later that year, there were no military honors or special recognition for the seemingly omnipotent leader who had ruled the country for more than a quarter of a century. His body was cremated hurriedly and his remains were tossed in the Rangoon River.

Whether their endings are precipitated by natural causes or dastardly plots, few of Burma's top generals have been able to retire peacefully in recent years, and there are plenty of other examples of Burmese leaders meeting a sticky end.

Saw Maung, who took over leadership of the army in 1988 before Than Shwe, began to behave erratically in public and then retired for health reasons (rumors at the time suggested he had been poisoned with drugs that made him insane, or that he had been given a lobotomy). He died five years later of a heart attack.

When Lieutenant General Tin Oo was killed in a helicopter crash in 2001, he was the fourth most senior general; though no investigation results were ever released, the helicopter reportedly went down after a grenade exploded onboard.

In 2004, the all-powerful head of military intelligence, Khin Nyunt, was ousted from his position as prime minister. He was charged with bribery, corruption, and high treason, among other crimes. His military intelligence unit was dismantled from top to bottom, allegedly resulting in the arrests of over six hundred intelligence officials and the sacking of hundreds of lower-ranking members of his staff. There were reports that soldiers took over Rangoon's main crematorium to burn the bodies of intelligence officials who had not survived their interrogations.

And the man who replaced Khin Nyunt as prime minister did not last long. In October 2007, Lieutenant General Soe Win died of leukemia at the age of fifty-nine. Soe Win was dubbed the "Butcher of Depayin" for his role in organizing the attack on Aung San Suu Kyi's cavalcade in 2003, in which an estimated seventy people were killed. Many people I spoke to in Burma believed that his death was karmic retribution. In a macabre fairy-tale twist, Soe Win's twin brother died just a month before him of the same disease.

It was the same for Burma's kings. The palace chronicles tell of men from humble origins who rose up to slay the monarch and assume the crown. The royal courts were rife with wicked princes and evil queens scheming to overthrow the throne. King Thibaw, the last of Burma's kings, ordered a massacre to eliminate any contenders to the throne, which ended in the deaths of over eighty of his royal siblings and cousins.

Life in the upper echelons of today's military is just as treacherous. Than Shwe, who rose to power under Ne Win, has picked up the late general's tactic of keeping his most loyal supporters close while expelling rivals or moving them to inactive posts. Of the nineteen original generals in the State Law and Order Restoration Council set up in 1988, Than Shwe is one of only two remaining generals; most of the others were demobilized in a mass purge in 1997. Regional commanders, who can accumulate great power and wealth from their fiefdoms, are periodically reshuffled to neutralize any potential threats.

Yet enemies lurk around every corner, and even the most trusted of comrades must be viewed with suspicion. The Burmese man whose family had military connections once told me of a dinner described to him by a high-ranking officer. Seated at the table was the spy chief Khin Nyunt and another leading general, Maung Aye. The dinner was convivial and Maung Aye displayed great deference to Khin Nyunt by spooning curries onto his plate in the traditional meal-time sign of respect for a senior. Maung Aye, however, was involved in a plot to unseat his fellow general, and the very next day Khin Nyunt was ousted from the junta.

Aung San Suu Kyi has spoken and written about how life in Burma is controlled by fear. While fear pervades civilian life, it is also prevalent in the army, from the lowliest private right up to the most senior general. Than Shwe must look back at the kings (of whom he may or may not be a reincarnation) and his predecessors in the military (some of whose downfalls he has plotted) and wonder what his own fate will be. In a sense, the senior general is trapped by the unforgiving cycle of Burmese history. If he relinquishes power and the regime falls, he could face a Nuremberg-style trial for war crimes. If he holds on to his position, the possible outcome may be assassination or deposition. According to the cruel logic of legend, the aged king must inevitably lose his grip on power and be usurped by the younger, stronger prince.

I was in Burma not long after Khin Nyunt was placed under house arrest by his colleagues and was amazed by how quickly all reminders of the general's existence were removed. Photographs of the general were excised from the Defense Services Museum along with any references to him. Plaques detailing the many donations and renovations he oversaw at pagodas around the country disappeared. It was even thought that the personal jewels he once placed on the *hti* at the top of the Shwedagon

Pagoda had been taken down, thereby removing any vestiges of a quasi-spiritual source of strength. Khin Nyunt, once one of the most influential men in the ruling junta, had effectively vanished.

The Burmese phrase *thoke thin ye*, which means "to wipe clean or eliminate," is used to describe the eradication of rivals and pretenders to the throne. *Thoke thin ye* can be likened to pulling a weed out at the roots so that no strands are left to grow anew. It is a vanishing so complete that it is almost as if nothing had ever existed.

MY EFFORTS to understand the Burmese junta required a significant amount of homework on Burmese superstitions. Astrology is taken seriously by the ruling generals. When Ne Win's family was brought down, their astrologer was also put in prison. Likewise, Khin Nyunt's downfall saw the arrest of his favored fortune-teller, Bodaw Than Hla. Among Than Shwe's primary seers are an elderly nun and a boy visionary who also happens to be his grandson. It is often said that Than Shwe does not make any major decisions without first consulting his soothsayers.

There are a great variety of specialists in Burma for those who dabble with the occult. There are alchemist monks, shamans who can conjure up love potions or fatal poisons, and practitioners of black magic known as *auk-lan saya* (literally, a "specialist of the lower path," or "one who has chosen the way of darkness").

One of the most popular forms of magic, practiced by many, is *yadaya*. Similar to voodoo, *yadaya* are ritualistic acts prescribed by an astrologer to prevent bad luck. Each *yadaya* is particular to a person's date of birth and the type of calamity that needs to be averted. Pocket books can be purchased at pagodas detailing simple *yadaya* for everyday challenges such as minor illnesses, school exams, or the construction of a new house. If, for instance, a person born on Sunday is suffering from an incurable stomach ache, he or she might be advised to offer nine candles and nine flowers to a Buddha image. Especially knotty problems might call for a certain species of flower, a designated pagoda, and a specific date or number of repetitions.

It was just after September 2007 that Kyaing Kyaing, the wife of the senior general, was said to have performed a *yadaya* ritual in which she circumambulated the Shwedagon Pagoda with a dog and a pig. I have never been able to fathom the precise significance of the animals in this odd ceremony. One theory was that they had been chosen to weaken Aung San Suu Kyi's magnetic hold over the people of Burma. The first letter of the word for dog (*khwe*) signifies Monday, and the first letter of the word for a pig (*wet*) signifies Wednesday. As Aung San Suu Kyi was born on a Tuesday, the day in between, walking the animals around in a circle symbolically binds her until she is unable to move and is therefore powerless.

Another theory had it that the ritual was conducted to reverse a prophetic saying in which a running dog and pig represent cowardly people fleeing from trouble. By leading the animals, the first lady could negate the effect of perceived troubles faced by her family and would no longer need to flee. In some versions of the story, Kyaing Kyaing actually sits astride the pig and rides it around the pagoda. Whatever the rationale, everyone I spoke to agreed it was dark magic, and that it meant the ruling family must be very afraid.

Pho Yaza, a Burmese scholar and expert in shamanistic spells, once tried to explain to me the connected practice of *ket kin*, the form of magic to which some attribute Kyaing Kyaing's midnight dog walking at the Shwedagon. *Ket kin* is premised on the idea that each letter in the Burmese alphabet is connected to a day of the week that, in turn, indicates a number and a planet. If the correct occult rituals are conducted, letters and words can influence the planets and the fate of human beings.

Ket kin was thought to have driven broad-reaching public policy in 2006, when an order was issued for people to plant physic nuts, a shrub with toxic seeds that goes by the scientific name of *Jatropha curcas*. According to state media, physic nut oil could be used as biodiesel fuel and would help the country meet its own energy needs. Mass plantings were conducted along roadsides and around schools and government buildings. Many townships were ordered to produce a required amount of physic nuts and had to either cultivate scrubland to fill the quota or replant existing arable land. Not only do the physic nuts provide fuel, the authorities claimed, but the branches can be used as firewood, crushed physic nut makes a wonderful fertilizer, and the oil even has medicinal properties. Kyaing Kyaing herself, along with other wives of the top generals, oversaw a physic nut planting event in Rangoon in which she ceremoniously watered a sapling as if she were anointing a new shrine at a favored pagoda.

To date, the physic nuts have failed to reap the miraculous rewards promised, and few people harbored any delusions that there had been agricultural or economic experts involved in the great physic nut push.

In Burmese, the physic nut is known as *kyet suu*. The first letter of *kyet* represents Monday and the first letter of *suu* represents Tuesday. If the last two parts of Aung San Suu Kyi's name, Suu Kyi (an oft-used shortened version) were reversed they would achieve the same numerical and planetary sequence as *kyet suu*. So the mass planting of *kyet suu* throughout the country neutralizes her power by figuratively reversing her name. Pho Yaza explained all this to me with a disdain that implied hardly anyone really believed this mumbo jumbo could ever do any damage to Aung San Suu Kyi's power base.

Essential to the practice of *yadaya* is numerology. Burma's calendar is filled with numerologically significant dates, such as the start of the nationwide uprising on August 8, 1988 (a date known as *shit-lay-lone*, or "the four eights"). For the regime, however, nine seems to be a luckier number and many dates relevant to the generals are coincidentally divisible by nine:

After the 1988 uprising, the SLORC took control of the country on September 18, the ninth month of the year (9 + 18 = 27, 2 + 7 = 9).

Armed Forces Day is held in the third month of every year on March 27 (27 ÷ 3 = 9).

Aung San Suu Kyi was first put under house arrest on July 20, 1989 (7 + 20 = 27, 1 + 9 + 8 + 9 = 27), a doubly auspicious day (2 + 7 = 9, 2 + 7 = 9).

A British reporter who covered Burma during and after the 1988 uprising timed his visits to Burma with what he called "power days" that were divisible by the number nine in order to have a better chance of catching news events. Though it wasn't a fool-proof system, he said it worked as well as any method used to analyze what could happen next in Burma.

Quite a few people I spoke with after September 2007 commented on how the crackdown against the monks was largely completed by September 27, 2007 (a most auspicious date that can be rewritten as 9/9/9).

In Burma, a person's date of birth is essential to diagnosing problems and charting a pathway through life. Working with this key to unlocking an individual's future, astrologers can help people decide what day to get married and even whom to get married to. It is thought by some that the date officially given as Than Shwe's birth date (February 2, 1933) is not correct. Burmese leaders have often kept their birth dates secret for reasons of personal safety; lethal magic can be practiced against you if your enemies have this key to work with.

I know a keen amateur astrologer in Burma who works not with palm-leaf manuscripts and cabbalistic squares, but with a computer program that he uses to calculate the astrological outcomes of political events. Like the reporter, he has found following the astrological forecast of the senior general a fairly reliable way of understanding decisions made by the regime. To plot the course of the general's life, it helps to have an accurate date of birth, and he methodically sifted through the calendar and times until finally arriving at one that matched up to significant events in Than Shwe's life. For the record, the date he decided on is April 1, 1932 (6:00 A.M.).

It didn't matter how much I read or how many people I talked to about the practice of magic, there was always an element that defied explanation. The new Buddha image at the Shwedagon Pagoda was a case in point.

A visit to the Shwedagon is often part of the itinerary for visiting dignitaries and, in recent years, government minders have led their guests to a new shrine placed on the pagoda platform—a sculpture of the Buddha hewn from a large hunk of white jade streaked with emerald green. Various Asian leaders have knelt in front of this image, and worshippers have included the United Nations secretary-general Ban Ki-moon, who was photographed bowing before it with his hands held together in prayer, and the UN undersecretary-general Ibrahim Gambari, pictured grasping the knees of the cross-legged image and gazing up at its face with a happy grin.

Curiously, the Buddha image does not conform to any traditional style or period in Burmese art history. The image is seated and wears a golden headdress studded with nine large rubies. It has a short neck and a broad and rather pugnacious face. Buddha images usually depict the Buddha's serenity and grace, but this one seems to highlight less flattering features. On closer inspection, the flat nose and hooded eyes bear an uncanny likeness to the country's ruler, Senior General Than Shwe.

The resemblance may be pure coincidence or another extravagant *yadaya* to secure the general's future. Or, it may just be a really good joke that keeps the boys in Naypyidaw amused and provides plenty of photo ops for ridiculing foreign leaders.

THAN SHWE'S PAGODA is visible from all over Naypyidaw. In keeping with monarchical tradition, it is a suitably enormous religious edifice constructed to provide the new capital with a spiritual heart. Known as the Uppatasanti, the pagoda is a replica of the sacred Shwedagon in Rangoon. The proportions of the new pagoda are almost identical to its ancient model, but the Uppatasanti was initially reported to be one deferential foot shorter than the Shwedagon. A *New Light of Myanmar* article, however, stated that the pagoda was 325 feet high, which would actually make it very slightly *taller* than the original.

It was early evening when I visited the Uppatasanti during my trip to Naypyidaw. Floodlights were trained on the recently completed pagoda, and it was an impressive sight. The fresh gilding was lustrous and un-earthly against the deepening indigo of the night sky. Around the pagoda endless plains stretched toward dark horizons that were lit up by shards of lightning, heralding the approach of a storm.

Unlike the Shwedagon, the Uppatasanti is hollow and visitors can enter the cavernous interior. Not all of the decorations had been com-pleted, and female workers lay on bamboo scaffolding with their faces pressed close to newly hewn carvings as they used toothbrushes to gently polish the bas-relief sculptures in the entrance archways. High up on the green walls of the inner dome, the Buddha's principal teachings are displayed in both Burmese and English. Etched onto golden plaques are the Noble Truth of Suffering and the Eightfold Path, which state that all life is suffering and counsels that solace can be found in correct conduct that includes right intention, right speech, and right action.

The construction of a pagoda, especially one of this size and stature, is an extended affair laden with ritual. The process begins with the choice of an auspicious site and ceremonies to purify the land. Foundation bricks made of gold and jade are symbolically laid at the center of the site, and sacred relics have to be acquired and enshrined within the edifice. Each step, including the actual construction, must be taken on an opportune date at a time calculated by an astrologer.

The Uppatasanti was built in keeping with these rituals, only some of which were well documented. According to the *New Light of Myanmar*, each of the ruling generals made offerings of sacred items to be enshrined at the heart of the pagoda. Among those provided by Than Shwe and his wife was a sacred tooth relic of the Buddha obtained from China. Vice Senior General Maung Aye and his wife also donated a sacred tooth relic, from Sri Lanka. (Presumably, both were replicas, as the limited number of tooth relics believed to be authentic has been accounted for.) The published list also made vague mention of "other offertories," which left many wondering what else may lie beneath the Uppatasanti.

When the body of one of Burma's most revered monks, Thamanya Sayadaw, disappeared from its resting place in April 2008, there were allegations that the generals were behind the heist. The details of the case were bewildering. One night, men wearing military uniforms stormed into the chamber where the venerated monk had been laid to rest since his death in 2003. They smashed his glass tomb and removed his body. A few days later the monastery received an anonymous message that the

Sayadaw's body had been cremated and his ashes could be picked up at a nearby village. His holy remains were duly collected and have since been securely locked away, but the case was never solved.

It is believed that when the corpse of an enlightened monk is cremated, sacred crystals or jewel-like remnants of his earthly form will be found among the ashes. These relics are called *dat-taw* and are worshipped by followers as a direct link to the deceased monk. Only a truly enlightened being, known as a *yahanda*, can leave behind such relics, and only a very few monks ever reach such spiritual heights. To be a *yahanda* is to no longer be influenced by the illusions of material life on this earth. It is the last stage of being, and upon death the *yahanda* attains Nirvana, or eternal enlightenment.

Supernatural powers are attributed to *yahanda*, such as the ability to read minds, become invisible, and even to fly. By extension, those in possession of *dat-taw* may also be able to acquire certain powers. It is not surprising, then, that the generals are said to take a keen interest in *dat-taw*. Rumor has it that the generals are putting together a collection of the *dat-taw* of nine monks from around Burma. In an interpretation of the historical practice of burying sacrificial victims to protect the citadel, the relics will be buried at various points around Naypyidaw; once all nine have been sunk into the earth, the generals believe they will have the power to rule Burma forever.

Pho Yaza, the scholar who studied shamanistic practices, was as dismissive about the cult of *dat-taw* worship as he was about the *ket kin* word magic, explaining that such relics have no traditional merit in Burmese culture, and that the actual stones were nothing more than gallstones or metal chelates trapped in the body after death. He did, however, think that the story about the generals was perfectly plausible. The fact that the case of Thamanya Sayadaw's stolen corpse had yet to be solved was evidence enough for him. "Their eyes are everywhere," said Pho Yaza of the regime. "If someone so much as sticks up an anti-government poster in the middle of the night, the authorities will put all their resources toward finding out who did it and, more often than not, they will succeed in finding that person. They can catch the players who stick up a poster, but they cannot catch the organized gang of soldiers who stole the body of one of the most famous monks in all the land? I don't believe it!"

I once went to see the *dat-taw* of a revered monk at a monastery in Rangoon. For the monk's followers, these remnants of his time in human form were a direct link to his life and teachings. Small miracles had been happening since the monk's death. During his cremation, two pythons slithered into the monastery compound and stayed for the duration of his funeral ceremony. The area around the *dat-taw* shrine had been arid before but was now fertile. A mango tree of a strain linked to the royal palace had, for the first time in living memory, begun to bear fruit.

The relics themselves were rather unimpressive; there were smooth bluish pebbles, white crystal toothpicks, and a green ball that looked like a marble. But they were housed in an ornate structure, mounted high on a large golden plinth. Each *dat-taw* had been placed in a little glass cylinder perched on a red velvet stand and topped with a tiny pagoda. Twinkling with gold and silver spires, the display was like a miniature mythical kingdom.

The monastery custodians were taking no chances with their precious legacy; the entire shrine was locked behind a sturdy metal grille with multiple padlocks.

The Uppatasanti Pagoda in Naypidaw was consecrated in a grandiose ten-day ceremony in March 2009. Each stage of the religious ceremonies was led by one or all of the top generals, depending on the importance of the ritual. Monks recited prayers for five continuous days. Extensive offerings were presented to monks by the generals and their wives. For the public, there was a fun fair, a bouncy castle, a Ferris wheel, a live circus, and dramatic performances at an outdoor theater each night.

The festivities culminated in a ceremony to raise the *hti*, or finial crown, on top of the pagoda—a ritual conducted, of course, by Than Shwe himself. With much pageantry, the *hti* was hoisted on a gilded rope pulled by Than Shwe and his wife, Kyaing Kyaing, along with close family members. Like the *hti* on top of the Shwedagon, this one was similarly studded with gems, jewelry, Buddha images, and minuscule replicas of famous pagodas carved from precious metals.

The *New Light of Myanmar* dutifully stated that paying homage to the Uppatasanti was just like paying homage at the Shwedagon. But, for all the fanfare and finery, the new pagoda seemed tawdry and tainted by its makers. The kings of Burma built pagodas to atone for their sins, and there was no doubt in people's minds that the Uppatasanti was Than Shwe's attempt to wipe his spiritual slate clean. The ambitious grandeur of both the pagoda and the city that surrounds it was clearly an architectural statement of dominance and longevity. The hulking constructions of Than Shwe's vision had been writ large upon the central plains of Burma and looked as if they were built as a stronghold intended to last for generations to come.

On the evening I visited the Uppatasanti, there were few worshippers at the pagoda. Most of the people circling the platform had come as sightseers to inspect the mammoth construction that had formed a new, glimmering mountain in the landscape. No one seemed to stay very long, but that may have been because the surrounding plains were darkening and the storm that had been hovering on the horizon had begun to head toward Naypyidaw.

It was already raining when I left the interior of the Uppatasanti and decided to head back to my hotel. As I hurried to the stairs, I saw that the golden pagoda was reflected on the glistening tiles of the platform and had cast an astral glow beneath my feet. I was momentarily reminded of the unholy magic that may have been employed in the construction of the Uppatasanti and the mysterious forces that were believed to emanate from the deep recesses beneath the pagoda.

I reached the stairwell and started to climb down alongside other fleeing visitors. The rain fell more heavily. Bolts of lightning snapped across the sky, accompanied by cataclysmic claps of thunder. But we were unable to hasten our descent, as the marble steps had become slippery with rain. Together with the other visitors, I gripped the metal handrails and made my way slowly down to ground level. By the time I looked back up at the pagoda, its brilliant form had been almost completely enshrouded by the dark and delirious fury of a monsoon storm.

PART THREE

EVERYTHING IS BROKEN

AUGUST 2008

Hardly anyone notices the solitary monk as he makes his way through the crowd. It is the day of the full moon and hundreds of visitors have come to the Shwedagon Pagoda to pay their respects. The pagoda platform is sizzlingly hot in the midday sun. Everyone who comes to this holy site must remove their shoes before entering, and worshippers are skipping quickly across the tiles to avoid scalding their bare feet. Children giggle and shriek as they race around looking for pockets of shade beneath the overhanging roofs of the prayer halls and in the crevices between the smaller shrines.

The monk seems impervious to the searing heat beneath his feet. His pace is steady and unwavering as he walks around and around the pagoda.

At one point, the monk passes a group of American tourists gathered in the shade of the southern entrance. In lilting Burmese-accented English, a tour guide recounts the legend of the Shwedagon Pagoda, which tells how two brothers from Burma traveled to India during the time of the Buddha and returned with a golden casket containing eight hairs from the Buddha's head. When the casket was opened at this site, the guide says, a miraculous light radiated throughout the land—the blind were able to see, the lame began to walk, trees blossomed and bore fruit, and precious jewels rained down from the sky . . .

A few of the tourists absently train their cameras on the passing monk, and his slow moving form is multiplied in miniature on their digital screens. The cameras automatically adjust to the stark contrasts within the frame— the deep burgundy of the monk's robes, the black-and-white marble tiles, the dazzling gold of the pagoda, the cloudless blue sky.

No one knows how many times the monk circles the pagoda before he stops, reaches into his robes, and pulls out a small knife. The knife looks like a barber's razor, the kind a monk might use to shave his head. He turns his face up toward the peak of the golden mountain and, with one long deliberate stroke, draws the blade across his throat. A moment or two passes as the monk remains standing and immobile. Then, with a sudden ungainly lurch, his body slumps heavily to the ground. A woman screams. Parents instinctively pull their children closer to them. People begin to back away as they notice the pile of robes, the limp arm, the blood seeping out across the sunbaked marble at the foot of the pagoda.

SEVEN

Seen from above, the Irrawaddy Delta is a patchwork of varied shades of green. There are swaths of velvety moss green and areas of pale jade, a color so translucent it is hardly green at all. The latticework of waterways that draw random patterns through this greenery is etched with tangled carpets of water hyacinth and spills over into the spiky neon-green expanse of the paddy fields. Villages of thatched houses are nestled within the curves of larger rivers, partially hidden beneath groves of palm trees. The entire landscape seems to undulate softly, rippling as if the surface of a pond were being disturbed by a light breeze, and it is impossible to distinguish land from water; seen from above, the delta seems to be both land *and* water.

Even three months on, the path of destruction carved by Cyclone Nargis is still clearly marked. The verdant green gives way to brown, and the delta's fertile lushness is replaced by a dying landscape. In the cyclone zone, the waterways course sickly gray and dark, brackish water seeps across the paddy fields and plantations. There are no more cozy clusters of huts and palm trees, only the remnants of villages—the hint of a dirt road beneath stagnant floodwater, the tilted skeleton of a rice warehouse that has no walls or roof, slight indentations where homes once stood. Though the original villages are gone, there are signs of rehabitation—tarpaulin tents and scrap-wood shacks—dotted here and there. But there are fewer people living in these areas since the cyclone and, beyond the tiny squares of orange and blue tarpaulin, the empty villages spread out in a ghostly imprint of life that is no longer there.

It was in this bleak and barren stretch of the delta, in early August 2008, that I visited Pyay Chaung, a village that had stood directly in the cyclone's path. The storm surge triggered by the cyclone was high enough to submerge all but the tallest palm trees in the area, and the fearsome deluge swept away the entire village and everything in it; all the people, all the houses, the wooden school building, and the jetty that once marked the entrance to the village. Even the monastery, the only structure made of concrete, crumbled beneath the weight of the water. When the flood finally receded, after twelve long hours, there was nothing left. All signs of life and habitation were gone. Pyay Chaung had, quite literally, been wiped off the map.

I had traveled to Pyay Chaung together with a Burmese aid worker and, when our boat docked at the waterfront and the boatman cut the engine, it was eerily quiet. There were no other boats and the area looked as if it had been abandoned. Once I climbed up out of the boat, though, I saw a narrow strip of frail, tentlike huts strung out along the riverbank. As I stood uncertainly on the bank there was some slight movement among the huts. Tarpaulin sheets were folded back and people began to emerge from their dwellings. They walked slowly toward us and, before long, we were surrounded by a crowd of silent, staring villagers.

The Burmese aid worker I was with had been to Pyay Chaung before and identified the village leader, explaining to him that I wanted to hear people's stories and find out what had happened to them after the cyclone. The headman told us that there had been around 360 people living in Pyay Chaung, but the cyclone had killed over 200, more than half the population. He pointed to a dark-skinned, barefoot man standing at the edge of the crowd and told us that twelve members of the man's family had perished in the storm. The crowd parted slightly so I could get a better view. The man bowed awkwardly toward me. Not knowing quite how to respond or what to say after such an introduction, I bowed back.

Then a woman in a ragged and faded red *tamein* was singled out. She had lost her husband and only child. Her baby had been just ten months old, one villager said. When I looked at the woman, she quickly pulled down the edge of the broad-brimmed straw hat she was wearing and hid her face.

A farmer told me that his wife and daughter had been killed. He explained that he had one surviving daughter but she was living elsewhere, farther north. He had no family left in the village and was unable to muster the will to begin working his fields again. "I am trying hard to overcome this," he said, "but I'm not sure that it's possible."

The introductions continued. It was a miserable litany of loss and I found myself wishing it would stop, but the villagers kept on pointing out the bereft. There were parents who no longer had any children and children who had lost both their parents. There were individuals who were the sole remnant of their entire family. And there were fifteen families with no survivors at all. The villagers had erected their shelters on the same land each family had lived on before the cyclone, and they ushered me along the narrow dirt track to show me the gaps: the plots that belonged to families that no longer existed.

In the days immediately after the cyclone, the surviving villagers had been picked up by rescue boats sent by private citizens and the authorities in the town of Bogale. Though Bogale was also badly hit by the cyclone, the storm surge had not been so high and the sturdier cement structures had been able to weather the storm. At Bogale, the villagers were able to gather together in a monastery where monks had erected large tents to shelter them and thousands of other villagers. People traveled down from Rangoon to bring them food and blankets. They drank water from plastic bottles supplied by the Red Cross and other charitable organizations they had never heard of before. Some townspeople gave them secondhand clothes to wear. A doctor and two nurses came to check on them, stitching up wounds and tending to broken limbs.

But then, after two weeks, the township authorities came to the monastery and told the villages they had to return home. Before leaving Bogale, each person received one *tamein* or *longyi*, a sizable tarpaulin sheet, a thirteen-pound sack of uncooked rice, a packet of biscuits, four portions of dried noodles, and one bottle of drinking water. Together with their supplies, they were loaded onto a boat and taken back to their village. Or, to be more accurate, they were taken back to the land on which the village had once stood.

As I followed the villagers farther along the dirt track, I looked inland and saw that there were no other signs of habitation around Pyay Chaung. Fields and swamps stretched out, endless and flat, toward a rain-smudged horizon. I was struck by how isolated the village was, here in the center of the Irrawaddy Delta. Even before the cyclone, Pyay Chaung did not have a telephone line or any electricity. Just as the rest of the world had not known what was happening in the delta during and after the storm, so people in villages like this had little idea what was going on beyond the limited part of the delta they could see before them.

I asked the assembled villagers if they had heard about the U.S., French, and British navy ships that had been moored offshore, waiting to deliver aid and provide assistance in the aftermath of the cyclone. Some of the villagers looked confused. "Wasn't that just a rumor?" one man asked.

"No, no," said another, "I heard through the radio that the ships were there, but the government would not let them land on Burmese shores."

There was a harsh laugh from the back of the crowd and someone said, "What the government wants and what the people want are often quite different!"

"So it *was* true?" a woman standing close to me asked incredulously. "The ships were really there . . . ?"

Since those fraught days in May, an unofficial détente had been declared between the aid community and the regime, and the ability of aid agencies to help cyclone survivors had been greatly increased. Building upon efforts made in those first few weeks, aid agencies were able to provide more systematic deliveries of food, shelter material, water purification equipment, and other supplies necessary for the rebuilding of homes and villages. Goods from outside the country, as well as those sourced in Burma, were being funneled through Rangoon and delivered to hubs set up by United Nations agencies and NGOs at the bigger delta towns of Pyapon, Bogale, Mawlamyainggyun, and Laputta. From these towns, supplies were being sorted and transported onward, farther into the delta.

The tide had begun to turn in the first week of June, around the time that the UN World Food Programme was finally granted permission to bring helicopters into Burma. Helicopters are usually deployed in the first few days after a natural disaster, when they can deliver immediate lifesaving supplies and conduct search-and-rescue missions in areas that are difficult or impossible to reach by land or water. It was four long weeks after the cyclone before the regime allowed the helicopters to enter Burmese airspace. Even then, permission was granted begrudgingly and with caveats; each helicopter was only allowed to be operational for three days, after which time it would have to leave the country. Daily flight plans had to be submitted and agreed to in advance, and the helicopters had to return to Rangoon each night—an order that resulted in wasting costly fuel that could have been better used flying sorties to the villages where help was still urgently needed. Eventually, though, the authorities seemed to accept the presence of the helicopters, as the three-day restriction was lifted and the fleet of helicopters was able to remain in-country, ferrying aid workers and material throughout the delta.

Aid was finally getting through to those who needed it, and NGO situation reports and press releases published three months after the cyclone recorded the results. The World Food Programme had dispatched over 25,600 metric tons of food to be distributed through local and international NGOs to almost 733,500 people. World Vision wrote that it had established its largest ever number of children's programs in a single country and had, among other activities, set up eighty-four "child-friendly spaces," which were equipped with toys and learning material for 10,000 children in Rangoon and the delta. Supplies sent by Caritas to the delta included 8,500 mosquito nets and tens of thousands of pots, pans, plates, and cups. CARE distributions included 4,000 yards of plastic sheeting and 20 metric tons of rice seed.

The increased ability of aid organizations to ramp up their emergency response was partly attributable to a diplomatic mechanism set up by the Association of Southeast Asian Nations (ASEAN) during a meeting held a couple of weeks after the cyclone. According to an ASEAN press release, the mechanism would "facilitate trust, confidence and cooperation"; it would also provide a less threatening and face-saving way forward for the Burmese government. The result was the Tripartite Core Group (TCG), which consisted of three representatives each from ASEAN, the United Nations, and the Burmese government. Based in Rangoon, the TCG held weekly meetings and acted as a sort of humanitarian broker for negotiations between the Burmese regime and the rest of the world.

One of the TCG-negotiated efforts was the Post-Nargis Joint Assessment, or PONJA, a survey of the cyclone-affected area conducted by 250 enumerators recruited from all the parties involved—ASEAN, the UN, NGOs, and the government. The PONJA collated data from a sample of 291 villages spread out evenly in the cyclone's path and was the first effort to compile comprehensive data on what had happened in the delta since Cyclone Nargis.

I happened to be in Rangoon in late July 2008, when the survey was released, and went to the ceremony launching the completed PONJA report at one of the city's plush business hotels. It was a relatively grand affair attended by foreign ambassadors and the heads of UN agencies and aid organizations. A simultaneous launch was also held at the ASEAN ministerial meeting that was taking place in Singapore. The Burmese government was represented by the deputy minister of foreign affairs, Kyaw Thu, who called it "an auspicious and milestone event." Camera flashes went off across the hall as the deputy minister spoke, and the ceremony had a strangely celebratory air, as if he were opening a new school or launching a ship rather than releasing a document detailing the losses and damage caused by a natural disaster.

For all the hype and publicity, the PONJA report was an unsatisfying document to read. The section describing "The Immediate Response" skips neatly over the month of May and focuses on June, blithely ignoring the initial weeks after the cyclone. The text was airbrushed substantially with sentences like "[T]he armed forces provided services that assisted the government, the private sector, civil society organizations, local community and international aid workers for more effective and timely delivery of aid supplies and services to the victims of the cyclone." Such descriptions were, to say the least, a euphemistic interpretation of events.

Despite mumbled criticisms, however, aid workers I spoke to in Rangoon said the PONJA was a useful tool for convening with the various ministries. It meant that they didn't have to deal with the government's usual denials (*yes, we have no disasters today*), and they had a working document everyone could refer to that stated, yes, there is a problem, and, yes, we need to prioritize, say, the treatment and distribution of clean and drinkable water.

It still was not easy for foreign aid workers to get into Burma and work in the delta, but it had, at least, become possible. The first hurdle was simply getting into the country. Though many more visas were being granted (by early August, the UN reported 358 of its staff had received visas), not everyone was allowed in. Outside Burma I had had countless conversations about how to secure a Burmese visa. There seemed to be no rhyme or reason to the process, and the information we exchanged was often contradictory:

> *I heard the embassy in Australia isn't giving out any visas.*
> *Go to Canberra—the ambassador there is sympathetic and it's the best place to apply.*

> *Passports without any previous visas to Burma are being rejected.*
> *Apparently it looks bad if you have too many Burma entry stamps in your passport.*

Some aid workers thought it might be easier to apply for tourist visas and enter the country unofficially, but it was a hit-or-miss tactic. One aid worker who tried that method had her passport returned with a Post-it note stuck above a Pakistan entry stamp dated 2005, the time of the Kashmir earthquake. The word "earthquake" had been written on the note, and it must have been assumed by eagle-eyed embassy staff that the timing of her visit to Pakistan was no mere coincidence.

Once in the country, the next hurdle was gaining access to the delta. Special travel permits had to be requested from the TCG and whichever government ministry the aid agency was affiliated with. I was able to obtain permission to travel since I had been hired to compile reports on conditions in the delta for international aid agencies, and they applied on my behalf. When I went to the delta, I still had to return to Rangoon to request additional permission letters for each township I visited. My arrival and departure needed to be signed off by the township authorities, and though I was able to travel to the villages by day, I had to return each evening and spend the night in the town where I was registered.

The bureaucracy involved was maddening, but I was finally able to meet people who had lived through Cyclone Nargis; though they had been at the epicenter of recent events, their voices had remained mostly unheard. In between compiling the specific information I needed for the aid agency reports, I spoke to as many people as I could wherever I went.

I had to leave Pyay Chaung, the village I was visiting, by late afternoon so as to get back to Bogale before nightfall, but the headman wanted to introduce me to the local noodle vendor before I left. Mya Win was in his late forties and used to have a family business making the popular noodle soup *monhinga* to sell to villagers. He had lost his entire family during Cyclone Nargis, his wife and four children, ranging in age from fourteen to twenty-two.

So that we could chat away from the crowd, Mya Win invited me into the hut he had built after the cyclone. It was a small structure, the size of a child's playhouse, with just enough space for one man to lie down on the floor and a roof so low that I had to stoop to climb inside. The rickety shelter was made from donated tarpaulin and mismatched planks Mya Win had retrieved from the storm debris.

As we sat squeezed inside the cramped hut, Mya Win talked about what happened to him and his family when the cyclone passed over the village. His face had a naturally stern expression that made him look as if he was concentrating especially hard on remembering something, and he spoke in an unhurried monotone. When the river began to overflow its banks, Mya Win moved his family to his brother's larger house, where he thought they would be safe. About thirty people had gathered in the house, and they sat together, chanting Buddhist prayers and praying for protection as the wind grew louder and the water rose up through the floorboards. The water rose so rapidly that before they could decide what to do they were standing in a waist-deep flood inside the house. Adults hoisted small children onto their shoulders and women clutched at their billowing *tamein*. Then, without warning, the roof flew off the house and the whole structure collapsed.

"It was like an explosion," said Mya Win. "People were thrown everywhere—into the water and into the air . . . I fell in the water and tried to swim, but it wasn't possible, because the waves were too rough. I grabbed at a floating piece of wood—it had come, I think, from the buffalo shed near my brother's house. I called out to people, to my family, but I couldn't hear anything above the noise of the storm . . . After that, I never saw anyone from my family again."

I had thought Mya Win would carry on speaking, but he ended his story there. One of the villagers standing at the entrance of his hut filled in the rest on his behalf, explaining how the storm surge had carried Mya Win far away from the village and how he had walked back the next day to find that there was nothing left of his family or his home.

Mya Win reached into a corner of the hut where a sleeping mat was rolled up and extracted a photograph that was tucked inside a folded blanket. It was a picture of his wife that he had come across while helping fellow villagers clear corpses from the fields. He never found the bodies of his wife and children, and this was all he had left to remember his family by. He handed it to me. The photograph was the size of a postage stamp and must once have been attached to an ID card—it was a small miracle that Mya Win had been able to find such a tiny picture amid the vastness of the demolition that had taken place around him. A water stain had spread across his wife's broad cheekbones and the black-and-white image was already beginning to fade.

"How will you make a living now?" I asked. Mya Win answered that he couldn't go back to selling *monhinga*, as it was a family business and he no longer had any family to help him. There was a small plot of land belonging to his in-laws, and they had spoken about helping him start a plantation, perhaps some areca palm trees, the seeds of which can be sold to betel nut vendors—the market for betel nut was always steady, especially in the delta where so many people still liked to chew betel for its mild narcotic effect. But as Mya Win spoke it was clear that he wasn't that interested in farming, or areca palms, or the economics of betel. I couldn't begin to conceive of what it must be like to summon the strength needed to start life all over again.

The cramped space we sat in was filled with items Mya Win had found in the wreckage of the village or goods that had been given to him since the cyclone. There were a few tools and some building materials—a hammer, a machete, coils of old rope, some plastic tubing of varying lengths, and a rusting sheet of corrugated iron. On a plank of wood, a simple shrine had been set up consisting of a Buddha image, a few candles, and two wooden rosaries for meditation. Also on the shelf was a flashlight with three Chinese batteries placed in a neat row. Together with the sleeping mat, a tin cup, a few melamine plates, and a cooking pot, they represented the sum total of Mya Win's possessions.

When we stepped out of the hut, Mya Win tied the door shut and looped a padlock through the knot. I wondered why he was locking up so fastidiously; I had seen nothing of value that anyone could possibly have wanted to steal and, besides, a thief could easily pull away a loose plank or cut through the tarpaulin. As he slipped the padlock key onto a string around his wrist, Mya Win followed my gaze and explained. "This is everything I have," he said. "I have to try and protect it as best I can."

AT A TRADITIONAL village funeral in Burma, the body of the deceased is bathed, wrapped in white cloth, and laid out on a bamboo mat. A coin is placed into the dead person's mouth so that he can pay his way to the afterworld. A meal of curry and rice is laid out next to the body and, if the person was a smoker, cigarettes or cheroots and a lighter are placed within easy reach. Merit-making ceremonies are performed at a monastery during which family members offer meals to the resident monks. In some cases, lengths of thread measuring exactly the same as the deceased person's children may be laid out beside them—a symbolic protective measure to ensure that strong emotional attachments do not enable them to snatch the souls of their children to take with them into the next life.

The body is either cremated or buried, after which someone from the family will snap a twig off a tree and take it into their house in the belief that the dead person's spirit will follow them. For a further seven days, the spirit stays temporarily in the home as it adjusts to the afterlife, and then a final farewell ceremony is held to accrue additional merit for the deceased and signal his release from earthly attachments.

It is a Buddhist belief that those who die while still attached to people or possessions will enter the realm of *peta*, or hungry ghosts, where they take on a ghostly form and remain trapped on earth, unable to move to the next realm. Some believe that all those who died a violent death are relegated to this realm, as they were killed suddenly without time to mentally prepare for death and relinquish their attachments to family and material possessions. The correct funeral arrangements are conducted not only to help the deceased by providing them with increased merit for their next rebirth, but also to ensure that they do not reappear as ghosts and remain to haunt the living.

The dead have returned in many forms since Cyclone Nargis, most commonly during the night. Sometimes people hear distraught cries for help. Terrible screams echo across the paddy fields. At other times, the noises are more gentle; a newlywed couple is often heard murmuring to one another in the corner of one village, though they both died during the cyclone. Lights flit along pathways where no one is walking. People wake up with the sensation that someone has been grasping at their arms or legs, in the same way people held on to each other during the storm.

Some people see members of their family. Early one evening, in the melting light that follows sunset, a man heard his name called from above. He looked up to see his dead aunt sitting high up in a coconut tree; she waved at him and kicked her legs as if she were playing on a swing. Lost children repeatedly walk through their parents' fitful dreams. Though they sometimes linger after their mother or father has woken up, they never stay long enough to provide any solace. Mostly the dead manifest themselves in disturbing ways that imply they are not there to help the living.

The bodies of those who died in Cyclone Nargis were never systematically cleared or properly buried. They decayed where the storm had left them or were disposed of without ceremony. Twenty unpaid workers from a village south of Laputta were given an incomplete set of masks and gloves by the township authorities and sent out to clear away any corpses that remained some two weeks after the storm. They were instructed that any bodies found close to the river should be thrown into the water and that those too far away should be buried or burned. A navy boat was said to have collected bodies in a net and sailed out to sea to disperse them in deep water. A man from Ah Mat village described how the corpses had piled up against a low hill. The surviving villagers had tried to cremate them, but they wouldn't burn—there were too many of them and what kindling could be found was too damp. The villagers left to seek shelter in Laputta, and when they returned to the village a month later, the pile of decaying bodies was still there.

For survivors living in the delta, it was impossible to erase these gruesome images. In a village not far from the delta town of Mawlamyainggyun, I walked past a large fresh-water pond that seemed to me a beautiful and tranquil spot. It was early morning and vivid pink lotus buds were opening on the surface of the water. But the villagers shuddered as they passed it. Many dead bodies had been found floating in the pond after Cyclone Nargis and, no matter how many times the pond was cleaned and washed out with lime powder, people still found that the water had a peculiar taste. As no one in the village was willing to use the water for drinking, cooking, or even to wash their clothes, it had become an ornamental pond—an unmarked and unintentional memorial to those who died there.

The dead were indelibly etched into people's memories and onto the landscape. The bodies of people and carcasses of farm animals that floated in the waterways during the weeks after the cyclone had now sunk beneath the surface, but at low tide the waters would recede and reveal anonymous piles of bones slick with the fertile, alluvial mud of the delta.

As I traveled from village to village, mostly by boat, I imagined that the riverbeds must be lined with bones. After a while, I began to see the dead everywhere, even in places they were not. When we sailed down a deserted creek, I mistook a fallen coconut embedded in the mud for a human skull. Blinking into the midday sun, palm fronds on the ground looked to me like rib cages, and fallen sun-bleached branches took on the appearance of femurs, ulnae, loose vertebrae.

AFTER LONG DAYS in the villages, it was with a guilty sense of relief that I returned each night to Bogale. In contrast to the desolation of the villages, the activity on the streets of Bogale felt enlivening and gave the impression that the aid effort was progressing and that life could somehow recover, even after so much had been lost.

Once a trading outpost for the agricultural and fishery products of the delta, Bogale had a well-worn, old-world atmosphere. Aged houses built of timber had been weather-proofed repeatedly over the years and now had an obsidian glow. The paint on Soviet-style concrete shop-houses constructed in the 1960s had faded beneath the harsh delta sun to pastel blushes that contained barely a hint of the original green, blue, or yellow. The few more modern structures were scrappy low-rise buildings no more than three or four stories high, with tiled exteriors and cheap, tinted windows. There were still reminders of the cosmopolitan mix of people once drawn to the delta for its business opportunities—in the center of town there was a mosque, a Hindu temple, and a number of Chinese shrines carved with writhing, rainbow-colored dragons.

The wreckage of Cyclone Nargis was still very visible, especially on the edges of town, where thatch houses had been resurrected and pieced together from disparate strips of paneling and cloth. Almost all of the town's trees had been felled by the storm, and logs and branches were chopped up and stacked in yards and at street corners. On a few buildings, gleaming tin sheets were used to replace old roofing and shingles that had been blown away.

The heyday of the delta was long past. Before World War II, when Burma was the largest rice exporter in the world, the delta had been the pulsing agricultural heart of the rice business and Bogale was a town of thriving traders and brokers. Farmers, fishermen, and plantation workers sold their produce in town, and from there it was then traded within the country or exported abroad. But years of deprivation and mismanagement that began under military rule and the socialist policies of the 1960s decimated the rice industry, and today Burma exports just one-tenth of the three million tons that used to be loaded onto ships at Rangoon, or at Pathein on the western coast of the delta, and sent out of the country each year.

The glory days of the rice trade may be over, but Bogale still functions as a somewhat dilapidated clearinghouse for the produce of the delta farmlands. Aid material moving through Bogale—initially emergency relief supplies and then more sustained deliveries for rehabilitation and longer-term aid programs—had reenergized the economy and the town. Disused warehouses colonized by sparrows and rats had been cleaned up, and sacks of rice and other commodities were once again piled high within the dark, cavernous interiors. The rickety walkways of the wooden jetties were crowded with laborers off-loading barges that had sailed down from Rangoon. They jostled one another to hand their colored sticks to tallymen as they redistributed the supplies onto smaller boats capable of navigating the narrower creeks and waterways farther south.

Boats moored along the riverfront flew the flags of aid organizations. Attached to a fishing boat was a white flag bearing the circle of yellow-and-orange handprints that is the CARE logo, while another vessel flew the red-and-white standard of Médecins Sans Frontières, accompanied by the organization's ever-present "no guns" symbol. In the town, grimy guesthouses had been given a new lick of paint to cater to the incoming international and local aid workers. Houses had been rented out to aid organizations and UN agencies to use as temporary offices. Outside each office, generators as big as cars thundered continuously throughout the day and late into the night.

Maps of the delta were stuck on the walls inside, listing town names, population figures, and ongoing needs. A color-coding system was used to indicate the locations where each organization was working, and the delta was shown carved up by new boundaries; there was a United Nations Development Programme area, a Pact zone, and World Vision villages, among others. Within this booming industry, townspeople had found work as office staff, cleaners, cooks, and laborers.

Each day, when the World Food Programme helicopters landed at Bogale, people gathered at the old football stadium that was being used as a helipad. Though soldiers guarded the entrance to the field, spectators were allowed into the brick stands to watch the helicopters land and take off. It was undeniably exciting to listen for the distant drone of the helicopter engine in the empty gray skies; whenever a helicopter appeared out of the gloom, the waiting crowd would often clap and cheer. The helicopter engines were usually kept running in Bogale, as they hurriedly dispatched aid workers from Rangoon and loaded up on cargo to transport to the villages. The rotor blades set up a whirlwind that flattened the overgrown grass of the football field, blowing hats off laborers and forcing women to laughingly hold down their *tamein* and blouses.

At night, evening tea shops and beer stands spilled out from the shophouses in the center of town. Against the roar of generators that powered the fluorescent bulbs dangling above them, people exchanged the news and events of the day, swapping rumors and the occasional fact. One evening I joined a table of international aid workers, who sat at an open-air stand drinking lukewarm beer and munching on crispy fried eel dipped in ketchup.

To begin with, their conversation revolved around work. More logistical challenges had arisen that day. Cooking oil destined for the village of Kone Gyi had taken too long to load due to the afternoon rainfall and the boat wasn't able to set sail before dark; the eight-hour journey would have to begin the following day, which would set the whole boat schedule out of whack for the rest of the week.

The continued movement of people across the delta was also causing major headaches for those in charge of distributing aid. As cyclone survivors left villages that had been completely destroyed and fields they were no longer able to farm, they moved from village to village in search of work. Aid agencies struggled to keep up with the ever-changing population figures and often delivered too much or too little.

One agency had been summoned by the tactical commander, a military officer overseeing the relief effort in Bogale Township. The commander wanted to know exactly how much tarpaulin they had given to a cluster of villages along the coast; until he received a breakdown of the exact length and number of sheets donated, he was prohibiting all future deliveries. Someone would have to go and see him first thing in the morning.

I asked the aid workers how they found working with the authorities and was surprised when they unanimously agreed that it wasn't as bad as one might have expected. "It's the people at the top of the pile who cause problems," said one New Zealander used to working in combat zones. "But out here in the field we don't have many problems with them. They live here, and their families suffered from the cyclone too, and they seem to want to help."

Those at the top of the pile, however, seemed to be conjuring up policies that were explicitly designed to further complicate the delivery of aid and movement of aid workers. In June, the regime released a set of NGO "guiding principles" that was in fact a series of convoluted rules and regulations. At the end of the six-page document, the guiding principles were summarized in ten not-so-easy-to-understand bullet points, some of which were grammatically incomplete. Among them were the following:

- The items of the relief supplies have to be described in-kind, in quantity and value, including the identification of lists that are to be provided to the storm survivors and those to be used for their agency/organization.
- The list of township-wise distribution of supplies including quantity, their value and prior consent from the focal Ministry for the distribution arrangement.
- The distribution arrangement within the townships is to be coordinated between the local coordinating committees and responsible personnel from the respective UN Agencies, IGOs, INGOs and NGOs at the respective areas and distributed according to the arrangement.

Though the document declared that its aim was to coordinate efforts and prevent duplication of supplies to areas where they were not needed, most agencies had difficulty simply trying to decipher the new rules and working out how to abide by them.

In July, it came to light that the regime was profiting directly from the influx of aid dollars through the country's dual-system currency exchange. Though black market rates averaged around K1,100 to the U.S. dollar, the official exchange rate had remained stuck at K6 to the dollar. Even the authorities seemed to acknowledge that this difference was ludicrous and allowed international agencies working in Burma to exchange incoming dollars into Foreign Exchange Certificates, known as FECs. In the months after Nargis, however, the FEC was valued lower than the dollar when changed into Burmese currency. UN officials admitted that the discrepancy may have resulted in a serious loss of 25 percent of relief funds, amounting to as much as US$10 million. It later transpired that the amount was far less, and was estimated to be around US$1.56 million. Still, it was a substantial bonus for the regime's coffers from money that had been earmarked for charitable contributions.

The regime also made money from other transactions. Shortly after the cyclone, aid agencies were informed that mobile phone and radio communication was prohibited in the delta. The May 16 edition of the *New Light of Myanmar* ran a small article noting that the Burmese minister for communications, posts, and telegraphs had accepted a donation of thirty thousand CDMA mobile phones, which operate on an alternative cellular technology to GSM, and fifteen base stations worth US$3.3 million from a major Chinese telecommunications company. Not too long after that, the authorities offered an alternative form of communication for aid agencies in need of mobile phone systems: CDMA phones that could be purchased from the government for US$1,500 per unit.

An Indonesian aid worker I met in the delta, who had worked in Aceh after the Indian Ocean tsunami of 2004, told me he was trying hard to see things from the perspective of the ruling generals. "I have to understand them if I'm going to work here," he explained. "Their thinking, as I have processed it, goes like this: My child is sick and my neighbor comes along with some large, shiny apples. These apples are maybe imported fruit or some such thing, and they are better than any apples I could ever give my child. So I feel bad because I cannot provide for my child as well as my neighbor can. I don't want my child to know this, so I prevent my neighbor from giving my child the apples. This is how I think the generals are thinking now—they didn't want us to help at first because they thought the apples we would bring in would be so much better than theirs."

In the sticky heat of the moment I thought there could be some wisdom to this theory; while Than Shwe might have Granny Smith and Golden Delicious apples flown in for his own fruit basket, he probably wouldn't want farmers in the delta getting a taste for imported fruits. Perhaps the regime closed off access to the delta to prevent itself from being seen as the governmental equivalent of a bad parent in the eyes of its people.

I later tried out the theory on a Burmese friend, who snorted with derision. "And what if your child is not just sick?" he asked. "What if your child is drowning in the river and you don't know how to swim? If your neighbor knows how to swim, or has an inner tube that he can throw to your child, don't you think you would *want* him to help?"

Indeed, even taking into account the regime's ruthlessness, I found it difficult to understand its cruel negligence after the cyclone. The most convincing explanation I had heard was that the regime was driven by fear and self-protection. The generals live in a rarified atmosphere; the very air they breathe is clouded with paranoia and the ground they walk upon is riddled with the fault lines of treachery. The thought of hordes of Western aid workers with their airy-fairy ideals of democracy and equality pouring into the country and running around remote and hard-to-police areas must have been anathema to them. With the September marches still fresh in everyone's mind and commodity prices on the rise again, they would have been especially wary of taking any steps that might compromise their control.

The regime's reluctance to open its doors may have been further exacerbated by the foreign navy ships waiting offshore; the threat of invasion could have looked very real to a pariah dictatorship sitting in the isolated splendor of its fortified capital. Under such conditions it was unlikely that the generals would acquiesce to allowing large numbers of foreigners into the country. To Than Shwe, U.S. troops were potentially hostile. The day before the cyclone struck, President George Bush had imposed more U.S. sanctions against Burma and stated that he was committed to helping the people of Burma "free themselves from the regime's tyranny."

Almost all the top generals were old enough to remember previous invading forces—the British in colonial times, the Japanese during World War II, and the Kuomintang incursion from China in the 1950s. While the junta views itself as the only mechanism able to hold the country together in times of crisis, its rhetoric also emphasizes the maintenance of national sovereignty at any cost. The Three Main National Causes, printed in the frontispieces of books and on billboards throughout the country, are:

Non-disintegration of the Union
Non-disintegration of national solidarity
Perpetuation of sovereignty

A Burmese friend, who had been helping a company owned by the son of a top-ranking general to organize an aid operation in the delta, managed to glean some direct insight into the regime's perspective. The general's son explained that his father and fellow generals had been deeply concerned by the fact that Western governments chose to send naval ships to Burma. He said that they had prevented aid from entering the country because they were afraid that foreign aid personnel and troops would use the relief mission as a cover to invade Burma and overthrow the junta.

Another theory came from Min Lwin, the editor I visited back in May. "I think this is something very ancient," he said. "It is like we are returning to the time of the old, old kings. Our senior general is the king and the people are his subjects or slaves. The king does not consider it his role to look after the condition of his slaves—they are only slaves, and he has so many of them that their death or hardship is not his concern."

The self-protection could also have been purely personal. The amateur astrologer whose hobby was to run Than Shwe's birth date through his computer and calculate the ruler's astrological forecast had noticed early on that 2008 was going to be an extremely bad year for the senior general. It was written in the stars that the general would be faced with many challenges and threats to his rule throughout the year. As a result, the astrologer reasoned, the superstitious general was doing everything possible to protect himself—from black magic rituals conducted by his wife at Burma's most holy Buddhist shrine to locking down the country in its hour of greatest need.

The aid workers I was sitting with at the beer stand in Bogale weren't that interested in debating the finer details of the regime's intentions or the moral ramifications of what had occurred. Done with discussing work-related issues, the talk drifted from the day's hurdles to the inability of Bogale beer stands to store beer at an adequately chilled temperature, and on to favorite bar snacks (even with the addition of ketchup, the crispy fried eel didn't make it into anyone's top five).

At the end of the evening I left the table feeling woolly-headed after too many glasses of tepid beer. With thoughts of french fries, salt-and-vinegar chips, and herbed olives in my head, I traipsed back through the dark streets to the guesthouse. The generator was turned off every night at 9:00 P.M., and without the electric fan my windowless room was humid and airless. Too hot to sleep, I lay on the bed swatting away mosquitoes and waiting for dawn.

EIGHT

O ver a hundred years ago, only wild animals roamed the lower
stretches of the Irrawaddy Delta. Elephants and tigers lived within
the forest, and crocodiles and snakes flourished in the grassy swamplands
and creeks. Toward the end of the nineteenth century, plucky cultivators
were enticed to this wilderness by the British colonial government. Burma's rice trade was expanding, and the government, keen to increase the
acreage of cultivatable land, offered farmers tax incentives and other lures
to try their luck in the area.

But carving a living out of the wetlands of the delta was no simple
task. Would-be cultivators first had to hack down dense forests of tenacious *kanazo*, or Burmese grape trees, and the tough swamp grass had to
be burned off and then uprooted. It took years before the land was ready
for planting, and even once paddy seedlings had been sunk into the
ground, they were vulnerable to numerous hazards. The low-lying land
was prone to severe flooding and in some parts remained underwater for
many months each year. Bunds and embankments had to be constructed

to protect the rice fields from inundation; saltwater floods could kill off a crop and crabs carried along with the water could chomp their way through entire fields of young shoots. The area was also dangerous for new cultivators, who had to build stockades around their dwellings to prevent tigers from entering, and who lived in fear of the poisonous snakes that slithered through the undergrowth. Mosquitoes bred easily in the fetid air, and farmers often succumbed to malarial fevers and other potentially fatal diseases. In short, the rich and savage soil of the delta had been ploughed with a great deal of hardship.

One day I traveled some hours south of Bogale with Shwe Ya, a farmer who wanted to show me the land he had not been able to farm since Cyclone Nargis. Shwe Ya sat in the prow of the boat directing our way through the winding creeks—with so many trees and visual markers torn down by the storm, boatmen found it hard to navigate the watery maze they once knew so well. To me, the nuances of the scenery were indistinguishable, and all the boat trips I took merged into one long, monotonous journey. The land was relentlessly flat. The trees that remained after the storm had been stripped of their foliage, leaving behind dead and contorted branches. The monsoon rains had leeched all color from the landscape; the river was always the pale brown of watery tea and the sky was a leaden white-gray that was more like an absence of color than any describable hue. Every boat I sailed on in the delta seemed to wind its way through the same post-apocalyptic landscape.

At first, Shwe Ya's land looked to me like any other part of the delta, but as he spoke I began to see it through his eyes—the possibilities and losses that had been bestowed upon it. Shwe Ya showed me where his house had stood before the cyclone. All that remained were a few stumps of the wooden posts and the slight depression of a foundation, no more than a soft shadow on the land. Nearby lay the shards of a smashed earthenware rainwater jar. It was like an ancient site recently excavated; proof that people had once settled there.

Shwe Ya wore only a *longyi* and had a sinewy body topped by a thick head of hair that looked like it had recently been trimmed with gardening shears. He strode barefoot and purposeful across his land, pointing out its boundaries and telling his story in a matter-of-fact way, as if it were an everyday affair for your house and community to vanish into nothingness. Shwe Ya and his family had been homesteaders, living out in the fields with four other farming families. The houses had not been close together but were spaced along the riverside so that each one was just visible and within yelling distance. There had been nowhere to run when the river began to flood; one family lost eight members to Cyclone Nargis and another family was killed off entirely. Shwe Ya's wife and child survived because they had been away from the land, visiting Bogale.

After the cyclone, the farmers took the remaining members of their families to live in a nearby hamlet. A few weeks later, the men returned to inspect their land and found the fields strewn with corpses. The land was still sodden with daily rains, so they weren't able to cremate the bodies. Instead, they carried them to the river, reciting all the Buddhist prayers they knew and trying hard not to breathe in too much of the cloying smell of decay. "What a miserable task," I said, half to myself. "None of them were people we knew," Shwe Ya responded in his pragmatic manner, as if that made it somehow not so bad. "They came with the flood, from villages farther south."

Shwe Ya showed me the bodies that still remained—the ones they had missed or that had washed up on more recent tides. In a hollow at the river's edge lay a disconnected skeleton that appeared to have been picked over by wild animals, or the bones may have been pulled apart by the to and fro of the river. Farther inland a yellowing thigh bone protruded from beneath a sheer floral blouse, and not far from there was a lone skull matted with black hair and mud.

"Normally at this time of year you would see nothing but green," said Shwe Ya, dragging his toes through the soil to indicate he was talking about his land. Had the cyclone not disrupted the agricultural cycle, the farmers would have spent the previous few months preparing rice seedlings and turning over the earth in readiness for a new crop. The rice seedlings would have been planted by then and should have sprouted into a field of neon-green shoots. But nothing was growing here, and the muddy land stretched out as far as the eye could see.

The farmers had no equipment with which to replant their fields. The three buffalo Shwe Ya once used to plough the land had disappeared in the cyclone, probably drowned. The seed stocks he had stored were also gone. Neither did he have any money to replace what was lost; like most Burmese who have no access to bank accounts or insurance polices, all that he owned had been kept in his house.

At the nearby hamlet where he was now living, he and his family had been given tarpaulin sheets to construct a shelter and were receiving regular rations of uncooked rice and other basic necessities from various aid organizations. The township authorities had distributed rice seeds and two power tillers to be shared among the farmers. It was nowhere near enough. The farmers in the hamlet worked a total of four hundred acres of land. With just two tillers, Shwe Ya explained, each farmer had to wait his turn and was only able to make use of the tiller for an average of two days out of every ten. Those two precious days were usually frustratingly unproductive; the farmers were unused to motorized equipment and found that buffalo were better equipped to work the excessively muddy fields. Tillers also needed diesel oil, and, though Shwe Ya had borrowed money to purchase the fuel and farm a quarter of his land, the crop had failed. He thought the failure was due to a combination of poor quality seed and badly prepared soil; the land had been inundated with saltwater during the storm surge, and the high saline content was not conducive to nurturing seedlings. "I know the food that people are giving us now will not last forever," he said. "I want to get working. I want to survive off my own land. I just don't know how."

Farmers across the delta faced the same predicament. In each village I stopped at, people pointed out the mismatch between the number of farmers and the number of implements donated.

Daung Chaung village
    Farmers: 32
    Tillers: 5
Po Thin Kan village
    Farmers: 18
    Tillers: 2

Both the government and some aid agencies were reportedly transporting buffalo from Arakan State in northwestern Burma to the delta, but there simply weren't enough to go around. Some farmers were able to rent buffalo for the planting season but livestock are not easily interchangeable from region to region. Arakanese buffalo didn't understand the commands uttered by delta farmers who speak a different dialect from their counterparts in Arakan State, and the animals were unused to the oppressive heat of the delta. In one village I came across a couple of buffalos standing beneath a specially built shelter. A young boy lay on the ground fanning them with a large leaf. It looked a little like he was paying homage to holy beasts, but further inquiry revealed that they were not deities; just Arakanese buffalo, easily tired in the delta heat.

Fishermen had similar problems: unable to replace equipment that had been damaged or lost during Cyclone Nargis, they could not resume their work. People across the delta depend on a variety of fishing methods to make a living and supplement their diet. Most families practice some kind of small-scale fishing, such as collecting shrimp and tiny fish from the saturated paddy fields during the rainy season. Women tip the contents of nets onto bamboo trays and patiently sort through the muck, sifting out whatever is edible. People sail along the edges of rivers in wooden canoes leaving traps or casting nets among the reeds and shallows. Professional fishermen go out to sea for days at a time to fill the holds of their boats, while large-scale commercial farms breed fingerlings and shrimp. The cyclone not only sank boats and destroyed nets and traps, but also damaged cold stores and ice factories.

Efforts to help fishermen have resulted in similar shortfalls:

Nee Laung Ye village
   Households: 60
   Nets: 17
Aung Hlaing village
   Households: 61
   Boats: 9

Even when they did receive equipment, it was sometimes inappropriate for the task; I met fishermen who had been given nets that were too fine, useful for dry-season fishing in the creeks when the water was low but useless for river fishing in the rainy season. The government did set up a boat-building program, and fishermen who were able to pool enough cash could begin yearly payments for a new boat, but the fishing industry faced additional challenges. When I admired the midnight-blue shells of crabs caught in a bamboo trap, the owner of the trap insisted I take them as a gift. He wouldn't accept my offers to pay him and walked me back to my boat, where he deposited the snapping, irritable crabs in the hull. When I thanked him profusely, he told me not to worry; it wasn't easy to sell delta crabs anymore, as there was talk that they had been feeding on a macabre diet since the cyclone. He wasn't sure whether a finger had ever really been found inside a fish, but the story had done its damage and the delta's fishing industry had yet to recover.

It was early evening by the time I headed back to town after visiting Shwe Ya's land. I lay sprawled in the bottom of the boat and watched the dreary delta landscape slip past—the water, the unchanging scrubland, the dead sky. A wooden canoe emerged from a patch of twisted grass. A woman sat in the prow wearing a turban wrapped around her head and holding a thick white cheroot between her fingers. A man in a conical straw hat and faded mustard-colored *longyi* stood at the back of the canoe. With dignified, slow-motion strokes, he punted along the river's edge like a gondolier. As I gazed lazily toward the canoe, I noticed an exact mirror image of the scene reflected upon the still, glassy surface of the river. Against the washed-out brown of the water, the reflection looked like a sepia photograph that might have been taken over a hundred years ago.

AT THE BEGINNING of 2007, a secret letter-writing campaign had been launched in Burma. Known as the "Open Heart Letter Campaign," it was run by the 88 Generation Students group, the organization made up of key leaders from the 1988 uprising who had been released from prison. Their aim had been to create a safe outlet through which people from across Burma could voice their concerns publicly. The organizers called for letters via underground contacts within the country and exile-run radio stations broadcasting programs into Burma, including Voice of America and the BBC. People were encouraged to write on a wide range of topics, such as politics, the economy, the education system, health care, and corruption. The 88 Generation group wanted to emphasize the importance of documenting abuse and injustice. To write down your grievances does not, they later wrote, "amount to breaking any law or committing any crime." And yet the process of writing, sending, collecting, and compiling the letters had to be done clandestinely. In a country where voicing a complaint can put you in danger, this was revolution in written form.

A total of 2,649 letters were received; others were intercepted by the authorities. Written and sent from across Burma, the letters now serve as a catalog of the everyday worries and underlying fears that characterize life in a military dictatorship. People from all walks of life wrote in: a housewife with seven children; a Christian minister in Chin State in the northeast; a high-school janitor; a shopkeeper. Civil servants wrote in too, along with headmasters, teachers, and students.

Read together, the letters tell the story of a people pushed to their limit. Parents cannot afford to send their children to school due to the unofficial bribes they have to pay for entrance fees and the inflated price of textbooks and uniforms. Patients at hospitals have to purchase overpriced medicines and sometimes even pay for the equipment necessary to treat their illnesses. People across the country are impoverished by random and illicit taxes charged by the township authorities for common amenities such as street lighting, which, as one letter writer made sure to point out, often don't even work anyway.

People who can't afford the exemption fees are forced by their township or neighborhood authorities to work on various projects. Townspeople in the Irrawaddy division had to build a new road, working long days to break rocks and lay tarmac. Not only did they have to contribute their time and labor free of charge, abandoning their usual places of work, they also had to pay for their own transport to and from the construction site and supply their own food for the day.

In Kachin State, in the north of Burma, forty-five farmers were seconded to a conservation forest to plant teak trees for the local authorities. Each farmer had to complete two acres—it cost them seven days' hard labor during the harvesting season.

One teacher wrote about the final straw after all this forced labor. When senior military personnel came to open a new road or bridge or school, people were herded into the local sports stadium at around 5:00 A.M. to welcome them. But the military VIPs always arrived late, sometimes not until 3:00 P.M., and the townspeople, who had already wasted their day waiting for people they didn't want to see, all had to contribute to the cost of hosting the event.

The letters detail a wide variety of injustices, from forced labor and the confiscation of land to travel prohibitions and lack of political freedom, but the main concern voiced in the majority of the letters is about the rising cost of living. According to this incomplete poll, the biggest fear in Burma is, *How am I going to feed my family?* It was in August 2007, soon after the Open Heart Letter Campaign, that the 88 Generation leaders organized the demonstrations against the fuel price hikes. Their attempts to point out that the government's policy was having a direct and devastating effect on people's ability to put food on the table landed most of them back in prison.

There is a silence that has settled over Burma; people can talk quietly about their everyday concerns, but as soon as they try to bring their complaints into the public sphere, they draw the ire of the regime. Occasionally, though, the silence becomes too much for an individual and he or she is driven to making a lone stand. These solitary protests do not happen often and, when they do, they are fleeting affairs, destined to be hurriedly swept off the street by police or plainclothes *Swan Ah Shin* thugs.

In July 2006, a former army sergeant stood in front of Rangoon city hall and called for an increase in pensions for war veterans.

In April 2007, an HIV-positive man handed out leaflets at a busy intersection in Rangoon, asking the government to offer treatment to people living with HIV.

A month later, a sixty-two-year-old woman walked up to city hall and demanded the release of Aung San Suu Kyi.

Each of these protesters knew they would be arrested and sent to prison, and yet they still decided to speak out. Ohn Than, the activist who went to the United States Embassy in Rangoon with a placard protesting against the rise in fuel prices in August 2007, was later sentenced to life imprisonment under Section 124 (a) of the Penal Code. Section 124 (a) is the regime's handy catch-all law that states:

> Whoever by words, either spoken or written, or by signs, or by visible representation, or otherwise, brings to or attempts to bring into hatred or contempt, or excites or attempts to excite disaffection toward [the government established by law] shall be punished with transportation for life or a shorter term, to which fine may be added, or with imprisonment which may extend to three years, to which fine may be added.

To his credit, sixty-one-year-old Ohn Than reportedly went down fighting by announcing in the courtroom that his sentencing was illegal. His logic was based on the fact that he was being incorrectly charged. Section 124 (a) of the Penal Code punishes actions taken against a "government established by law"; the current government of Burma was *not* established by law and, as Ohn Than's actions were therefore taken against a government that had been established illegally, he had in fact been acting in accordance with the law.

I have always been captivated by these solitary outbursts. What drives people to speak out when they know they will be arrested, and that their story will vanish with the next day's news? Whenever I hear of a lone protester, I collect the news clippings and as much information as I can find on them. But there is never very much, as the trail of information is always quickly snuffed out by the authorities.

In 2008, two solo protesters went so far as to attempt suicide on the platform of the Shwedagon Pagoda. It was the first time in living memory that people had tried to kill themselves at Burma's most sacred landmark. It was an act of absolute despair to end life at the spiritual heart of the nation, a focal point that so many millions look to for hope.

On the day of the full moon in mid-March 2008, Kyaw Zin Naing, a twenty-six-year-old man, stood on the platform of the Shwedagon Pagoda. Shouting words to the effect of, "Down with the military regime!" he doused his body with gasoline and set fire to himself. He was still alive when the flames had been extinguished by pagoda trustees and was taken to hospital where he was kept under armed guard while being treated for burns that covered more than 60 percent of his body. He died just over three weeks later. Though Kyaw Zin Naing had chosen a good day to make an impact—on the day of a full moon the pagoda is often crowded with worshippers—his act of self-immolation went mostly unheard-of beyond those who witnessed it. The news never made it past the censorship board in Burma and only a few brief articles appeared outside the country in the exile-run media.

Then, in September 2008, around the time of the first anniversary of the monks' protests the previous year, a lone monk stood on the platform of the Shwedagon Pagoda and slit his throat. The monk survived, but his story was suppressed almost instantly. Staff at Rangoon General Hospital, where the monk was taken for treatment, refused to divulge any details to local journalists. One journalist managed to get a pagoda trustee to speak off-the-record, and he was told that the monk had tried to kill himself because he had been having financial difficulties. But it was an unsatisfactory explanation given the timing of the suicide attempt and the fact that monks live for free in their monasteries and are supported by the community.

Aside from the monk's attempted suicide, the September anniversary was marked by only a few incidents that were of little consequence. A bomb exploded near the Sule Pagoda in downtown Rangoon. It was not a big explosion and nobody was killed. There was speculation that the regime itself had planted the bomb to distract public attention from the anniversary and provide an excuse for an increased security presence on the streets; it was just another in a series of sporadic small explosions that no one ever claimed responsibility for. One night, truckloads of riot police surrounded the Botahtaung Pagoda, a rallying point during the marches the previous year. They conducted a number of crowd-control exercises among themselves, going through choreographed sequences in which they pinned each other to the ground. There was no reason for them to be there and it must have been simply a show of force, a kind of *haka* perhaps. The rest of September went by in relative silence.

It had been the same during August 2008, the twenty-year anniversary of the 1988 uprising. The Burmese calendar showed that there would be an unusual astrological phenomenon in August 2008, as two new moons, or "black moons" as they are also known, would occur in a single month—one on the first day of the month and one on the last day. Astrologers pointed out that the last time this configuration was in place, over a century earlier, it had ushered in an era of catastrophic change for the country; it was 1885, and the king of Burma was forced from his throne by the British army. Fortune-tellers traded in doomsday predictions, and people spoke with nervous excitement about the calamity that was expected in August, but the anticipation was wasted, as nothing happened and the month passed without incident.

By maintaining an effective gag order on all public forums, the regime ensures that there is no space for any collective remembrance. Only the regime's version of the truth remains to be seen and read. As a result, recent historical events—no matter how earth-shattering or all-consuming—are remembered only in private. Because people cannot compare their experiences easily or openly, past events become distorted and intensely personal. In isolation, these memories evolve into the kind of twisted secrets that can end up breaking people.

I saw this after the marches of September 2007, when people began shutting off and shifting into hibernation mode while the regime searched through the population for witnesses and reconstructed the course of events by arresting people or silencing them. During the trips I made to Burma afterward, I began to see in my friends a weariness that I hadn't seen before, a kind of deep-seated fatigue that lay behind the jovial banter and tea-shop debates. Many of them had gone out in the streets to join the protests in September. Many had taken great risks to get information and photographs out of the country. A Rangoon resident told me he had used up his last reserves of hope. "We had so much hope then," he said. "My whole family was out on the streets, but it came to nothing, and now I wonder why we even bothered."

Events happen in Burma, and then they are systematically *un*happened. Ko Ye, my publisher friend in Rangoon, pointed out the depressing sequence to me when we chatted in September: life goes on, economic conditions become untenable, the people rise up (individually or together), and the army cracks down. It is a relentless, unforgiving, and utterly exhausting cycle.

It was around the first anniversary of September 2007 that I paid a visit to the Taukkyan War Cemetery just north of Rangoon. Funded and managed by the Commonwealth War Graves Commission, the cemetery contains the remains of members of the Allied forces who died during the Burma campaign of World War II. I had been before, but on this occasion it was one of those rare and glorious Rangoon afternoons when the dinginess of the monsoon season breaks into the clear blue sky and crisp air of an English summer's day, and I spent an entire afternoon walking among the graves.

The War Graves Commission held that the dead should be commemorated by name, and that no distinction should be made on account of military or civil rank, race, or creed. As a result, all 6,374 graves look identical. They are laid in symmetrical lines across a vast manicured lawn intersected by pebbled pathways and neatly trimmed bushes. Each marker bears a plaque inscribed with the name, rank, regiment, and service number of the deceased. At the center of the gravestones stands a long, open colonnade in the form of a mausoleum which was constructed as a memorial to the 26,857 members of the commonwealth forces who died in Burma during the war but whose remains were never found and who have no known grave. It is a haunting and humbling commemoration of all the sacrifice and loss of life.

While I was at the cemetery, I made sure to seek out a grave I had discovered on a previous visit. It took me a while to locate it amid the thousands of uniform headstones, but eventually I came across the grave of J. J. Curley, corporal of the Queen's Own Royal West Kent Regiment, who was killed in 1944 at the age of twenty-nine. There was nothing remarkable about the grave itself; it was like all the others, a small block with a plaque stating his name and rank. It was the inscription that I wanted to see. It was just one sentence, but its sentiment summed up the entire place and put the overwhelming number of casualties into dreadful perspective:

To all the world you were only one, to me you were all the world.

The line was most probably chosen by the corporal's wife or girlfriend back in England, and I have long wondered whether she was ever able to go to Burma and see his final resting place.

As long as the generals remain in control, there will be no memorial to the martyrs of 1988 or 2007, or to the lone protester who went up in flames at the Shwedagon Pagoda. It is even unlikely that the victims of Cyclone Nargis will be honored with a memorial. To my mind, this is one of the great tragedies of life in Burma: that recent historical events—both large and small—cannot be honestly and openly acknowledged, debated, or even remembered within the country. Instead, the exact opposite takes place, and Burma's history is swallowed up by a strictly enforced collective forgetting.

THE NINETEENTH-CENTURY Burmese monk Thingaza Sayadaw liked to collect and create stories that he could use to teach people various wisdoms and essential truths. Though composed and preached over a century ago, these stories are still relevant today. There is one that explores the nature of reality called "The Abbot Is Frying Eggs." It is similar, in some ways, to the European fairy tale, "The Emperor's New Clothes." In the European tale, a young boy is the only one among the crowds who dares to speak out about the fact that the emperor has no clothes on. The Burmese take on the tale, however, has a melancholy slant; the person who is the equivalent of the brave boy is reprimanded, and he soon learns to stop his pesky, truth-telling ways.

"The Abbot Is Frying Eggs" features a merchant who has accumulated great wealth. He and his wife have more than enough to live on, and they have decided to devote themselves to making merit. The retired merchant builds a monastery and invites a respected abbot and a retinue of young monks to take up residence there. In order to live a worthy life in accordance with Buddhist principles, the merchant and his wife become vegetarians, vowing that they will refrain from killing all living beings.

On religious days, they prepare a banquet of meatless dishes and host the abbot and monks at their home. The merchant leaves much of the cooking to his wife and her helpers; at his advanced age he is not so interested in the flavor of his meals, and he has become accustomed to the bland vegetarian fare served in his home. The abbot and the young monks, however, normally consume a broad variety of dishes—they eat whatever is placed in their alms bowls each morning and are used to the spicy, pungent meals offered to them by most Burmese housewives. Though none of the monks say anything when they visit the merchant's house, they all acknowledge that the meals produced in his kitchen are disappointingly tasteless.

On one particular religious day, the monks arrive at the merchant's house as usual, but this time the abbot is not present. The merchant immediately asks the monks where he is. The monks glance at one another and say nothing, but the merchant keeps pestering them; he believes his merit making and perhaps even his future lives are compromised by the venerable monk's absence, and he wants to remedy the situation. With great reluctance, one of the monks eventually ventures the information that the abbot is unwell.

Concerned that the abbot might be seriously ill, the merchant leaves his home and hurries to the monastery, where he finds the abbot alone in the kitchen. To the merchant's astonishment, the venerable one is standing in front of the cooker frying eggs. He seems quite happy as he listens to the pop and sizzle of the eggs cooking, and the merchant watches him for a moment just to be sure of what he sees.

But there is no mistaking the fact of the matter, and it only gets worse; the abbot picks up a fork and begins, brazenly, to eat the eggs straight out of the frying pan. As eggs are an animal product, it becomes devastatingly clear to the merchant that the abbot—the leader of the monastery he funded as a spiritual investment for his retirement and future lives—is not, in fact, a vegetarian.

Dismayed, the merchant hurries home to tell his wife: "The abbot is frying eggs!" His wife refuses to believe him. She tells him it cannot be true as the abbot is a holy man, a religious leader, and a follower of the Buddhist precepts.

"But I saw it with my own eyes!" insists the merchant. "The abbot is frying eggs!"

His wife becomes convinced that some evil spirit has taken hold of her husband. How could he imagine that an abbot, a respected and robed man of the religious order, is frying eggs? She calls her neighbors and asks for help. The neighbors understand the urgency of the situation and recommend a traditional remedy used to temper delirium and febrile delusions. Desperate to cure her husband, the wife agrees. A mixture of tobacco leaf and salt is pounded together and rubbed into the sick man's eyes. The merchant screams, but the neighbors do not relent, and, after some time, his wife is greatly relieved to see that his demeanor becomes calm and placid.

That night, as he lies next to his wife in bed, the merchant is again consumed by an urge to tell the truth. With his eyes red and stinging, he turns to his wife and describes what he saw in the monastery. In the privacy of their bedroom he hopes that she will listen to him, but her reaction is unexpected. She becomes perturbed and frightened by his speech and threatens to call the neighbors again. Unable to bear the painful administrations of tobacco and salt, the merchant acquiesces.

With a heavy sigh, he relinquishes his hold on the truth: "All right," he says. "All right. It's true. The abbot is *not* frying eggs."

I **SPENT SEVERAL MONTHS** traveling back and forth between Rangoon and the delta. After a week or so in one of the townships, I would return to the city to apply for permission to visit the next township, and gradually was able to work my way across the cyclone zone. I enjoyed the days in Rangoon as they gave me a chance to regroup. I could write up my notes, catch up on e-mail, do my laundry, and make the most of having an air-conditioned hotel room after so many hot and sleepless nights in the delta.

It was during one of those Rangoon trips that I heard about Myat Su Mon, a university student who died after being bitten by a snake in August that year. Burma has some of the deadliest snakes in the world and produces antivenom against bites by the most lethal: viper and cobra. The denuded health-care system, however, is unable to provide sufficient supplies of antivenom, and village clinics have only a couple of vials in stock at any given time. As a result, Burma has one of the highest incidences of death by snakebite in the world, with nearly eight hundred deaths each year and speculation that many more go unreported. Myat Su Mon's death would not have been unusual but for the circumstances that followed it.

After she was bitten, Myat Su Mon was taken to a nearby hospital, but the hospital had run out of antivenom serum and was not able to treat her. The doctor in charge transferred her to a larger hospital in the Insein district in northern Rangoon, but that hospital was also out of serum, and she was transferred again, this time to the country's main hospital, Rangoon General, where she reportedly died shortly after arrival. Even by Burma's abysmal health-care standards, people were shocked that the bigger hospitals like Insein and Rangoon General were not equipped to treat a snakebite victim.

What was even more surprising, though, was the government's reaction. The minister of health himself became involved and oversaw an investigation into Myat Su Mon's death. It was unprecedented for a minister to handle an individual case like this or, indeed, for the Ministry of Health to demonstrate any public interest in casualties of the health-care system. Most people I spoke with in Rangoon at the time were convinced that there must be something more to the story; something that wasn't being reported in the state media.

What *was* being reported in the media had the dual effect of erasing the incident from public record and portraying the Ministry of Health in a beneficial rather than negative light. Intended to meet these ends, the results of the health minister's investigation were predictable. He reported that all the hospitals Myat Su Mon had been taken to were actually fully stocked with the necessary serum. It was, he stated, the fault of the doctors; they had been careless and negligent in their haste to transfer the patient. The minister announced that one doctor had been fired and a medical superintendent was retired. Other medical personnel involved received strong warnings. The Ministry of Health went on to provide assurances that health-care workers were chosen only from those who loved, and were willing to serve, their country.

As always, the subtext of Myat Su Mon's story was to be found in the rumors rustling behind the newsprint. There were stories that students at Rangoon's Technological University, where she had been a second-year student, organized a demonstration to protest against a health-care system that was unable to deal with snakebites in a country filled with poisonous snakes. Supposedly, the demonstration was quelled by local security forces. But when I asked a young friend to question any friends she had at the university, she was told that there hadn't been any demonstrations. According to her source, many students had attended Myat Su Mon's funeral, and it may have been the large gathering that started the rumors and spooked the regime.

Whatever had happened at Myat Su Mon's university, the minister's reaction and public statements seemed to illustrate that the event had rattled the rulers in Naypyidaw. The nationwide uprising of 1988 was triggered by a seemingly inconsequential incident—a brawl in a tea shop—and the authorities were now always alert for possible catalysts that might unleash the widespread dissatisfaction that lay concealed beneath the surface of Burmese society.

Though it was one of those frustrating half stories I could never quite get to the bottom of, the incident opened my eyes to the fact that there were potentially incendiary sparks flying off all the time—sparks that were constantly being contained by the dogged force of the regime and its security apparatus. To maintain its control, the regime had to be ever watchful, as it was not always the overtly political elements or events that could trigger a mass outburst. It was more likely to come from one of the many day-to-day injustices: a farmer's order to contribute labor to the construction of a new road; the late arrival of a military VIP at the opening of a school; or an empty vial of antivenom serum.

NINE

It was quiet in the center of Laputta during the morning rush hour. There was only the gentle percussion of bicycle bells, sandals scraping the dirt road, and the hushed babble of the tea shop. Laputta had the atmosphere of a frontier town: it was dusty, worn down, and storm battered. Aside from the patched-up tractors used for hauling heavy loads, there were few motorized vehicles on the streets.

After spending a few days there, I found a hole-in-the-wall tea shop I liked where I could go for breakfast each morning. It was a simple establishment, with just four low tables surrounded by plastic stools and walls streaked with mildew and the shredded residue of old posters. The kitchen area was fenced off with a blackened sheet of corrugated iron and had a single charcoal brazier above which an extra-large tin kettle was always steaming. The shop served only one dish: a plate of rice and split peas flavored with fried garlic that was known as the poor man's breakfast. The tea maker was a surly, wiry man whose arms were branded with tattoos and fading track marks. The tea was always a bit too strong and sloshed messily in the saucer when he slapped it down in front of me, but I liked the no-nonsense atmosphere; it was a tea shop in which people studiously made a point of minding their own business. I could sit undisturbed at a little table by the entrance, drink my tea, and watch the pleasantly quiet rush hour slip past.

The streets of Laputta were filled with the industrious signs of construction. A group of barefoot children pushed a wheelbarrow filled with bricks. Two women strode by in unison with long bamboo poles balanced on flat rolls of cloth on the tops of their heads; with their graceful posture and synchronized strides they looked as if they were modeling exotic headdresses. The occasional tractor juddered past, its wooden trailer loaded down with sacks of rice, a cloud of black smoke following behind it. One man had dry fronds of *dani*, the nipa palm that is used for roofing material, strapped like an enormous fan to the back of his bicycle, and he wobbled his way precariously around the potholes.

Like the surrounding countryside, the town was devoid of any color, and everything seemed to have been bathed in a brown rinse. Even the clothes people wore had taken on dull shades of brown, as if the mud of the Irrawaddy River had dyed the fabric after so many riverside washings. Every so often, one of the bright, white Land Cruisers used by the United Nations agencies hurtled past, its shiny newness at odds with the dust-covered, mud-soaked town.

It was at the tea shop that I arranged to meet aid workers or townspeople I had been introduced to, and I spent much of my time there collecting stories. Amid the chronology of inconceivable loss, I had begun to pick out miraculous tales of survival and had acquired a mild obsession for stories that involved animals. The animal tales seemed innocent and fable-like, and they allowed me to write brief moments of redemption into notebooks that were becoming weighted down in misery, scrawled over and over with the same words I kept hearing: *I have nothing left; everything is broken.*

The animal tales included stories about a boy who had been rescued by a crocodile, a girl who had survived by holding on to a goose, and a woman who managed to catch hold of a python as it navigated the storm surge. Snakes were everywhere in the saga of the cyclone; people spoke with awe of how poisonous snakes had become entwined around their necks in the rising water but had not bitten them. Driven out of their holes by the turbulence and flooding, snakes coiled themselves around trees. In the darkness of the storm, one woman grabbed on to a branch, only to find that it was, in fact, a cobra. The venomous snake didn't strike her; it simply slid along her arm and moved farther up the tree. These stories were biblical in tone, depicting an epic flood in which man and beast battled the elements and long-time enemies chose not to fight each other in the interests of mutual survival.

Over a few cups of tea, I chatted with a local trader who was convinced that some animals had known the storm was coming. We swapped stories we had heard about animals and natural disasters. Indigenous tribes on the Nicobar Islands in the Indian Ocean were said to have known a disaster was imminent when they noticed a day or two before the Indian Ocean tsunami of 2004 that ants had begun to leave their nests and were marching, en masse, to higher ground. In Thailand some years ago I talked to tsunami survivors who told me that working elephants living along the coast had become agitated well before anyone was aware of the wave and had, in some instances, broken their chains in their attempts to flee. The trader said he too had noticed something strange. Each evening at dusk bats fill the sky above Laputta, chasing insects through the air. One night he had looked up, expecting to see the usual balletic spectacle of black shadows darting above him, but the sky had been empty. Cyclone Nargis struck the next day. "Now," he said with an acquired sagacity, "I am always watching for the bats."

I had come to Laputta toward the end of October 2008 and was planning to visit villages in the area and travel to the coastal town of Pyinzalu, one of the worst-hit parts of the delta, near where the cyclone made landfall. Restrictions were still tight on the movements of international staff, and I had to stick to my established routine of going to villages by day and returning to town each evening. By then the processing of foreigners in the delta had become more formalized. When I arrived in Laputta I had to submit my travel-permission letter in person to a committee of military officers. The three men on the committee were all dressed in crisp olive-green uniforms that had an unpleasant sheen from too much starch or too much ironing. They seemed a little like the UN Land Cruisers, incongruous and overdressed.

My passport and papers were handed from officer to officer, and each man took his time examining them in detail; looking at my passport photograph, looking at me, looking back at my photograph. They flicked slowly through the passport, turning over each page and examining old visas to other countries. For reasons I was unable to discern, one officer gazed intently at an entry stamp for Marseilles from a holiday I'd taken eight years ago. My permission letter, endorsed by the Ministry of Social Welfare, Relief, and Resettlement, was given the same fastidious attention before being handed back to me with a curt nod of dismissal. Only later did I realize that I had accidentally shown them a previously used and out-of-date permission letter. They clearly had not bothered to read the details. The whole exercise had been for show, another kind of *haka* but performed in the seated position and designed to intimidate, or perhaps just to make it look like they were doing their jobs.

Laputta was farther into the delta than Bogale, and the town had been harder hit by the cyclone. Along the waterfront I saw houses that had tilted dramatically to one side or collapsed almost intact into the mud, as if exhausted by the effort of remaining upright. Even six months on, storm debris was still strewn around the outskirts of town. I watched a young girl picking through rotten palm fronds and broken planks in an abandoned neighborhood. Balancing on fallen logs, she crossed the swamplike terrain like a tightrope walker. She didn't seem to find anything—whatever was salvageable was no doubt picked up long ago—and after a while I got the sense that she was looking for something specific. I saw her conducting her careful search most days when I passed by, and once she looked up and caught my eye. Yellow circles of *thanaka*, the cosmetic paste made from tree bark, had been swirled all over her face, and she looked pale and ghostly amid the surrounding desolation.

The only accommodation I was able to find in Laputta was a grim shoebox of a room at a guesthouse situated above the town video parlor. Each night the generator-fueled entertainment featured back-to-back Chinese gangster movies. Falling asleep to the sounds of screams, crashes, and gunshots gave my dreams a violent edge, and I often awoke with a start, thinking that something awful had just happened. Whenever I opened the door in the hope of catching a nonexistent breeze, Burmese men staying along the corridor would gather in the doorway and gaze unabashedly into my room. One of the guesthouse workers, a young boy no taller than my waist, would often come and rescue me in these situations. He was small but tough, and he strode down the corridor with the same swagger as the gangsters shooting one another to pieces on the television screen below, snapping his cleaning rag in the air and chasing off the unwanted sightseers.

His name, he told me, was Gam Ba Ri. It didn't sound like a Burmese name, and it took me a while to work out that he had been nicknamed "Gambari" after the Nigerian UN negotiator to Burma because he had dark skin and similar wide-set eyes, which gave him a permanently startled expression. Gambari and I made small talk whenever we bumped into each other. When I asked how old he was, he looked flustered and held up six fingers before turning to another worker, who was napping on top of the check-in desk, and asking, "How old am I?" The drowsy reply came that Gambari was twelve, but he looked no more than eight, even taking into account the malnutrition that stunts the growth of so many children in Burma.

After a few days, Gambari took to lingering in my room in the evenings. He chatted aimlessly and played with the camera on my mobile phone (though my phone didn't work anywhere in Burma, I still carried it around out of habit). He would take pictures of me, or the ceiling fan that didn't work, or my bag lying in a grubby corner, and marvel at the out-of-focus results. Gambari told me one night that his parents had been killed by Nargis. After their death, he and his older siblings had traveled to Laputta in search of work. Gambari had started off as a serving boy in a tea shop but later found a cleaning job at the guesthouse, which he preferred as the money was better (K6,000, or about US$6.00, a month) and the work was less hectic.

One day Gambari said, "Auntie, your Burmese isn't up to much, is it? How come it's no good?" Having grown up in the isolation of the village and not gone to school, he had little comprehension of other languages and that there were people in the world who might *not* speak Burmese or the more familiar languages of neighboring countries. I tried to teach him a bit of English—*Hello. How are you? What's your name?*—but he always collapsed into a giggling fit when he tried to repeat the words, claiming they were the silliest sounds he'd ever heard.

According to official figures, 833 orphans or children separated from their parents had been registered since Cyclone Nargis. With so many people dead, some aid workers estimated that the true number must be a great deal higher. Either the orphans were not being registered properly or they were being absorbed back into their communities through relatives. There were rumors, too, of course. People said that some orphans were being taken to military camps, where they were forced to join the regime's dreaded orphan brigade and be trained as ruthless fighters who had no families to worry about or to worry about them.

Many of the redemption tales I scribbled down in the village and at the tea shop had to do with mothers and the almost inhuman strength they had shown when it came to trying to protect their children during the storm. There was the story published in a Burmese weekly about a woman who had gone into labor just as the storm struck. She managed to last through the night holding on to a tree, but when she climbed down the next day, she felt her legs give way beneath her, and she ended up giving birth where she was, alone in the middle of a field strewn with corpses. Another woman gave birth during the cyclone while holding on to a tree in the storm surge. When the newborn was tugged away in the flood, he was still attached to his mother by the umbilical cord and she was able to pull him back.

One mother had no way to hold on to her seven-month-old baby when she climbed a tree to escape the rising waters, so she put his shirt between her teeth and bit down hard while clasping her arms around the tree. Once the storm had passed and she had climbed down to the ground, she was unable to open her mouth and release her child. Other survivors had to help her unclench her jaw and stem the flow of blood that poured out.

And then there was the popular tale of the baby found inside a pot. A toddler placed inside a pot had somehow floated through the waves unharmed. Later found bobbing calmly on the water, the baby was reunited with his parents. Such a miracle could not go unacknowledged, and the overjoyed parents renamed their baby O, or "pot" in Burmese.

Inevitably, for each story that had a happy ending, so many more ended painfully. In Laputta, I met a thirty-two-year-old woman from Pyinzalu who had not seen her husband and ten-year-old daughter since the cyclone but still held out hope. "I keep hoping that maybe they are still alive," she said. "And that maybe they are looking for me, too." The woman had heard rumors of cyclone survivors washing up on the shores of Bangladesh and had been told that a boatload would soon be returning to Burma. "Is it true? Have you heard this too?" she asked. If she hadn't found her husband or daughter after amost six months of searching, it seemed unlikely she would find them now, but I didn't have the heart to say anything. Before we parted, she asked me to write down her daughter's name. With her house and everything she had owned taken by the storm, I realized it was all she had left. There were no possessions or photographs—just a name. She spelled it out with care and repeated it a couple of times to make sure I wrote it down correctly. I did so and added the few extra details I knew:

Mi Mi Zaw, ten years old, still missing from Pyinzalu. October 2008.

WHENEVER THE WIND whips up and a storm moves across the delta, survivors of Cyclone Nargis become nervous. People were sleeping badly at night. Children were woken up by nightmares, and many of those who were in school were unable to concentrate on their studies. Both children and adults carried with them a heavy listlessness that they couldn't shake off. Some started crying at odd moments, like when they mistakenly handed over the wrong fare for a ferryboat or when they realized they had forgotten to bring the laundry in before the rain. People found themselves in the middle of heated arguments they didn't mean to begin. Palm toddy, the local brew that stings the back of your throat but aids temporary memory loss, was selling well.

An aid worker who had been in Sri Lanka during the Indian Ocean tsunami pointed out that the traumatic effects of the cyclone were different from those caused by the tsunami. Though people suffered similarly sudden and devastating losses, the experience of the actual disaster was quite distinct. The tsunami lasted minutes; it was short, intense, and horrendously violent. People's experience of Cyclone Nargis, by contrast, went on for hours—in some cases people were buffeted by the storm for up to twelve hours. And during those long hours so much happened. Mothers let go of their children, husbands were unable to protect their wives, aged parents were left in their homes to drown. One woman I spoke to told me how a crying toddler was swept into her arms while she was holding on to a tree during the storm surge. She let go with one hand so she could hold on to the baby, but she was rocked by a series of waves and the child was swept away again. She didn't recognize the child and will never know whose it was, but the image of it floating into and out of her arms haunts her still.

Along with the immense and incalculable loss—of people, houses, whole villages—was the shame that descended the morning after the storm. As their clothing had been torn off by the tumultuous waters, many survivors ended up naked and had to scavenge for rags to cover themselves the following day. In the very conservative village society of Burma the sense of shame this caused is hard to forget. Almost everyone I spoke to mentioned the loss of their clothes. A tall, thin man told me he had ended up wearing a mud-soaked child's dress wrapped around his waist. A young woman who had clung on to a tree for the duration of the storm refused to climb down when other survivors called to her because she no longer had any clothes on; she waited all day, until nightfall, and climbed down in the darkness.

The traditional methods people might have used to alleviate trauma and shame were in many cases no longer available. Buddhist monks and Christian pastors were among the dead, and monasteries and churches were damaged and destroyed. Mya Win, the man I met who had lost all his family and padlocked his hut of salvaged belongings, has nowhere to turn for help in his village; the monastery was washed away and the three monks in residence were killed. Villagers there had searched for the large Buddha statue they had all contributed to purchasing for the monastery, but it too was gone, buried somewhere beneath the mud.

Psychological trauma was erupting all over the delta in ghastly and unnerving ways. When one Burmese aid worker arrived at a village to oversee the monthly food distribution, a teenage girl ran up to her and threw her arms around her, declaring that she had known all along her sister was still alive. Villagers told the aid worker that the girl's sister had died in Cyclone Nargis, and that they had tried to make her understand that fact, but she refused to believe them. When it was time for the aid worker to leave, the girl clung on to her. "How can you leave me?" she cried. "You're my sister, and I have waited so long for you to come back."

I met an eighteen-year-old in Ka Pyo who was the sole remaining member of his family. During the storm he, his four sisters, and their parents had all climbed into one tree. The water rose around them and the wind grew fierce; it stung their skin, lashing them with sand and grit. As the hours passed, they grew weaker and, one by one, fell off the tree and were consumed by the waves. Unable to see where his family was, the father had shouted out their names in the darkness to check that everyone was still there, but the answering calls became fewer until, finally, only his son was responding to his hoarse cries. The two survived the storm, but a couple of days later, the father killed himself by banging his head repeatedly against a tree.

In a sense, Nargis was still raging through the delta; people were mentally trapped inside the cyclone. In Thama Thu village, I had sat down with ten villagers in a ramshackle shop. The shop's interior was suffused with a rosy glow from the red tarpaulin sheet that served as part of the roof. There wasn't much for sale, just hand-sized portions of dried fish, chips inside small plastic bags stapled shut, and palm toddy sold in old beer bottles with wads of rolled-up newspaper used as stoppers.

The owner of the shop, Nwe Nwe, was in her twenties and had lost twenty-three relatives to Cyclone Nargis. During the storm most of her family had sought shelter in a rice warehouse on the riverside while she had run farther inland to the monastery. The warehouse had flooded and everyone inside it had drowned. Nwe Nwe said she had heard them hollering for help and banging on the roof of the warehouse before they died, but the villagers sitting around her said there was no way she could have heard anything above the noise of the storm.

"What did the cyclone sound like?" I asked.

A young boy eagerly recalled the bulletlike sounds he had heard when coconuts from the palm trees began falling into the floodwater. *"Pow! Pow!"* he said, putting his hands together in the shape of a gun and ducking into the trenches behind some rice sacks. *"Pow! Pow! Pow!"*

A man began emulating the fierce winds with a deep *whoo-whooing* noise, but the woman next to him said the wind had made more of a screeching sound. It sounded, she said, like a pig being slaughtered. As the man continued with his deep bellowing, she launched into a series of high-pitched squeals. Another person started banging out a frantic and random beat on the mismatched wooden planks that made up the floor, and the whole structure began to shudder. Soon everyone had joined in, and the tarpaulin tent filled with an unbearable cacophony of clapping, shouting, and wailing.

The noise didn't stop until people noticed that Nwe Nwe was crying, and that her body was convulsing with uncontrollable sobs. One by one, the members of the strange orchestra fell silent.

IN A VILLAGE south of Mawlamyainggyun, there was one villager who everyone missed. He was an older man, a carpenter known as Uncle Zin. His grown-up children had left the village to seek work elsewhere, and his wife had passed away some years before the cyclone. The villagers remembered him as a friendly, talkative man who loved a good joke and was also an excellent carpenter. Uncle Zin could take a few discarded planks and transform them into a smart knee-high table for schoolchildren to use while doing their homework. He could fix doors that wouldn't shut properly and smooth down splintered floorboards. Often he'd do the smaller jobs for free (not counting the bowls of fish curry and endless cups of tea that housewives were coaxed into serving up for him), and he was a popular man in the village.

Uncle Zin had had the foresight to keep a flashlight with him during the cyclone. He had probably tied it to his wrist when he realized the storm was getting stronger; he was organized with things like that and had a knack for finding practical solutions even when resources were scarce. In the pitch black that followed the storm, Uncle Zin had been able to locate people with his flashlight. He had waded through the mud and clambered over felled trees looking for people from the village and checking that they were okay:

Ko Myo? Is that you? Are you okay? And your family—your wife and your two naughty boys?

Daw Kyu, is your sister not with you? Don't panic, I'll go and look for her.

Hey, Aung Kyaw Soe! I'm glad you made it. Stay calm, my old friend, the worst is over. . . .

Uncle Zin managed to find many survivors from the village, even though the storm surge had flung them far and wide across the area. The villagers recalled feeling a great sense of relief knowing that he had survived and would be around to help them as he always had done But later, when the villagers began to compare their experiences of the storm, they realized that Uncle Zin had not stayed long with anyone and that no one had actually seen him—they had only heard his voice and sensed his presence in the darkness as he shone his flashlight into their faces. When people thought hard about what they remembered, they had to admit that there had been only a bright light and the comforting and familiar sound of Uncle Zin's voice:

You made it, Sayagyi! Your house is a bit of a mess, I have to say, but we can spend some good times fixing it—as long as your wife rustles up some of her famous shrimp paste while we work!

Even odder, no one remembered seeing him in the days that followed the cyclone. No one had seen him when survivors gathered together in the bleak dawn after the storm, and no one had seen him in the desperate days as they waited for help in the mud and rain. Many villagers eventually made it to Mawlamyainggyun, where people from their village were directed to a particular monastery. As the surviving villagers were reunited at the monastery, they began to remark on how strange it was that Uncle Zin hadn't turned up yet.

It wasn't until some days later that they learned that Uncle Zin was dead. One of the villagers had joined a volunteer team moving through the area to clear away bodies from village sites, and he discovered that Uncle Zin hadn't survived the cyclone but had drowned in the storm surge—his body was found beached on a small sandbank about a mile and a half upstream from the village.

THOUSANDS OF PEOPLE who lived in and around Pyinzalu had decided not to return to the area and were still residing in camps outside Laputta. The authorities had begun clearing out unofficial shelters at monasteries and schools, and closing down government camps from mid-May onward and, by June, only a few camps were left. These remaining camps near Laputta were providing shelter to over seven thousand people who were either unable or understandably unwilling to return to the nothingness that awaited them on the coast of the delta.

In a move that was somewhat out of character, the authorities did not force these people back to their villages as they had done with everyone else. Instead, they decided to relocate the inhabitants to camps farther outside Laputta. The decision was unpopular with camp dwellers; the new sites were seven and fourteen miles out of town respectively, and the distance along a road poorly served by public transport would make it difficult for them to pick up day labor in town. To beg for a stay of execution, five women threw themselves down in front of the car in which Prime Minister Thein Sein was traveling when he visited the camp. A man wrote a letter to Naypyidaw explaining how relocating the camp would make it impossible for those sheltering there to earn the funds they needed to rebuild their homes and lives. The women were removed, the letter writer was arrested, and, at the end of August, the camps were moved to their new locations safely out of sight and earshot of the main road.

While I was in Laputta I was able to visit the camps with aid workers who were distributing supplies. The huts were uniformly laid out and relatively spacious, with white tarpaulin walls and ceilings and floors made of split bamboo rods. The inhabitants I saw were mostly elderly people or children—too old or too young to face the hard labor of reconstructing life from scratch. In one hut I met a seventy-five-year-old widow and her adult daughter who was deaf and dumb. They were sharing the space with a couple they had not known before the storm. The couple was old too and, as the wife put it, had "only one good eye and two working ears" between them.

This motley household wanted to stay at the camp permanently and told me they could earn a living by hiring themselves out as laborers in the fields come harvesttime. I sincerely doubted whether any of them were capable of physical labor, but they had run out of other options. "If we go back to our village we have to start again," yelled the old man with bad hearing. "Here, at least we have this shelter. We are old people. We don't have the strength to begin everything over again. I pray they will just let us stay here."

At the so-called Seven Mile Camp, closer to town, I met a group of fishermen from Pyinzalu sitting in a tea shop. It wasn't really a tea shop in the normal sense, just a sheet draped across bamboo poles underneath which you could buy a cup of tepid and lumpy Coffee-Mix, a store-bought sachet of coffee containing sugar and dried milk. I bought a round for the fishermen and we sat in the shade and chatted. They couldn't return yet, they said, because there would be no work for them in Pyinzalu. They were sea fishermen and needed big boats to go out to sea. With so many vessels sunk and fishermen killed, the fishing companies they used to work for had yet to resume operations. "Even if there was work, I don't know if I would go back," said one burly man with a permanent scowl etched across his features after so many years of squinting into the sun. "In my village, we had four hundred houses.

There were only four left after Nargis. Every single fisherman who was out at sea at that time died." He laid his large, calloused hand on his chest and concluded, "I feel as if my heart was broken by the cyclone."

As we were talking, a cardboard box walked up to me and leaned against my leg. The box had two muddy little feet sticking out of the bottom and was labeled USA Refined Vegetable Oil, Vitamin A Fortified. When I tapped the box it started giggling. One of the fishermen laid claim to the contents, saying that his son liked to pretend he was invisible. Though it was a bit sad to see a child playing with the throwaway remnants of aid supplies that adults in the camp were becoming dependent on, we all laughed. I carried on tapping the box until it got bored and ran off, disappearing from view behind one of the long line of identical white huts.

The final trip I took out of Laputta was to Pyinzalu, where most of the camp inhabitants had originally come from and were still avoiding returning to. Because Pyinzalu was so close to where the cyclone made landfall, it had taken the full brunt of the storm, and the surrounding scenery looked as if it had been blasted by chemical defoliants. The ground was slick with white-gray mud and littered with pale logs that looked like dinosaur bones. The monsoon clouds had begun to dissipate and a harsh sun glared down on the roofless boat I was traveling in. The water was calm, like handblown glass, and a gently blurred mirror image of the land was cast onto the surface of the river. Every so often the unchanging reflection was momentarily distorted by a swirling eddy or hidden current.

As the boat neared Pyinzalu, we passed the salt fields that the area was once famous for. Though there was absolutely no sign of any life, it was clear that some substantial industry had once been conducted there. Concrete poles protruding from the water were all that remained of the large steel jetties. The abandoned, unworked fields were encrusted with

salt and gave the disconcerting impression that a touch of frost had
settled upon the hot, sticky delta. The boatman told me that as many as
thirty thousand salt workers had perished along this stretch—a tragedy
impossible to prove or disprove, as many of the people who worked these
fields were illegal seasonal migrants from elsewhere in Burma and were
not registered with the local authorities.

Before Cyclone Nargis, Pyinzalu was a trading town, dealing in fish,
salt, and other coastal produce. There were ten ferries a week direct to
Rangoon. The town had a hospital, a school, and a police station and
functioned as a hub for its far-flung corner of the delta. But the cyclone
had demolished Pyinzalu, crushing all the buildings and killing a staggering 90 percent of the population.

The once busy pier was gone, and the boat I was traveling in with a
team of Burmese aid workers docked against a row of salvaged planks
that was loosely nailed together. The riverfront was lined with dead trees.
Where there was once a row of well-stocked warehouses for storing produce, there was now only swampland. Still, there was more activity than
I had seen in any of my other delta destinations. Companies owned by
cronies of the regime had begun rebuilding work in Pyinzalu. There were
also a hundred soldiers posted there, helping with reconstruction and,
perhaps, ensuring that there were no disturbances of any kind. They
were camped out in sagging, threadbare olive-green tents pitched along
a raised dirt embankment that was once a road.

In the flooded field that was the center of town there was a brand-new
one-story cement building with white walls and a sloping roof of green
tiles. This well-constructed bungalow looked out of place on the muddy
edges of the delta, and when I asked what it was, I learned why. The
building had been built with the sole purpose of receiving high-ranking
military visitors who had come to Pyinzalu in recent months. No longer
in use, it was empty when I visited, and a forlorn wooden barricade

indicated that it was off-limits. The shrubbery that had been planted along the walkway leading up to the entrance was wilted and dying. The building had the feel of a disused prop for the senior general's first Delta Disaster Tour back in May.

A housing project was being built nearby (courtesy of Max Myanmar, a crony company and builder of one of Naypyidaw's villa-complex hotels). There were rows of houses on stilts all exactly the same size and shape, with dark wood walls and tin roofs. The doorways and windows had been left empty, and people living in them had nailed up sheets of plastic or tarpaulin to stop the rain from coming in. I peeped inside a few houses and saw that none of them had any furniture, though there were towers of plastic buckets, folded blankets, and matching sets of aluminum kitchen equipment.

In one of the houses I met a fisherman and his wife who had lost all four of their children. "People here have changed," he told me. "We are all different now. Look at my wife: she used to talk all day long and now she hardly says a word. And me, I used to eat for the whole of the town, but now my wife has to force me just to take a little rice in the morning and the evening." He spoke of a sense of unreality that had settled upon the town: "Maybe I am dreaming this. Maybe I will wake up soon. Even people like you who come here and ask us what we need and write things down in your notebook . . . These people leave and I never see them again. I think sometimes that maybe they were never here and that I just imagined them."

As we spoke, some villagers had gathered nearby. They began to interrupt the fisherman, telling me their own experiences of the cyclone. I wrote down all their stories, each one a wretched tale devoid of any hope. By the time the stories were told, I had a cramp in my hand and could barely write. I asked the villagers around me what they would do if another storm came. They all had different answers; some had identified a tall tree that was still standing that they would run to, others talked about trying to ride the storm out in a boat. An older woman who had not spoken before shushed everyone. She lowered the cheroot she was puffing on. "What does it matter?" she croaked, as the sweet-smelling smoke wafted out of her mouth. "You can bring us food and shelter if you want, but when the next storm comes, we'll all be dead anyway!"

I had read an article in the *New Light of Myanmar* describing how Senior General Than Shwe had given "guidance" on disaster preparedness measures some months ago, but I had not yet seen any evidence of his methods being put into practice. In the photograph that accompanied the article, Than Shwe was pictured seated on an ornate couch with a small banquet of food laid out on the coffee table at his knees. He held in his hands a map of the delta and was using his finger to draw lines—perhaps randomly—across the area. A bevy of two- and three-star generals was crouched around him, notebooks in hand, avidly following his finger and awaiting their instructions.

Than Shwe's take on disaster preparedness consisted of a road network linking towns and villages across the delta. He mapped out over 186 miles of new road that would connect even the most waterlogged parts of the delta to the rest of the country by land routes. In keeping with the senior general's guidance, the road system was to be elevated so that it would not be vulnerable to flooding or high waves. He also wanted man-made hillocks in each town and village that were higher than the highest point of the storm surge during Nargis.

This vision was especially wise, stated the article, because it had a dual purpose: a road system in areas previously accessible only by water would boost trade routes and people's livelihoods and, therefore, their ability to recover from the disaster. A good idea in theory, but as one Burmese friend pointed out, how were people supposed to get up to roads floating fifteen or twenty feet in the air? "Are they going to build a ramp every mile or so? Or maybe they have plans to elevate the entire delta!"

Though the *New Light of Myanmar* featured a map detailing how the road network would link towns like Laputta, Pyinzalu, and Maw-lamyainggyun, nothing ever came of the ambitious plan. I saw no road construction anywhere in the lower reaches of the delta, and there was not a man-made hillock in sight. Neither was there any mention of the senior general's elevated road network in the government's final Program for Reconstruction after Cyclone Nargis, a plan for "Preparedness and Protection from Future Natural Disaster." Despite the eager posture of the generals around Than Shwe in the original meeting, his idea seemed to have been quietly ditched, though probably no one had yet mustered the nerve to mention that to the senior general.

A FEW DAYS after Cyclone Nargis, Laura Bush, then U.S. First Lady, issued a statement that said, "Although they [the regime] were aware of the threat, Burma's state-run media failed to issue a timely warning to citizens in the storm's path." Others followed suit, and before long it became a much-touted truism that orders had come from the capital, Naypyidaw, imposing a media blackout on weather reports so as not to cause a panic about the approaching storm, an order that also could be reinterpreted in its most simple and horrifying form as, *Let them die.*

In fact, the storm's path was not known with any surety until less than two days before it made landfall. When Cyclone Nargis was brewing in the Bay of Bengal, it was a middling-sized storm that appeared to be traveling north. The Bangladesh government issued a series of storm warnings and prepared for the worst; aid organizations began preparations to stockpile food and evacuate people from vulnerable coastal areas to storm shelters. It had seemed almost certain that the cyclone was going to strike the storm-weary shores of Bangladesh.

But cyclones are beholden to slight changes in temperature and the push and pull of distant winds; their movements can be erratic and hard to predict. For about twenty-four hours near the end of April, the storm stopped moving entirely and hovered ominously in the middle of the bay, poised between India, Bangladesh, and Burma. It was not until midnight on April 30 that the U.S. Joint Typhoon Warning Center recorded the cyclone making an abrupt turn to the northeast, after which it began to track a path that would have led to Arakan State in northwestern Burma.

But, as the hours passed, the cyclone spun farther eastward, lining up with the Irrawaddy Delta. Only in the final twenty-four hours before it hit land did the cyclone begin to intensify. Staff of UN agencies in Rangoon who monitored weather sites on the Web told me that on May 2, the morning of the storm, it was still unclear where it was going to hit land.

Local weather reports reflected this uncertainty. Beginning on April 27, the state media ran warnings that there was a cyclone in the region and (incorrectly) predicted a relatively mild storm with winds of 40 to 45 miles per hour. On the day of the storm, updated radio alerts warned of winds of up to 120 miles per hour. Villagers I spoke to in the delta said they knew of the cyclone's impending arrival—either through the newspaper or radio—but had assumed it wouldn't be too bad and thought they would be able to hunker down in their homes.

The head of Burma's Department of Meteorology, Htun Lwin, had a clear conscience. Though he didn't respond directly to the international accusations that appropriate weather reports had not been issued, he spoke to the local media in Burma and wrote articles designed to clear his name and that of his department. Htun Lwin stated that he had followed up his regular broadcasts with personal phone calls to authorities on Haing Gyi Island—the first piece of land in the cyclone's path—and had maintained half-hourly phone contact until the last possible minute. He also made it known that his department had been cleared of any wrongdoing by the World Meteorological Organization. Representatives of the UN's weather-monitoring arm had come to Rangoon and ascertained that the Department of Meteorology had done an adequate job, especially given the out-of-date equipment they had to work with.

The problem, said Htun Lwin, was not the lack of a warning; the problem was that there had been no effective system in place to tell people what to do in such circumstances. He reminded readers that the delta had never been hit by a storm anywhere near the size and ferocity of Cyclone Nargis, and it was unreasonable to expect there to be early warning systems or cyclone shelters in place to protect people in the area. In one article the weatherman wrote that it was an ill-fated combination of conditions that made the cyclone so lethal to so many people: the high population density; the low-lying land of the delta; the many waterways along which the storm surge could travel; the waterlogged land on which the cyclone could feed and maintain strength; and the denuded mangrove that could have absorbed some of the surge.

Throughout the time I researched the story of Cyclone Nargis, I always imagined that, one day, a great reckoning would come; not quite a thunderbolt from the sky that would strike all evil forces from the land, but at least some record or true assessment of what had happened in the wake of the storm. Given the international outcry after the cyclone—the accusations of a crime committed against humanity and the calls for delivering aid by force—I had assumed there would be some effort to establish exactly what had taken place and what the ruling generals were culpable for. But the outrage had somehow been retracted, and the crime, if it had ever been committed, was now forgotten or absolved.

Yet even the most basic questions remained unanswered. How many people had been killed during the cyclone? The final death toll used by both the Burmese government and accepted by the aid community and media was the official toll of 84,537 dead and 53,836 missing, considered to add up to over 138,000 dead.

Many people believe the death toll was much higher. A boatman in Bogale who had been hired by an aid agency to make deliveries across the township was conducting his own unofficial and private tally, and he told me that at least 100,000 people had died in Bogale Township alone. *"Minimum,"* he emphasized. The official number in Bogale Township was recorded as 34,744 dead and 3,198 missing.

Estimates of the true number of people killed by Cyclone Nargis were three or four times higher than the government's final count, which would bring the number of dead to over half a million.

There were also more complex questions that would always have been hard to answer: How many people died because of the regime's negligence and reticence in allowing foreign aid into the country? Many survivors I spoke to had witnessed deaths in the first few days immediately following the storm. People had died of injuries sustained during the storm, and those who were unable to walk to places where they could get help died of dehydration. Would these people have lived if the regime had acted more quickly, or if it had allowed foreign military helicopters to conduct search-and-rescue missions? A seasoned UN logistics expert who had worked in emergency operations throughout the region told me that thousands of people could have been saved.

As time passed, though, the possibility of a fair and comprehensive reckoning became less and less likely. The facts were already bloated with hindsight, overblown by rumor and sound bites from the more sensational elements of the international media and activist groups, and underplayed by the regime's own meticulously archived propaganda machine.

Perhaps I was spending too much time under the gloomy delta skies, but I did not share the optimism I read about in some of the international news stories written to mark the passing of six months since Cyclone Nargis. Headlines like "Hope Returns to the Delta" seemed trite, especially when everything I saw indicated the exact opposite. The UN's Food and Agriculture Organization stated that 97 percent of paddy fields had been restored. So I must have spent my time traveling exclusively in the 3 percent of the area with failed crops and speaking with farmers who were unable to properly plough their fields—a strange coincidence given that my travels took me to so many disparate parts of the delta.

Aid workers spoke to the foreign press about a new and improved relationship between the aid community and the regime. It was true that access had become possible in the delta, but assistance in other areas of the country was still subject to restrictions.

In Chin State, bamboo had flowered—an unwanted occurrence that happens once or twice in a century and causes a massive increase in the number of rats. The multiplying rats were munching their way voraciously through crops and food stocks, and the threat of famine was looming in Chin State. Yet the authorities would not allow international NGOs or the UN into Chin State to see what could be done to alleviate the disaster.

One aid worker I met at a UN office had been waiting over a month for permission to leave Rangoon and travel to Magwe in central Burma, where there were also reports of food shortages. These areas did open up eventually, once the regime felt confident it had enough control over the situation on the ground, but the initial restrictions were a replay of what had happened after Cyclone Nargis, albeit on a smaller scale.

Whenever a door opens in Burma, another one is surreptitiously closed. It seemed like a very military tactic:

Keep your enemy operating in an unpredictable environment; if land has been conceded in one area, send reinforcements to another.

It was the kind of move I would have expected to find described in Sun Tzu's *The Art of War*; some archaic wisdom that provided counsel on how to wrong-foot an opponent by keeping his attention fixated on one target so that he would not notice that other areas were being bolstered and strengthened.

I took my counsel elsewhere, in an anthology of poems called *The Way of the Hyacinth* by a late, great poet of the delta region known as Zaw Gyi. One of the poems describes the challenging journey made by the *beda*, or water hyacinth, that is ubiquitous in the delta's waterways. The *beda's* journey is not easy; it is tugged by tides and attacked by palm fronds and other haphazard flotsam. Yet, the *beda* always overcomes these obstacles, and even manages to flower in the face of adversity, displaying silky lilac petals above its tangled raft of verdant leaves.

Though the poem was published in 1960, long before Aung San Suu Kyi came to the fore in Burmese politics, it is sometimes read as a reference to her strength and grace; whenever she appeared in public she almost always wore fresh flowers in her hair. I also read the poem as a treatise on endurance in general—the kind of endurance people throughout the country had to exercise as they recovered, regrouped, and rose above the ruins. The poem's last verse portrays the hyacinth resurfacing after a spell underwater:

Back on the surface there's no relief.
A flock of ducks spills out from a creek.
They number hundreds, and the beda *is but one,*
Kicked and pulled by their paddling feet,
She holds up resolute, and keeps the flower in her hair.

I WAS LATE leaving Pyinzalu. The sun was already beginning to fade and the boatman was worried about getting us back to Laputta before nightfall. We set off, sailing rapidly back upriver past the empty salt fields. The late afternoon light threw long, twisted shadows across the land. The boatman gunned his engine against the setting sun, but he was fighting a losing battle. The sun had already turned a livid red and began to accelerate its descent as it neared the horizon. The waters flushed pink for the briefest of moments and then the light was gone.

For a short while the boatman was able to navigate in the gray half light by checking the black lines on either side of us that marked the edges of the narrow creek we were traveling along, but soon it was too dark to do even that. And then I realized why the boatman had been so concerned when we left Pyinzalu—the light on his boat was broken and large parts of the delta were entirely without electricity.

I had my headlamp with me, and we took turns putting it on and lying at the front of the boat peering out into the darkness, shouting if we spotted the bamboo poles of a fishing net or buoys that marked traps beneath the water. The boatman had slowed down and was moving at a walking pace. After about an hour, we saw a weak, yellow light in the distance. It turned out to be a flashlight used by a fisherman who was laying nets. He gamely climbed onboard to direct us to the nearest village. It was still a slow journey, and I leaned back against the side of the boat, my services with the headlamp no longer needed. As the boat engine puttered along, the setting took on a magical air: the black waters, the silent wetlands all around us, the star-filled sky above. I felt very far away from anywhere and oddly calm.

When we arrived in the darkened village, the Burmese aid workers I had been traveling with realized they had worked there before and knew some of the villagers, so we were able to arrange a room for the night. We were taken to a part of the village that had not been badly affected by the storm surge, where some of the bigger wooden houses had survived intact. The house we stayed in was empty that night—it was a one-room wooden house on stilts. There was little inside other than a couple of live chickens tied to a railing and some rolled-up, weevil-ridden, rattan sleeping mats.

We washed our sunburned faces in a rainwater jar and unfurled the mats. Someone found candles and lodged them in empty bottles that were then placed around the room. The chickens, initially alarmed by our arrival, settled into a wary watchfulness. We played tic-tac-toe in my notebook, scared one another with a few ghost stories, and then stretched out on the mats and went to sleep.

The next morning we wasted no time in leaving the village to return to Laputta. I was scheduled to be back in Rangoon that day, and I had no travel clearance to spend the night in a village far from town. I didn't speak to anyone as we walked through the village back to where the boat was docked. It was barely dawn and everyone was busy. Children were trotting along the dirt pathways to get to school on time. Two men climbed out of the river, mud-drenched, carrying traps filled with crabs. A woman and her daughter were preparing food beneath their stilted house, pounding pungent shrimp paste in a stone mortar and releasing the scent of freshly crushed garlic into the morning air.

When our boat sailed out onto the river I saw that fishermen were already punting their wooden canoes along the river's edge, slipping behind the newly sprouting *dani* that stretched out like a long green fence, as they made their way to the nets they had laid the night before. In the dewy post-dawn light, the water took on the rich, brown color of cocoa. Months of rainfall had brought some greenery back to the land. Unruly tangles of *beda* were beginning to grow along the edges of the creeks and stiller stretches of the rivers. The heat of the day had yet to descend, and when I dropped my hand into the water it felt cool and inviting. In that idyllic early morning, as the boat skimmed lightly above the surface of the river, it was hard to believe that anything terrible had ever happened there.

AFTERWORD

Whenever I think of Burma these days, the Buddhist parable of the blind men and the elephant comes to mind. In the age-old teaching, a king summons a group of blind men and places an elephant before them. Each sightless man is led to a different part of the elephant's body to touch the animal and feel what it is like. The king then asks each in turn to describe the elephant.

The man who felt the rounded head says confidently that the elephant is like a water jar. Another, who felt the cylindrical foot, says the elephant is like a pillar. The man who felt the tusk says it is like an iron rod, and the one who felt the tuft of the tail says it is like a broom. Before long the blind men are arguing over their description of the elephant, since each one is convinced that his description is correct.

It is the same in Burma today. Given the regime's restrictions on information and association, it is difficult to form any public consensus or verifiable version of the truth. While certain events can be accounted for with certainty, there is much that remains unknown. Like those blind men in the parable, it has become impossible for anyone to see or fathom the beast in its entirety.

In a society where nothing can be taken for granted, distorted truths, half stories, and private visions are, by necessity, woven into the popular narrative of events. Burma is a place where the government hides behind convoluted smoke screens. It is a place where those who sacrifice themselves for their country must go unrecognized and can only be lauded or remembered in secret. It is a place where natural disasters don't happen, at least not officially, and where the gaping misery that follows any catastrophe must be covered up and silenced. In such an environment, almost anything becomes believable.

IN THE EARLY HOURS of a muggy Rangoon morning in May 2009, exactly one year after Cyclone Nargis, a fifty-three-year-old American man reportedly tied two planks to his sandals to improvise swimming flippers and ducked into the warm waters of Inya Lake. Using five-liter plastic water bottles for buoyancy, he paddled under cover of darkness to Aung San Suu Kyi's house. After spending two nights there, he swam back across the lake. At 5.30 A.M. on May 6, he was fished out of the water by a police inspector and was later charged with secretly entering Aung San Suu Kyi's house, violating his tourist visa, and breeching the restriction on swimming in Inya Lake under the Rangoon municipality's Water Supply and Sanitation Rules.

Aung San Suu Kyi was charged with violating the terms of her house arrest, under the law safeguarding the state against the dangers of subversive elements, for failing to report a visitor to her home. Her two female companions, a mother and daughter who live with her and help to look after her and the house, were also charged.

When the trial began later that month, it instantly became a favorite topic of conversation in Rangoon. I was in Burma at the time, and at some point in every conversation someone would inevitably ask, "So, what news of The Swimmer?"

We pieced together The Swimmer's personal details from international news sources and Burmese state media. His name was John William Yettaw. He was a retired bus driver from Missouri and a Mormon. He apparently had attempted to visit Aung San Suu Kyi in the same manner the year before, in November 2008, though her helpers had prevented him from meeting with her. Yettaw stated in court that he had believed Aung San Suu Kyi's life was in danger. It had been revealed to him in a dream that someone would attempt to assassinate her, so he had swum across the lake to warn her and to save her life.

During her defense, Aung San Suu Kyi told the judge that she had not committed any crime. According to her lawyer, she pointed out that the security detail around her compound must not have been working properly as no visitor should be able to enter unnoticed. She and her helpers pleaded not guilty.

There was plenty of detail available on the proceedings. State newspapers informed us that when Yettaw swam across the lake he carried with him a camera tightly wrapped in plastic, a pair of pliers, a screwdriver, a flashlight, and twenty-eight dry-cell batteries. Further peculiar and unexplained details were released, such as the items Yettaw had left behind at Aung San Suu Kyi's house, which included two black chadors, two pairs of gray stockings, and a volume of the *Book of Mormon*.

Yet, for all the minutiae, there was no satisfactory explanation as to what had actually taken place and why. All the discussions I had about the case were punctuated by unanswerable questions:

AFTERWORD

They say The Swimmer is asthmatic. There's no way he could have swum over a mile across that lake. Did the regime help him, do you think? Or is he just a crazy man?

And what of Daw Aung San Suu Kyi? It must have been a setup. Why else would she not report him to the guards at her gate? How could she have let him stay the night?

It can only be a drama staged at the command of the generals. They have done this for a reason. But what could the reason possibly be . . . ?

The one point that nobody questioned was that the trial would result in a guilty verdict for all parties concerned—the ending was pre-ordained. In August that year, Aung San Suu Kyi and her helpers were each sentenced to three years imprisonment with hard labor. Yettaw was sentenced to a total of seven years, receiving an additional three for breaking immigration law and an extra year from the Rangoon municipality for breeching the water sanitation restrictions on swimming in the lake.

Immediately after the sentencing, the minister of home affairs strode into the courtroom and read a last-minute order of clemency granted by Senior General Than Shwe. The women's three-year prison sentences were reduced to eighteen months under house arrest on account of Aung San Suu Kyi being the daughter of Burma's national hero, Aung San.

It was just long enough, people noted, to keep Aung San Suu Kyi under lock and key until after the general elections that were scheduled for 2010.

During the last general election, held in 1990 and considered to have been relatively free and fair, the generals suffered a humiliating defeat. Though Aung San Suu Kyi and other key members of her party were under house arrest or in prison at the time, the National League for Democracy fielded 447 candidates and won 392 seats. The National Unity Party, a proxy of the regime, fielded 413 candidates and won 10 seats. The figures allowed no room for ambiguity; the people wanted the military out and the NLD in.

Having utterly misjudged the will of the people, the regime disregarded the results and continued to rule. With the hindsight of twenty years it is unlikely they will make the same mistake again. The determination with which the referendum was pushed through in the wake of Cyclone Nargis and the dubious methods used to garner the final 92.48 percent positive result was evidence enough that there was little sincerity behind the government's so-called Road Map to Democracy.

Besides, Than Shwe had made it clear that no one should expect democracy in Burma anytime soon. "[G]iven that the kind of well-established mature democracy that is the end result of two or three centuries of development cannot reasonably be made to appear overnight, all-round consideration and thoughtful action will be advisable," he said during his address for Armed Forces Day in 2009. "Democracy in Myanmar today is at a fledgling stage and still requires patient care and attention."

Than Shwe further cautioned more than 13,600 troops standing to attention at the Naypyidaw parade ground not to let down their guard: "We must be combat-ready forever to defend the nation and protect the life and property of the people."

Come 2010, all main contenders and rivals to the throne will be safely behind bars or, in the case of Aung San Suu Kyi, under house arrest.

Most of the 88 Generation Students group who organized the protests against the rise in fuel costs in August 2007 will still be in prison, as they are serving sentences that are sixty-five years long. Among those condemned to a lifetime in prison, are Mie Mie, a thirty-five-year-old zoology graduate and mother of two, who was transferred to a prison in the far north, and Nilar Thein, a former political prisoner who gave birth to her first child just before the 2007 protests. Min Ko Naing, a prominent leader during the 1988 uprising who had already spent seventeen years in prison, mostly in solitary confinement, was also sentenced to sixty-five years, with an additional six months for contempt of court.

It is estimated that 220 monks are incarcerated in Burmese prisons and will undoubtedly still be in prison during the elections. For his role in the September 2007 marches, U Gambira, a twenty-eight-year-old leader of the All Burma Monks' Alliance, was sentenced to sixty-eight years, twelve of which will be served with hard labor.

Harsh punishment was also meted out to bloggers and journalists who sent information about the marches out of the country. Nay Phone Latt, a man in his twenties whose blog was widely read around the world during September 2007, was sentenced to twenty years for using electronic transactions to harm national security, among other charges.

Zargana, the outspoken comedian arrested for his high-profile involvement in relief efforts after Cyclone Nargis, was sentenced on various charges to fifty-nine years (though his sentence was later reduced to thirty-five years).

Most people I spoke to in Burma viewed the upcoming elections as just another tactic for the military to hold on to power with less international condemnation and the cultivated appearance of legitimacy. There was a joke doing the rounds that the generals would discard their military uniforms and don *longyi* so that they could reemerge after the elections dressed as civilian politicians and continue to rule the country. As the joke goes, the new constitution and elections *will* bring change to Burma—a change of uniform.

John Yettaw left Burma shortly after his verdict was read. He had suffered numerous health issues related to his diabetes and epilepsy. U.S. senator Jim Webb arrived in mid-August and was granted meetings with both Senior General Than Shwe and Aung San Suu Kyi. After the senator's visit, Yettaw was released and taken back to the United States. Since his return, Yettaw has denied any accusations that the regime sponsored or aided his swim to Aung San Suu Kyi's house. When asked by *Newsweek* magazine whether the junta had put him up to it, he said, "I've been accused of being CIA, of being on the books of the junta. The idea is just ridiculous."

Senator Webb's visit to Burma, the first by a high-level U.S. diplomat in many years, marked a turning point in U.S. policy toward Burma. A few months later, Kurt M. Campbell, the assistant secretary of state for East Asian and Pacific affairs, used the phrase "pragmatic engagement" to describe his government's revised approach. While economic sanctions would remain in place until the regime displayed the necessary commitment to change (such as releasing Aung San Suu Kyi and all other political prisoners), the United States intended to pursue active dialogue with the generals. Campbell later visited Burma together with his deputy, Scot Marciel. During an open meeting held in Bangkok, Thailand, after their visit, Marciel repeatedly stressed that the dialogue was in its infancy and offered few details of their meetings in Burma or their expectations for future engagement. As Campbell had stated earlier, "We expect engagement with Burma to be a long, slow, and step-by-step process."

A FEW DAYS AFTER The Swimmer was arrested in May 2009, Kyaing Kyaing, the wife of Senior General Than Shwe, held a ceremony at the Danok Pagoda, not far from Rangoon. For the previous couple of years, members of the regime had been donating funds to refurbish the ancient pagoda, and the work was nearly completed. As one of the primary patrons, Kyaing Kyaing made the customary offerings to the religious order, and monks recited the *Paritta*, or Buddhist scripture of protection. Holy objects were enshrined inside the reliquary of the *hti*, and it was hoisted to the top of the pagoda in a sacred carriage. Before Kyaing Kyaing left, she performed a few acts to accrue additional merit. She planted and watered a Bodhi tree, the sacred fig tree under which the Buddha gained enlightenment, and she released a flock of birds into the air.

Just over three weeks later, a crack appeared in the 2,300-year-old pagoda, and the entire edifice collapsed in on itself. Reports varied as to how many people were killed. Though the state media reported that only two people died, Burmese exile-run news sources outside the country claimed there were up to twenty dead.

A Burmese journalist in Rangoon showed me photographs he was able to take the day after the accident; the pagoda had been reduced to a large mound of bricks, dirt, and splintered bamboo scaffolding. He said the authorities were sifting through the rubble, looking for the *hti* and its diamond-encrusted orb.

The *New Light of Myanmar*, which had chronicled Kyaing Kyaing's ceremonial visit three weeks earlier, ran a terse article blaming shoddy and rushed renovation work.

Everyone else, of course, knew that there were other causes for the accident. The symbolism was not difficult to interpret. As the *hti* is the crown on top of the pagoda, the fact that the crown had tumbled signaled the imminent demise of the king. It was a fearful omen for the regime; an irreversible and supernatural declaration of dissatisfaction with Burma's current rulers. Call it wishful thinking or the manifestation of unvoiced hope, but there was no doubting the frisson of excitement that ricocheted through Rangoon as the story of the pagoda's collapse spread across the city.

A NOTE ON SOURCES

In piecing together the story of Cyclone Nargis, I relied mostly on first-hand information and interviews. For backup, I used news clippings from the time and various reports released by NGOs and the United Nations. Situation reports by the UN Office for the Coordination of Humanitarian Affairs helped me chart the international emergency response. The OCHA-run Web site, www.reliefweb.int, and the UN-supported Myanmar Information Management Unit (MIMU) served as portals for documents, maps, and other material on the cyclone collated from a wide variety of sources.

The main official document on the effects of Cyclone Nargis is the Post-Nargis Joint Assessment (PONJA) report, which was launched in July 2008 by the Tripartite Core Group. *Post-Nargis Analysis—The Other Side of the Story* by Yuki Akimoto (Another Development for Burma, October 2008) and *After the Storm* (Emergency Assistance Team, Burma, and the Johns Hopkins Bloomberg School of Public Health, March 2009) were written to provide an alternative view to the PONJA, while

A NOTE ON SOURCES

Listening to Voices from Inside: Myanmar Civil Society's Response to Cyclone Nargis (the Centre for Peace and Conflict Studies, Cambodia, May 2009) detailed the extraordinary determination of private citizens in Burma to provide assistance to cyclone victims. Also useful was issue 41 of the *Humanitarian Exchange Magazine* (December 2008), which took the response to Nargis as its theme. A frank interview with the comedian Zargana, who was imprisoned after speaking out about the failing relief effort, was published online by *The Irrawaddy* magazine ("Zargana's Relief Role," June 2, 2008).

Among sources I turned to in search of background information on the regime were Mary Callahan's *Making Enemies* (Cornell University Press, 2004), which documents the early years of the Burmese military, and *Burma's Armed Forces* by Andrew Selth (Canberra, 2001), as well as Selth's working papers on recent events such as "Even Paranoids Have Enemies: Cyclone Nargis and Myanmar's Fears of Invasion" (*Contemporary Southeast Asia*, vol. 30, no. 3, December 2008). I came across the profile of the soldier who enlisted at the same time as Than Shwe in *The Caged Ones* by the late Burmese journalist Ludu U Hla (reprinted by Orchid Press, 1998). Further details were sourced from reports such as *Neither War Nor Peace* by Tom Kramer (Transnational Institute, July 2009), which offers a recent analysis of ethnic minority politics, and *Total Impact* (EarthRights International, September 2009), which covers Total and Chevron gas projects in Burma.

Before I traveled to Naypyidaw and while I was writing about it, I examined the capital from an aerial perspective on Google Earth and read *The Road to Naypyitaw* by Maung Aung Myoe (Working Paper Series No. 79, Asia Research Institute, National University of Singapore, 2006). I often found myself returning to Dominic Faulder's articles; he is the foreign correspondent who timed his Burma visits against "power days," which he describes in a 2001 article entitled "Predictions, Observations and the Power of Nine: Why Myanmar Confounds Outside Analysis." In a 2004 issue of *The Irrawaddy* he recalled trying to report on a fire that took place in Mandalay in 1981. His words became startlingly prescient as I reread the piece in the wake of Cyclone Nargis: "A town of 10,000 people could burn to the ground here and nobody would ever know about it."

An article entitled "A Preliminary Study of Burmese Prophetic Sayings" by Saw Tun (*The Journal of Burma Studies*, vol. 7, 2002) provides a concise history of *dabaung*. For more on Burmese superstition and magic I dipped into *Burmese Supernaturalism* by Melford E. Spiro (University of Chicago, 1967).

I read "The Abbott Is Frying Eggs" in *Burmese Monk's Tales* by Maung Htin Aung, now sadly out of print outside Burma. Juliane Schober's papers, "Buddhist Just Rule and Burmese National Culture" (University of Chicago, 1997) and "Venerating the Buddha's Remains in Burma" (*The Journal of Burma Studies*, vol. 6, 2001), informed my explorations of the regime's appropriation of regal attributes.

For an understanding of the events that led up to September 2007, the findings of the Open Heart Letter Campaign (The Burma Fund, March 2008) were illuminating. Thanks to the work of brave and diligent Burmese journalists, there is some astounding footage available online of the various events that were key to the September marches. Short films taken by the Democratic Voice of Burma (DVB), an exile-run Burmese media organization, and others can be seen on YouTube. I was particularly moved by footage of the solo protests conducted by Ohn Than, who stood alone outside the U.S. Embassy in Rangoon in August 2007 and was later sentenced to life imprisonment.

The haunting audio recording of monks invoking the *thabeik hmauk*, or overturning of the alms bowl, was obtained by the Asian Human Rights Commission and can be listened to at the Web site www.ahrchk.net.

There have been some excellent reports written on the September 2007 marches, compiled at considerable risk to the researchers and their sources. Particularly helpful to me were *Bullets in the Alms Bowl* (National Coalition Government of the Union of Burma, March 2008); *Crackdown* (Human Rights Watch, December 2007); *The Resistance of the Monks* by Bertil Lintner (HRW, September 2009), which has additional historical context and interviews with monks who fled to the Thailand–Burma border; and the Asian Legal Resource Centre's special report, *Burma, Political Psychosis & Legal Dementia* (article 2, vol. 6, October-December 2007). For up-to-date information on Burma's prisoners and their sentences, I used the Thailand-based Assistance Association for Political Prisoners (Burma) Web site, www.aappb.org, which has an extensive and regularly updated database.

For insight on Buddhism in Burma, I looked at *Mental Culture in Burmese Crisis Politics* by Gustaaf Houtman (it was he who used the phrase "Aung San amnesia" to describe the phenomenon of how the generals rewrite their own history) and *Burma's Mass Lay Meditation Movement* by Ingrid Jordt (Ohio University Press, 2007).

When checking points on Burma's modern-day history, I referred often to *Living Silence in Burma* by Christina Fink (Silkworm Books/Zed Books, 2009) and *The River of Lost Footsteps* by Thant Myint-U (Farrar, Straus and Giroux, 2006). Two other recently published books that serve as good introductions to Burmese history are *Burma/Myanmar: What Everyone Needs to Know* by David I. Steinberg (Oxford University Press, 2009) and *A History of Modern Burma* by Michael W. Charney (Cambridge University Press, 2009). I garnered otherwise hard-to-find descriptions of the early settlement of the Irrawaddy Delta from *The Burmese Delta* by Michael Adas (University of Wisconsin Press, 1974).

For daily updates I turned to my old favorites, *The Irrawaddy* magazine's online version at www.irrawaddy.org and Burmanet at www.burmanet.org, which compiles news sources from around the world. Indispensable to my research was the online edition of the *New Light of Myanmar*, the regime's de facto mouthpiece; I made good use of the archive available at www.myanmargeneva.org.

ACKNOWLEDGMENTS

I owe enormous thanks to the following people: my loyal agent Jeffrey Simmons; my editor Janie Fleming for her patient guidance and the wonderfully diligent team at Granta—Michal Shavit, Christine Lo, and Daphne Tagg; SB, who got me started *and* finished (though her role in the making of this book is absent from the text, it is there in memory!); K for offering shelter from the storm to myself and others; Paul Wyatt for creative logistical support; Ko Ba Hein and Khin Khin Lay for their wise and lyrical insights; LB for generously sharing her endless knowledge of, and enthusiasm for, all things Burmese; my trusty undercover researchers in Rangoon, No. 2 and No. 3; Hla Thein for kind Burglish assistance; also "Ko Ye," "Aung Moe," MG (the *peh nanbya* fairy), ZL, and Nic Dunlop; my parents for their unflagging support, particularly my father, who allowed me to fall asleep on the couch during hospital duty; and, finally, Justin for having faith that broken things can be fixed.